The Literate Imagination

QUALITY IN SECONDARY SCHOOLS AND COLLEGES SERIES

Series Editor, Clyde Chitty

This new series publishes on a wide range of topics related to successful education for the 11-19 age group. It reflects the growing interest in whole-school curriculum planning, together with the effective teaching of individual subjects and themes. There will also be books devoted to management and administration, examinations and assessment, pastoral care strategies, relationships with parents and governors and the implications for schools of changes in teacher education.

Early titles include:

Geography 11-16: Rediscovering Good Practice
Bill Marsden
1-85346-296-9

English and Ability
Edited by Andrew Goodwyn
1-85346-299-3

Active History in Key Stages 3 and 4
Alan Farmer and Peter Knight
1-85346-305-1

English and the OFSTED Experience
Bob Bibby, Barrie Wade and Trevor Dickinson
1-85346-357-4

Partnership in Secondary Teacher Education
Edited by Anne Williams
1-85346-361-2

Shaping Secondary Schooling: Talking with Headteachers
Edited by David Hustler, John Robinson and Tim Brighouse
1-85346-358-2

The Literate Imagination:
Renewing the
Secondary English Curriculum

Bernard T. Harrison

David Fulton Publishers
London

David Fulton Publishers Ltd
2 Barbon Close, London WC1N 3JX

First published in Great Britain by
David Fulton Publishers 1994

Note: The right of Bernard T. Harrison to be identified as the author of this work has been asserted by him in accordance with the Copyright, Designs and Patents Act 1988.

Copyright © Bernard T. Harrison

British Library Cataloguing in Publication Data

A catalogue record for this book is available from the British Library

ISBN 1-85346-300-0

Typeset by Harrington & Co
Printed in Great Britain by BPC Books and Journals, Exeter

Contents

Contributors

Denise Aitken is head of the English Department at Penistone School in Derbyshire. She has completed an investigation of the impact of National Curriculum requirements in English on classroom reading.

Dr Janet Collins is a research fellow in the School of Education, University of Leeds, following a teaching career in Sheffield middle schools. She is engaged on research into special-needs education.

Sue Dymoke is head of English at West Bridgeford School, Nottingham. She is a coursework moderator for A-level English literature, and has contributed to PGCE tutorial programmes in the University of Sheffield; she has published four volumes of her own poetry.

Kath Green is a lecturer in the faculty of Education at Nottingham Trent University, where she has special teaching and research interests in mathematics education.

John Hodgson is head of the English Department at Bideford School, Devon. He has researched and published on media studies in English, is a member of NATE National 16–19 Committee and is an A-level coursework moderator in English literature.

Beth Mercer took early retirement, following disablement, from her work as a secondary-school teacher of English and special-needs pupils. She is now engaged on research at the University of Sheffield, into the needs of socially disabled pupils in schools.

Dr Eve Richards has taught at the Universities of Minnesota, Cambridge, Salonica and Nagasaki; she now teaches in further education, and has recently completed research at the University of Birmingham, on classroom metaphor.

Muriel Rubin has taught in London secondary schools and for the Open University. She is now engaged in developing Distance Learning Programmes in Namibia.

Alan Thornsby teaches in Wisewood Junior School, Sheffield; he is completing postgraduate studies in the field of children's reading responses.

Series Editor's Foreword

The title of this book has been chosen with great care though also, as the other author himself admits, with a feeling of some regret that other worthy contenders had to be abandoned along the way. Within its particular and valuable focus on literacy and imagination in the teaching of English, the book is also concerned with the wider issues of language, learning and values in education, and has a practical objective in seeking to influence the on-going and urgent review of the 1988 National Curriculum. While the value of literacy might appear to be self-evident – literacy standards having obvious implications for the promotion of material well-being in our society – a case is also made in the chapters that follow for the importance of the imaginative life in any curriculum programme that is truly serious about generating energy, resourcefulness and autonomy among learners.

Drawing on evidence from colleagues and students, as well as from his own field studies, Bernard Harrison seeks to celebrate creative teaching linked with creative learning. Rejecting the barren concept of curriculum 'delivery' to be found in so many government-inspired National Curriculum documents, he is concerned to highlight the ideals of meaning and joy in discovery and of adventure and risk-taking in learning. By endorsing a creative role for teachers in sharing responsibility for the curriculum that they teach, he provides what amounts to a manifesto for a genuine professionalisation of teaching in this country.

Clyde Chitty
Birmingham,
August 1994.

The child:

> ...Protean in your elements,
> You are all time shaped into flesh;
> You fashion sand, water, stars and paint to
> your own use, making the fresh
> connections behind innocent
> eyes where others cannot follow.
>
> About your superiority Wordsworth was right.
>
> (Barrie Wade, 'Poem for a Child', in Linklove, 1985)

The grown-up:

> ...his nature is such that he requires to be drawn out by kindness and encouragement...but if love be shown to him and he be treated really well he will accomplish things that will make the whole world wonder.
>
> (from a reference in support of Michelangelo, for the commission to paint the Sistine Chapel, quoted in Wilson, 1990, p. 11)

A 1990s view:

> I feel it is in some way a result of the lack of competitive ethos these days that children are not taught that they are bound to fail sometimes, and when they do they cannot cope with it.
>
> (coroner's comments on a girl who killed herself after failing to gain the grades she expected at GCSE, quoted in *Times Educational Supplement*, 10.9.93)

Preface

This book identifies principles and strategies for improving the quality of language and literacy in learning. Its particular focus, therefore, is on English studies. Yet its themes are of concern to all teachers, as well as all learners, their parents and all who are concerned with learning processes. The book appears in a decade when the education of new teachers has become distinctively the responsibility of schools themselves; therefore, it does not deal exclusively with fine details of classroom practice. It aims, rather, to be both 'truthful' and 'useful' to teachers through discussion of broader issues of vision and policy, on which good practice may be developed, as well as providing examples from practice.

As a teacher, I have drawn on evidence from students, teacher colleagues and from my own classes; as a researcher, I have drawn on research evidence from my research students, researcher colleagues, and my own field studies. I am most grateful to all those who have contributed directly to the chapters or who have kindly given permission for their work to be cited. I also acknowledge, with thanks, all those writers to whose published work I have referred.

In deciding on a title for the book, this had to highlight its two principal concerns – literacy, and imagination in learning; and also its main utilitarian purpose – to influence reform of the National Curriculum for English in schools. It was with reluctance, that several terms which had contended for inclusion in the title were eventually not used. These included: 'creating meaning in learning'; 'realising value'; 'autonomy for the learner'; 'whole language and whole learning'; 'empowerment through learning'; 'integrity in language and learning'. Yet, in focusing on literacy and imagination in English teaching, the book cannot help but be concerned also with the much wider issues of language, learning and values in education that are indicated by those other terms.

The intervention in 1993/4 of the Dearing Committee into policy-making for the National Curriculum showed that government, at last, was willing to take action to make the National Curriculum more flexible and less bureaucratic; less knowledge-bound, and with more emphasis on where to go for knowledge and how to use it; and more answerable to the local expectations of learners and teachers. Schools should, above all, be concerned with generating *energy* in learners, to be resourceful in taking increasing responsibility for their own learning; to think, and to know how to say and write what they think; and to develop the capacity to analyse problems, the vision to find solutions, and the courage to take action. In support of these aims, twin theses concerning literacy and imagination are proposed:

1. *Literacy* If there is any entirely common ground on which all members of the whole international community are agreed, it could be about the value of literacy – to 'developed', 'developing' or 'underdeveloped' nations alike. Today, as I wrote this, a familiar litany was reported on the radio, this time from America's Education Secretary Richard Riley, that 'nearly half of all Americans read and write so poorly that they are ineffective in the work place'. Similar concerns about literacy/illiteracy are, as the chapter in this book on reading will discuss, common throughout the world, and no less so in Britain. Standards of literacy have obviously close associations with standards of material well-being, as well as less tangible cultural standards. At best, the concern to improve literacy can lead to more effective investment in education, as an essential element in meeting community needs and planning for the future. At worst, it can lead to 'knee-jerk', anti-educational reactions which demand that teachers must cut-the-frills, get-back-to-basics and be-paid-by-results.

2. *Imagination* As with literacy, the case for imagination is long established, although it has not been usually as aggressively promoted by communities or governments, since its links with material well-being are less obvious – even though they may be shown to be just as strong. Charles Dickens chose to emphasise the 'higher' qualities of the imagination, when he claimed – to 'loud cheers' – that 'I hold it to be more than ever essential...that the imagination, with all its innumerable graces and charities should be tenderly nourished' (in Ackroyd, 1990, p. 699). Yet, as will be argued throughout the chapters to follow, it is the imaginative life which is most at stake in the National Curriculum debate, and which is most crucial to any programme of education that truly aims to promote energy, resourcefulness and effective thinking among learners. Moreover, it is essential to *all* areas – not least, material aspects – of human well-being.

Knowledge-packs or a civilised curriculum?

In pursuit of quality in literacy and imaginative learning, this book celebrates creative teaching, linked with creative learning. Helen Gardner, one of Britain's most notable literary researchers, declared in the last sentence of her book *In Defence of the Imagination* (1982, p. 162), that 'I would wish to be considered as a teacher or nothing'. She was not, of course, being 'anti-research': far from it, given her own eminent record as a critic-researcher. Rather, she was attacking drudgery in research. Academics in British universities are still paid to carry out research; they are, however, just as vulnerable to pressures for data-crunching and knowledge-packaging – and against the ideals of meaning and joy in discovery – as schools have been, in their 'delivery' of the National Curriculum.

Helen Gardner criticised the 'publish or perish' mentality in universities, which created a falsely busy drive for 'productivity' in research. There was, she suggested, a general failure of nerve in higher education, revealed in a feeling that they must justify themselves by easily measured research outputs. This drive for the measurable was crowding out time for reading, thinking and teaching (in the full sense of this, not just delivering knowledge-packs through lectures), and for richer modes of research (see, for example, the account of using personal histories in ethnographic research, in Chapter 4 of this book). If Gardner's was a dissenting voice in the early 1980s, the growing drive for academic performance indicators since then made her views seem downright eccentric, in the climate following the Education Reform Act of 1988. Especially outrageous to the prevailing academic opinion of today would have been her claim on behalf of 'blessed idleness, the true plot of thought' (p. 159).

Yet every respectable course on management earnestly advises its students to do just this – to take time out to think, and not to feel guilty about such 'idleness'; the best way that they can serve their organisation, after all, is to produce and implement good ideas. Both teachers and their learners must be managers of learning. They need personal space, to develop independence of thought and to take responsibility for learning; this principle should be at the heart of any debate about quality in research, as well as teaching. It was encouraging to note that the *Final Report* (Dearing, 1993) gave belated recognition to teachers' needs for time to reflect and plan. Perhaps more civilised principles may emerge, as educational policies prepare now for the third millennium.

Clearly, an imaginative and appropriate curriculum is of crucial importance in the good discipline of schools; moreover learners, as well as teachers require time and space to develop their capacities for learning. That discipline in teaching and learning is essentially a matter of civilised relations was confirmed in a study of school discipline by Gillborn, Nixon and Rudduck (1993). This study, published by the Department for Education, identified 'expectations, consistency, dialogue, engagement and respect' (p. 110) as essential dimensions of discipline in schools. In a concluding summary of their study they found that:

- Pupils are developing a clear sense of their own achievements, and of their own aspirations and needs.
- Pupils are increasingly involved in the assessment of their own work; they are also involved in thinking, with their teachers, about relevant tasks and appropriate targets, and about how the decisions they make may affect their future.
- Pupils are gaining a sense of how the various learning experiences they are being offered 'add up' and achieve coherence.
- Pupils know what to do – whom to approach, whom to talk with when they are experiencing a sense of failure or a lack of direction in their work or in their own lives (pp.116–17).

This positive picture gives good cause for optimism for the future. It reflects a fundamental principle, that all learners require the opportunity to reveal themselves as they actually *are*, not just in ways that are deemed to be useful to whatever educational or market policies may happen to be the fashion of the time. Constraints on achieving this picture in all respects do, however, remain – not least, through constraints imposed by the National Curriculum itself, and by other forms of government intervention.

To provide just one unpleasant example from English studies, well-established and successful syllabuses in English Literature A-level, which included a coursework component of up to half the syllabus, came under arbitrary attack in the 1990s from government, which decreed that, from 1996, coursework must be reduced to no more than one-fifth of the syllabus. The syllabuses were forced to return to old 'stand-and-deliver' modes of examining, that English teachers since the time of Quiller-Couch have found irksome. Following this, elements of optional original writing in English literature A-level syllabuses were suddenly rejected in 1994 by the Schools Curriculum Assessment Authority (SCAA), despite strong support for this from Examining Boards. This move showed further intolerance by SCAA of teaching approaches that had enabled students to experiment with forms of writing on their own terms – to take responsibility for their learning, as outlined in the picture above.

The need for good principles and practice in developing the curriculum is far too important an issue to be left to the arbitrary interventions of SCAA or other government-directed bodies.

Reform often involves giving new meanings to old terms (which is the opposite of disguising old thinking with new labels). Therefore, this review of literacy and imagination in learning involves 'going back to basics', in the sense of re-examining some first principles in learning. Take, for example, spelling – that pet subject of back-to-basics sloga-neers – and consider Margaret Atwood's account of her daughter's early efforts in 'spelling' (1981):

> My daughter plays on the floor
> With plastic letters,
> red, blue & hard yellow,
> learning how to spell,
> spelling, how to make spells.
>
> A word after a word
> after a word is power.

The play on meanings here – spelling, and casting spells, leads unobtrusively to thoughts about the power of words, and about demonic elements in learning:

> At the point where language falls away
> from the hot bones, at the point
> where the rock breaks open and darkness
> flows out of it like blood, at
> the melting point of granite
> where the bones know
> they are hollow and the word
> splits & doubles & speaks
> the truth & the body
> itself becomes a mouth.
>
> This is a metaphor.

Following her witty recognition of the monstrous inner powers to be released by learning, Atwood returns to the spelling task:

> How do you learn to spell?
> Blood, sky & the sun,
> your own name first,
> your first naming, your first name,
> your first word.

The learner takes possession of language and learning, just as language and learning take possession of her. It is a fierce, ransacking business, conducted with a relish that has little concern for niceties; such adventure in learning is not for the squeamish.

This is not everyone's view of language and learning, and it is unlikely to be celebrated in government-inspired National Curriculum documents. Yet serious purpose underlies the fun of this mythic account; it dwells on how learning involves soul, mind and body, in renewing the ancient quest to take whole possession of one's world. Atwood's poem provides, in fact, a welcome theme for this study of literacy and imagination.

The first, introductory chapter reviews the uses of a literate imagination. It looks, in particular, at the impact of the National Curriculum for English, in the light of issues raised.

This is followed by Part I, each chapter of which addresses a theme of general educational importance that is related to the main theses of the book – imagination in learning (Chapter 2, with a study by John Hodgson); the role of metaphor in language development (Chapter 3, drawing on work by Eve Richards and Muriel Rubin); and the learning process itself (Chapter 4, which includes a study by Kath Green). These chapters draw variously on a range of teaching and research evidence.

Part II investigates aspects of literacy development. While this Part follows a pattern as laid down by the National Curriculum for English – with successive chapters on reading (Chapter 5, drawing on work by Denise Aitken and Alan Thornsby); writing (Chapter 6, drawing on work by PGCE English/drama students); and talking and listening (Chapter 7, with Janet Collins) – it draws together issues of imagination in learning with issues of literacy. Again, these chapters are based on direct teaching and research fieldwork, as well as select readings in these areas.

Finally, Part III shows applications of principles established in the earlier sections. Chapters deal with language development for learners with special needs – (Chapter 8, which draws on work by Beth Mercer); creativity in learning (Chapter 9, with Sue Dymoke); and finding personal meaning through language and learning (Chapter 10, with John Hodgson).

CHAPTER 1

Introduction: Imagination, Literacy and the Renewal of English

Summary

The Introduction provides an overview of issues to be examined in the book. It reviews the place of imagination in education – especially its uses in literacy, language and learning. Having dwelled on the *liberating* powers of imagination, it argues for *personal space* in learning and teaching, so that these powers may grow.

These ideal conditions for imagination in education provide a critical focus on the National Curriculum, especially in English studies; the chapter offers a critique of both the established (1990) Order and the revised (1993) Order for English.

Having endorsed a *creative* role for teachers in sharing responsibility for the curriculum that they teach, and for learners in what they learn, the chapter moves from specific concerns in English teaching, to a wider context of curriculum development and professional responsibility in teaching. It highlights some essential professional competences for teachers, and also a manifesto for a genuine professionalisation of teaching, before the end of the present century.

The effort to find meaning

to know and not to act is not to know.

(Wang Yang-ming)

In Margaret Atwood's poem 'Spelling' (quoted in the Preface), her pun on activities of spells and spelling had much more than casual force;

through literacy, she declares, her daughter will gain power in and over her world. To link imagination with literacy is to insist on the potential in all learners, to take command and to make things happen in language and learning.

Yet, while there may be sudden magical effects, spelling requires patient, full absorption in the game. It is hard, perhaps impossible, to define this learning process, without invoking poetry, or art-language, as well as the language of reasoned observation (for example, of educational psychology).

Furthermore, the process itself may require learners to work in ways that are required of dancers, actors or painters, as well as those of the social sciences:

> the efforts of dancers warming up, of actors living themselves into a role, of painters' close attention to single strokes, of musicians struggling to find the right sound...require as much discipline, control and patience, knowledge and vision as that of any engineer, historian or scientist struggling to solve a problem, find the evidence or falsify a hypothesis.
>
> (Calouste Gulbenkian Foundation, 1983)

Given the amazing range of educational panaceas that are urged, year by year, to put education right, it will strike many as rash to place renewed trust in imagination, as just one key term. The habit of offering simple solutions that fail to work have, suggested John Wilson, reduced people in both the academic world and the worlds that it serves 'to a kind of despairing relativism' (1979, p. 131). Yet Wilson's book was, inevitably, followed by an even greater proliferation of new remedies throughout the 1980s.

Wilson, making a philosopher's commitment to Ockham's razor (which maintained that it is bad method to entertain more entities than is strictly necessary), rejected all competing educational ideologies, in moving to just one educational principle on which to base a philosophy of education. He called this the 'largely unexplored hinterland' of love, which lies behind all the facts, methodologies and subjects of education.

Few would dispute that love, in some form, is essential in education; this explains, for example, the choice of the three quotations that preface this present book. Yet the question, 'What *kind* of love?' should prompt lively debate. Turning, for example, to a case which has earned a place in educational folklore, that of J.S. Mill's *Autobiography* (1873), it is clear that Mill was 'loved' by his father. That same father, however, inflicted such an unremittingly harsh programme of education, based on Bentl .. s utilitarian ideas of education, on the young Mill, that it caused mental breakdown.

Reflecting on this crisis, Mill related how there was no basis of 'sympathy with mankind' in the educational programme that his father had devised. Yet Mill acknowledged, too, that the very seeds which grew into rejection of his father's system were sown in the informal, non-institutional learning that was his privilege in childhood. Garforth (1979) commented that Mill's childhood was where 'Greek and arithmetic and English history were mingled in his early memories with "green fields and flowers" – a delightful and enviable recollection'.

Mill was helped to recovery by reading Wordsworth's poetry (which will be a focus for the next chapter, on 'Imagination'). In his *Autobiography* Mill tells how he came, through pain, to identify the cause of his crisis as stemming from emotional and imaginative deficiencies in his education. Yet, in developing his own, independent viewpoint, he did not simply overthrow his father's influence. Instead, he sought to integrate paternal ideals of discipline and social responsibility with the admission of emotion, the play of imagination, and the enhancement of autonomous, individual life.

Mill's own educational thinking was based on the belief that the learner is a self-responsible individual; he emphasised 'the dignity of a thinking being'. The effort to understand was, for him, an effort of *imagination* – he envisaged the principle of a supreme art, 'unfortunately still to be created', which would bring together 'an art of life' from all the known separate arts and disciplines. His term for this art of life was 'Teleology, or the Doctrine of Ends' – a term which deeply influenced some key 20th-century studies in phenomenology on learning, knowing and meaning, such as Merleau-Ponty (1962), Polanyi (1975) and Grene (1969, 1974), and which were introduced directly into schools studies on English by Peter Abbs (1979), David Holbrook (1980) and others.

Mill's poetic concern for the imagination emerged in his attack, in an essay 'On Genius', against forms of instruction where 'things have only been taught and learned, but have not been *known*'. Here, his claim that individual energies must be released in learning is nearer to Merleau-Ponty's notion of learning as encounter, or to Polanyi's version of learning as bodily knowing, than to his own familiar adherence to Victorian association psychology. He declared, in 'On Liberty', that the notion of human nature as a 'machine to be built after a model' must give way to a view of humanity as a tree that grows 'according to the tendency of the inward forces which make it a living thing'. Mill was an experientialist, shaping his own world view on actual events of his time, but he also recognised events of the mind:

experience, instead of being the source and prototype of our ideas, is itself a product of the mind's own force working on the impressions we receive from without and has always a mental as well as external element.

(1984, 'Logic')

Through this recognition of what the poet Coleridge termed the 'esemplastic' powers of imagination, Mill was able to feel and think with sufficient complexity about the complexities of real living. A commitment to imaginative thinking and to reflective discourse exacted its price, however. In an early essay on 'Civilization' he wrote, with pessimism, that the loss of respect for individual vision in a mass culture meant that 'any voice not pitched in an exaggerated key is lost in the hubbub'. It is fair to say of Mill himself, though, that he won a wide public audience without loss of imaginative vision, intellectual rigour, or individual integrity – all of which qualities remain in the highest demand in educational principles, policy and practice.

Empowerment through learning

Compared to Wilson's claim for a hinterland of love, the choice of imagination as a first principle in education may seem far less daring. On the other hand, the case for imagination is asserted here from the beginning, rather than (as was Wilson's case for love) as a conclusion; its centrality will be justified in all the chapters to follow. Genuine learning is necessarily imaginative; its enemies are cliché and jargon (not unfamiliar in the discourse of education); or drily abstract discourse (where the live wires of argument are deadened through lack of metaphoric play); or simple philistinism (as in the case of the applause-seeking delegate at a political party conference in the 1980s who, in the spirit of that time, urged teachers to read less Wordsworth and promote more 'words work' in schools).

As for educational writing, the 'publish-or-perish' pressures on educational researchers have threatened to make this a disaster area, as far as vision and imagination are concerned. New papers, books and journals appear each month. Yet it is difficult, sometimes, to imagine an audience for these, apart from the incestuous attention of other researchers; or to find a message that is powerful enough to reach actual teachers, learners and parents. The problem, like many others, is not new:

> Many of the books which now crowd the world may be justly suspected to be written for the sake of some invisible order of beings, for surely they are of no use to the corporeal inhabitants of this world. Of the productions of the last bounteous year, how many can be said to serve any purpose of use or pleasure? The only end of writing is to enable the readers better to enjoy life, or better to endure it.

(Johnson, 1757)

How much discourse on education, it might be asked, would survive Dr Johnson's rigorous test of 'use or pleasure'? And, of much greater importance, how many of the millions of school and college lessons given during that time would pass that same test? In an incautious attempt to meet Johnson's requirement for quality in learning and literacy, this present book will:

1. address *real concerns* of learners, and their supporters and teachers;
2. raise questions, throughout, about the *why?* of learning and teaching – about *meanings* in these processes;
3. celebrate elements of *play, curiosity and natural enthusiasm* in learning; and
4. examine how learners may be *empowered*, not only to 'endure', but also to *change* their conditions of life.

To fulfil these aims, *imagination* must play its full part in the argument, in examining *literacy* (on which modern education depends), *language* (which learners share in partnership with teachers) and *learning* (where the active contribution of the learner will be reaffirmed).

The passage from Dr Johnson is from a hostile review of an otherwise forgotten book by Soame Jenyns. Johnson condemns the futility of effort in a writer whose 'shame is to impose words for ideas upon ourselves or others. To imagine that we are going forward when we are going round.' Words must be fuelled by ideas, and all must have access to these. Indeed, some of Johnson's most severe criticism is aimed against Jenyns' smug view, that the 'opiate of ignorance' might be better than the 'danger' of providing learning for those who are born to poverty. Johnson makes an impassioned plea for universal education, which he sees as an entirely liberating force. It would be unforgivable, he asserts, to side with envy and cruelty, or to exercise 'that malevolence which delights in seeing others depressed', by denying education to anyone:

> The privileges of education may sometimes be improperly bestowed, but I shall always fear to withold them, lest I should be yielding to the suggestions of pride, while I persuade myself that I am following the maxims of policy.

Yes, of course – though the argument needs to be taken further than Johnson's own caution permitted. A modern view of the uses (other than pleasure) of learning and literacy was provided by Willinsky (1991), when he wrote of the 'pleasure and power of an emerging working-class literacy in the years before English literature was a school subject' (p. 179). In emphasising the uses of *empowerment*, rather than just endurance through learning and literacy, Willinsky drew on the history of popular literacy in the times of Cobbett, to indicate what people 'can get up to with reading and writing':

> The factory workers of those industrial towns of the last century – man, woman and child – found themselves in a community of print buoyed by an oral and literate culture; they were able to turn the heads of the governing classes, through persuasive appeals to justice, outright verbal assaults, biting political satires, as well as simple heartfelt tales. Literacy was an open contest of social-class interests as the disenfranchised spent the century establishing an alternative political economy of print.

The power of rhetoric to bring about change was well understood, and there was keen appreciation for high quality of polemic in literary writing:

> In this inky milieu, literature held its own as the stuff of public entertainment and edification; Keats shared the page with cobbler-poets; people flocked to talks on literary greats and peasant revolts. Literature was simply part of the cultural bundle taken up by Sunday schools and coffee-houses. Culture was, in those days, very much a matter of self-cultivation...but also one of collective determination.

> (pp. 179–80)

While this is, arguably, to take an over-optimistic view of the enfranchising powers of literacy, Willinsky invokes persuasive accounts by Thompson (1963) and Simon (1960), of an 'active and varied literacy bent on learning and self-improvement...that had to argue its own right to exist' (p. 38). So effective was this argument, of course, that the government of the day imposed the infamous 'Six Acts' to curb freedoms of press and of assembly, the first of which was the Stamp Tax Act, aimed directly – and with notorious success – against the cheaper journals of the radical press. The opportunities for 'self-help', and the new directions in learning and literacy offered by radicals such as Cobbett and others were followed, eventually, by government provision of universal education.

Now, after several generations of schooling for all, and several years after the statutory imposition of a National Curriculum, in what ways may universal education be seen as 'liberating' – in a political as well as personal sense – for those who receive it?

Making personal meanings

In Angela Carter's novel *Wise Children* (1991), the narrator is an elderly actress; she recalls a production of *A Midsummer Night's Dream* which disappointed her in its attempts to provide a rich scene. It left nothing to her own imagination:

> When the artificial wind stirred the leaves and flowers, they were stiff enough to clank.
> What I missed most was illusion. That wood near Athens was too, too solid for me. Peregrine, who specialised in magic tricks, loved it just because it was so concrete. 'You always pull a *live* rabbit out of a hat,' he said. But there wasn't the merest whiff about of the kind of magic that comes when the theatre darkens, the bottom of the curtain glows, the punters settle down, you take a deep breath...none of the person-to-person magic we put together with spit and glue and willpower.

The trouble with Peregrine's production was that he was too preoccupied with prescribing the scene, instead of delighting his audience:

> This wood, this entire dream, in fact was custom-made and hand-built, it left nothing to the imagination.
>   You spotted snakes with double tongue,
>   Thorny hedgehogs, be not seen –
> And there they were, waiting in cages, snakes and hedgehogs, not to mention newts, worms, spiders, black beetles and snails, with snake handlers and hedgehog handlers ad lib at hand to keep them happy, waiting for their cue to scatter this way and that across the set as soon as the fairy chorus started up. It was all too literal for me.

(p. 125)

Could the theatre of education be making a similar mistake to Peregrine's, in trying too hard to 'deliver the goods' to its clients, the learners, and leaving no space for them to create their own vision?

Are we providing enough space for learners to bring their own minds and cultures into taking part in learning? Have we lost sight of essential qualities such as play, curiosity and friendship in learning? Whose 'production' *is* it, anyway?

The search for an honest answer to these questions requires a review of what learners need from education, and what spaces in learning should be left 'to the imagination'.

In his prophetic work *My Pedagogic Creed* (1897), the educationist John Dewey declared: 'Education is the fundamental method of social progress and reform'. A century after this ambitious claim for education, our present decade witnesses, in many ways, a search for continuity and consolidation. This is an understandable retrenchment of mood from Dewey's optimism, in response to a pace of change that put great pressures on all those concerned, in the late 1980s. Now, the wisdom of the moment is that humanity cannot endure too much change; we need at least two-thirds of our lives to be stable in order to cope with change in the third area.

The counter-truth, however, is that life itself cannot endure too much sameness. If we do not plan for change, we shall be overtaken by it. If we do not seek out fresh forms and fresh ways, then our lives – personal, cultural, commercial, academic – will atrophy.

During the 1960s – a period widely reviled in the 1980s – there were many books on education with titles and chapter headings about ' imagination', 'creativity', 'discovery'. In one of the earliest and most widely influential of these, *On Knowing. Essays for the Left Hand* (1962) Jerome Bruner included sections on 'The Conditions of Creativity', 'Art as a Mode of Knowing' and 'Myth and Identity'. His ideas won wide support in Western education. His government, stung by Russian success with the Sputnik space venture, was ready to hear criticism of 'unimaginative' Ph.D. theses in physics; education was due for a shake-up of an opposite kind to the 'framework and control' emphasis in 1980s Britain. Bruner argued that,

> just as there is predictive effectiveness, so there is metaphoric effectiveness. For the while, at least, we can do worse than to live with a metaphoric understanding of creativity.
>
> (p. 30)

Yet, predicting later reactions against creativity as some kind of anti-educational force, he also warned that 'there is, alas, a shrillness to our contemporary concern with creativity' (p. 17). Since no single educational movement is likely to achieve all that has been sought from education, it might be best to avoid extravagant claims. He still argued, though, for an essential element that he called *'effective surprise'* in education to be achieved through the operation of metaphoric effectiveness.

Once more, a concern to develop the imaginative life needs to be at the centre of issues on language and learning in schools and colleges. We have become too cautious in recent years, and too dependent on imposed frameworks, despite much rhetoric about freedom and enterprise. While noting the broad 'two-thirds' guideline for stability when one-third is changing, the need for metaphoric play in learning remains a fundamental requirement in education; it is especially obvious in language/English studies. Imagination requires that a third area of change, of unpredictable shapes, of antic play, should be in the very heart of mainstream thought on language and learning, and of curriculum planning. In developing literacy, learners and teachers together require personal space, not only to choose texts and stories, but also to choose their own kind(s) of response. Yet their particular needs may well come into conflict with the 'official' assessment demands of examiners who distress the pupil depicted in U. A. Fanthorpe's poem (1987), 'Dear Mr. Lee':

> they'll be looking for terse and cogent answers
> to their questions, but I'm not much good at terse and cogent,
> I'd just like to be like you, not mind being poor,
> See everything bright and strange...

(p. 22)

This wistful dream, that learning should make things 'bright and strange', highlights a fundamental premise in curriculum planning: that the 'responsibility' of learners and of teachers is not simply to 'deliver' whatever the curriculum decrees; there is also a principle of *self*-responsibility for learners, which invites them to choose, shape and develop their own directions. This principle, which involves a personal realising of realities, requires that learners should not be seen as so many pieces of lego, to be constructed according to the (changing) wishes of educational planners.

Individuality involves some essential unpredictability of response. In the struggle to get the world right for one's self, an imposed 'correct' answer may sometimes seem inappropriate to the real needs of a learner. Peter Abbs (1979, p. 91) described an apocryphal university seminar, where a student defended a point of faith by declaring, 'I know, because I feel it in my heart.' After a palpable pause, her tutor reasserted academic authority with the clinical reply, 'In which ventricle, may I ask?' Having been given space for reflection, the pupil who wrote the letter to 'Dear Mr. Lee' needs space and support – to wonder, to criticise, to resist and to choose personal directions according to personal need. Education, Abbs suggested, is

> the very act of consciousness struggling for adequacy and expressive existence. Education is that in which I am involved, the continuous effort to recreate myself within the context in which I exist...There can be no knowledge without knowers, and knowers in turn must, on analysis, dissolve into a multitude of individuals living in quite specific contexts, relationships and culture.

(1979, pp. 111–12)

The National Curriculum: time for a shake-up

While the view of education proposed by Abbs, above, became more rare in the 1980s, it virtually disappeared in the early 1990s, as planners set up the apparatus of the National Curriculum. Now, gradually, debate is being renewed about the dangers of imprisoning the curriculum in a bureaucratic framework. These are, though, well worn issues, as was shown in a parody called 'The Animal School' by Reavis (1939), of a prescribed curriculum that disregards individual difference and need:

> Once upon a time, the animals decided they must do something heroic to meet the problems of a 'new world'. So they organised a school.
>
> They adopted an activity curriculum consisting of running, climbing, swimming and flying. To make it easier to administer the curriculum *all* the animals took *all* the subjects.
>
> The *duck* was excellent in swimming, in fact better than the instructor; but he made only passing grades in flying, and was very poor in running. Since he was also slow in running, he had to stay after school and also drop swimming in order to practise running. This was kept up until his web feet were badly worn and he was only average in swimming. *But average was acceptable in school so nobody worried about that except the duck.*
>
> The *rabbit* started at the top of the class in running, but had a nervous breakdown because of so much make-up work in swimming.

and so on, until:

> The prairie dogs stayed out of school and fought the tax levy because the administration would not add digging and burrowing to the curriculum. They apprenticed their child to a badger and later (joined by the groundhogs and gophers too) started a successful private school.
>
> (pp. 39–40)

We should learn from history. Many years after the Renaissance had begun, there were monasteries where the number of angels who could sit on a pinhead was still being debated; this anachronism was matched by the pope who, having heard about the 'trendy' view of Copernicus that the earth moved round the sun, decided to summon him to Rome – but then discovered that the offending astronomer had died a hundred years earlier. Perhaps the debate in Britain on the National Curriculum for English should have included more ridicule, to attack the bureaucracy of National Curriculum planners, and to expose the authoritarian arrangement that politicians and civil servants should always be able to overrule any teacher representation in curriculum planning.

Now that debate has been renewed about the dangers of imprisoning constraints in the National Curriculum, we should take this opportunity to restore attention to *principles* in English studies. Such attention almost disappeared, in the glare of publicity about 'skills' in listening, talking, reading and writing, according to statutory requirements. Never was a spirit of *critical* enquiry more needed nor, it seems, more absent. Anthony Burgess, for example, throwing a stone or two at 'educational reformists' who 'deny the value of grammar in English' (1993, p. 334), conceded that the 'old grammar books...are, admittedly, no longer to be trusted'; instead, he advocated the 1970s fashion of Chomsky, who 'made transformational grammar not merely startling but newsworthy'. In his modest proposal to teachers, Burgess expressed the hope that

> our pupils will accept the concept of the morpheme as well as that of the phoneme. The free morpheme and the bound morpheme, the autosemanteme and the synsemantine make basic sense.

(p. 334)

Perhaps this should be enjoyed by teachers as Swiftian irony, whether or not this was intended. Yet, to invoke a further source from the 1930s, where irony is unmistakable: what Collingwood, in *The Principles of Art* (1938), declared about grammarians might also apply to NCC Committee work on 'structures' for English; he viewed the grammarian as 'a kind of butcher' who converted language from 'organic tissue into marketable and edible joints' (p. 257). Yet a language that lives and grows, Collingwood argued, no more consists of verbs, nouns and so forth, than animals as they grow consist of joints of meat. Offering some hope for language, however, he suggested that it takes more than a grammarian to kill a language; in a dry amendment to his original metaphor he recalled how in some parts of the world people may 'cut a steak from a living animal, and cook it for dinner, the animal not being much worse' (p. 259).

Similarly, it will take more than SCAA planning committees to have the final, or even main decisions on how language is taught and learned. Where there is powerful demand, we may find far more valuable (and succinct) accounts of English and language studies, which respect the 'living animal' of language. For example, in a chapter called 'Critical Language Awareness and People's English' Hilary Janks (1992) dwelled on the empowering qualities of a teaching approach to English studies which highlights 'Critical Language Awareness' as a key to language and learning development. She cited proposals which provide a refreshing vision of *learners in responsible ownership of their language*. These proposals were drawn up by the National Education Crisis Committee in South Africa, for a People's English where language competence must include the ability:

- to say and write what one means;
- to hear what is said and what is hidden;
- to defend one's point of view, to argue, to persuade, to negotiate;
- to create, to reflect, to invent;
- to explore relationships, personal, structural, political;

- to speak, read and write with confidence;
- to make one's voice heard;
- to read print and resist it where necessary;
- to understand the relationship between language and power.

(in Hayhoe and Parker, 1992, p. 50)

What is true for learners must, of course, also apply to teachers. The professional status of teaching depends on teachers making their own significant and independent contribution to all areas of educational planning and research, as well as curriculum matters. That contribution will not be exclusively made by teachers; indeed, its effectiveness depends on the best possible links with parents, commerce and industry, higher education, and other community interests. It needs, however, to involve a significant restoration, for teachers, of professional autonomy – a term which remains unpopular with government and its servants, such as SCAA and OFSTED.

Consider, for example, the high degree of empowerment, and the opportunities for flexibility in decision-making about the curriculum, that were offered to teachers, even at the beginning of the 20th century (at a time when teaching was still considered by the 'established' professions to be a menial occupation), in this passage from *Suggestions* to elementary school teachers from the Board of Education:

> The only uniformity of practice that the Board of Education desires to see in the teaching of public and elementary schools, is that each teacher shall think for himself and work out for himself such methods of teaching as may use his powers to the best advantage, and be best suited to the particular needs and conditions of the school.
>
> (1905, p. vii)

Clearly, the authors of these *Suggestions* not only wished to emphasise their respect for skills that teachers are known to possess; they also supported professional autonomy, inviting teachers to exercise their judgement, according to local needs. By way of contrast, both the undue tameness of response among us all to the original (1990) Order for the English Curriculum, and the ill-tempered disputes that rose on the handling of proposals for a new Order in *English for Ages 5–16* (DFE, 1993) characterised, in different ways, a lack of candid discussion between educationists and government. Something ought to have been learned from that earlier mode of exercising power in educational policy, by the 1905 Board of Education. We can see, now, that the Board was maintaining an essential principle of enlightened leadership. This principle was memorably expressed, at international level, in the European doctrine of subsidiarity, as formulated by Pope Pius XI in 1931:

> It is an injustice, a grave evil and a disturbance of right order for a larger and higher association to arrogate to itself functions which can be performed efficiently by smaller and lower societies.
>
> (quoted in Sayer, 1993, pp. 109–10)

What remains true for nations applies to all groups, and also to individual life; when authority becomes repressive and intrusive instead of enlightened and guiding it loses, paradoxically, its essential authority.

Old Order versus New Order in the National Curriculum

Since the 1960s, the professional concerns of teachers of English have been vigorously represented by the National Assocation for the Teaching of English. Through its many national and regional meetings, its widely distributed journal *English in Education*, and its highly successful national and international conferences, it has made a notable impact on policy-making in English studies. Nor has it been afraid to use authoritative argument and evidence, in taking on political power groups.

In a robust statement on *English for Ages 5–16* (DFE, 1993), for example, NATE criticised in 1993 the proposed revised Order for the English curriculum, for its lack of 'professional credibility and intellectual coherence'. While the NATE statement may have remained insufficiently critical of the original 1990 Order (which, in its view, 'strikes a workable balance between various traditions of language education'), it revealed that the Association had, at last, become thoroughly alerted to the dangers of government directives in which 'opinion and prejudice have been allowed to take precedence over knowledge and evidence'.

Certainly, there was cause for complaint about the further erosion of good principles and practice in English teaching, in the 1993 proposed Order. It specified, for example, several new, prissy prescriptions for the teaching of grammar; it revealed a sterterous anxiety about inserting fullstops; it was unduly preoccupied with 'phonics' at key stage one, rather than a proper concern for familiarity with stories; and it was eccentric in its tabulation of statements of attainment in 'reading skills', which made no value-distinctions between the three tables of 'comprehension', 'response to literature' and 'information handling'.

One may presume that the list, provided in Appendix C of the proposals, of worthy people and organisations who were consulted during the Review process, would be in no hurry to claim credit for the contents of that proposed new Order; perhaps it was only civil servants in the DFE who were to blame for the drafting of these unattractive changes.

Yet were they, in fact, so different from the 1990 Order? Brian Cox, whose 1988 Report laid the foundations for the 1990 Order, endorsed his own achievement, in advocating both 'unity' and 'diversity' in English studies: 'In *Cox on Cox* (Cox, 1991), in which I present my view of the National Curriculum in English' (Cox, 1992, p. 30). Cox certainly showed skill in selling the English curriculum package to NATE and to others; by 1993 it became clear, however, that those Cox/NATE voices of progressive reason should have been more vociferous in resisting the original 1990 Order. Instead, there had been widespread praise for an Order which facilely linked statutory requirements for 'skills' in speaking and listening, reading and writing, with requirements in the nonstatutory programmes of study, in order to encourage less measurable achievements such as highlighting meaning *(whose meaning?)* 'in a sensitive way'. For reasons that were highlighted in an editorial by Roger Knight in the journal *The Use of English* (1992), which contained one of the few attacks to be made on Orders both old and new, there should have been general outrage at the failure of the National Curriculum Council to consider 'either the value or the practicability of its prescriptions'. This editorial concluded that

> no coherent idea of literacy shapes their recommendations; no philosophy of English teaching disciplines their proposals, giving them practicable and intellectually defensible form. Literacy being simply assumed to inhere in the constituent elements of National Curriculum English, the Council's much touted 'rigour' nowhere exercises itself on questions of *value*.

> (p. 8)

Nor can it be claimed that the Consultation Report on English by Ron Dearing (who had been brought in hastily, to restore peace between the government and the teachers) had the desired effect. Proposals by Dearing (NCC, 1993a, b) were, for example, severely criticised by Myra Barrs, in an editorial for *Language Matters* (CLPE, 1993/4, p. 1). In particular she attacked Dearing's claim that 'the National Curriculum will need to occupy a greater percentage of time at key stage 1 than at other key stages'. Barrs estimated that this will represent up to nine-tenths of the early years English curriculum: 'this is back to basics with a vengeance'. In the same editorial she recalled an entirely different version of 'basics' that has characterised the best teaching in this field; this other version asserts 'the central function of the imagination, and the fact that play, story and creative arts are the true "basics" on which we build our later learning'. There were problems, too, at secondary level, with

Dearing's proposals in his *Final Report* (1993). Commenting on these in a BBC Radio Four interview (7/1/94), a senior NATE representative warned that the exclusion of drama or media studies from the National Curriculum framework for English would weaken their contribution to English studies. Given that a statutory framework now exists, this view would seem to be irrefutable. Yet it was brusquely rejected by a senior SCAA representative, Chris Woodhead, on the same programme, who dismissed with equal brusqueness the professional authority of NATE as a 'pressure/lobby group'. Woodhead claimed that teachers could not have the argument both ways; this meant, presumably, that they should accept without criticism the amended curriculum prescribed by SCAA, whatever it contains, and be grateful that the New Order is at least rather shorter than before.

When teachers were directed by law to work under the authority of the National Curriculum Council QUANGO (replaced in 1993 by SCAA), teachers of English shared, for better or worse, the same restrictions of choice that are imposed by government on any group which is on the receiving end of its policies, no matter how 'enlightened'. The sense of loss, for example, recorded by the Tribal Revival movement in the United States:

> Today we live in houses other people made,
>   the government made.
> Today we drink out of glasses
>   that are clean.
> Long ago we drank with our hands
>   from the Big Horn River.

(quoted in Salter, 1977, p. 219)

generated a will among indigenous peoples to resist the 'hand-out mentality'. Similarly, all who are involved in teaching and learning need to flex muscles – professional, political, academic – to reclaim some autonomy and essential rights in education.

Dearing may take some credit, at least, for initiating some action to simplify the framework of the National Curriculum. In his review of curriculum and assessment, he questioned the value of the 10-level scale of achievement in the curriculum; made proposals to reduce the range of compulsory subjects (though English will continue to be included); recommended less compulsory components and more space for teachers' choices; and reviewed external assessment, promising 'more manageable administration' for teachers. His *Final Report* (Dearing, 1993) was fully accepted by government, with the promise that these should set a firm pattern for the rest of the 1990s.

Yet, as has been noted, serious problems remained for the English Curriculum in Dearing's proposals – not least, and not only, in the first key stage of these. In any fresh review of requirements for the English curriculum, an essential premise should be, that intervention on natural processes in learning ought to be *minimal*. A first, obvious thing to remind ourselves about language development is that the outstanding human achievement of learning a mother tongue (or, even more impressively, of early fluency in more than one language) is a wholly natural process, which may happen entirely without tears. Yet, like many other natural processes, it remains an incomprehensibly complex phenomenon.

Despite an immense amount of research in recent decades, there is no clear answer to exactly what motivates virtually all children to speak a language, nor how they accomplish this most remarkable of intellectual feats. However, we do know, as Myra Barrs (CLPE, 1993/4) emphasised in her spirited editorial, that free and full access to the imaginative life through books, plays and poems is of the essence, in developing confidence in literacy among the young.

Understandably, teachers of English like to think that they have made at least some progress in schools, towards creating better conditions for developing all aspects of language – including National Curriculum requirements for speaking, listening, reading and writing. Fortunately, parents do not have to wait for all the answers from teachers; their own intuitions about how best to encourage their offspring to talk and listen may be seen to work well throughout the world, on the whole. Even where they do not, children will show remarkable determination in making themselves heard; for when they fail to do so, their very hold on the world is at risk. The requirements for confident early development in language and learning are, as Winnicott (1971), Wells (1987) and others showed, a matter of providing favourable conditions for exploration, within a supportive and flexible – not rigid – framework, which provides its own creative space for exploratory play. If there must be a National Curriculum for English, it should be guided by the fact that the great majority of young learners are already proficient in one language (or more), by the time that they arrive at school; and, until they are coerced to think otherwise, they feel a natural ownership of their mother tongue.

It is increasingly important that all aspects of the National Curriculum for English should, from now on, be rigorously reviewed by all concerned with it, to safeguard that ownership. This implies, especially with younger children, a new strength of partnership between teachers and parents in this area, so that teachers and parents may *inform each other* fully on language and learning matters. Some National Curriculum provisions have, let it be admitted, been unobjectionable. For example, many of the proposals for language competence among South African learners cited (earlier) by Hilary Janks appear in National Curriculum targets, even though it all sounds a good deal more cautiously neutral in National Curriculum-speak. In recognising the importance of talk in learning, for example, the single general attainment target proposed for the speaking and listening profile component was

the development of pupils' understanding of the spoken word, and the capacity to express themselves effectively in a variety of speaking and listening activities matching style and response to audience and purpose.

(DES, 1989)

Perhaps this was all that was needed, in terms of government advice on the matter.

Competence and partnership in education; taking part in future planning

This chapter has sought to identify issues of literacy, imagination and the teaching of English, in a wider context of teaching and learning in the 1990s. To be fully effective professionals teachers of English need, of course, to interrelate not only with learners, but also with the larger professional school-teaching team, with parents, and with community interests. If issues concerning imagination and literacy are to become the urgent policy issues that they deserve to be, then all teachers of English need to be competent managers – not only in the classroom and in their subject, but in these wider spheres, too – so that they may transform what they know into effective action.

To conclude this chapter, therefore, notes are offered on first, the *individual competences* that are required, for teachers to play a full professional role in the development of teaching and learning, and second, larger policy issues in the *whole movement for partnership in educational development*.

First, as far as *individual teachers* are concerned with issues of partnership in education, few of them would deny that a sense of ownership – which may include shared decisions concerning educational aims, targeting resources, or planning the curriculum – may be legitimately achieved only through proven *professional competence*. Trust in this leads to entrustment of responsibility.

While sensible notions of professional competence are to be welcomed, the voluminous 'professional competences' for teachers that developed during the early 1990s posed a danger that, like the engine-drivers' manual, more time would be spent reading them than enacting them. Jenkins (1991), however, provided a chaste checklist of just twelve essential competences; while he aimed these at headteachers, they may be seen to apply just as appropriately to student teachers, all kinds of classroom teachers and, indeed, to all managers (including secretaries of state for education). They deserve, therefore, the attention of all members of an English/language department in any school or college. In summary, and slightly adapted, these are:

1. PROBLEM ANALYSIS	(what to analyse, and how to examine complexities)
2. JUDGEMENT	(reaching 'high quality' decisions, skill in identifying and setting priorities)
3. ORGANISATIONAL ABILITY	(planning, scheduling, using resources well)
4. DECISIVENESS	(knowing when a decision is needed, and when to act)
5. LEADERSHIP	(able to guide those who need direction, and to interact in accomplishing tasks)
6. SENSITIVITY	(able to perceive others' needs, skill in handling conflict, tact in handling different kinds of people)
7. STRESS TOLERANCE	(able to work and think under pressure)
8. ORAL COMMUNICATION	(clear spoken presentation of facts or ideas)
9. WRITTEN COMMUNICATION	(able to express ideas clearly for different purposes and audiences)
10. RANGE OF INTEREST	(able to handle a range of topics – educational, political, cultural)
11. PERSONAL MOTIVATION	(able to find personal satisfaction in work; to self-monitor)
12. EDUCATIONAL VALUES	(holds a well-reasoned educational vision; open to new ideas and to change)

(adapted from Jenkins, 1991, pp. 159–60)

In endorsing these, I would add the need for *imaginitive vision*, and ability to *generate creative action* – perhaps within no. 12 of this list. More emphasis, too, might be placed on *enjoyment* of the work (in no. 11), and on the need for resources of courage, perhaps throughout all these competences. Readers can choose to make other such adjustments to the list – though it may be found to provide a remarkably comprehensive (and demanding) coverage of essential competences in teaching.

Second, moving from issues of individual teaching competences, to *the effectiveness of whole schools*, the movement for partnership and for progressive consolidation in education is well represented by John Sayer, in *The Future Governance of Education* (1993). Sayer, who is Secretary to the General Teaching Council Initiative, proposed in the concluding chapter a ten-point 'Charter–99' for a programme of development in education, 'to be adopted now and implemented by 1999'. In summary, his proposals are that there should be:

1. *a right of access for all to learning* – to be incorporated into any Bill of Rights
2. acknowledgement that learning is *'lifewide and lifelong'*
3. a fully *flexible education service*, to meet constant change
4. a new *partnership between education, parents and local community*
5. provision of the *new media, to transform access to information*
6. *integration of education* with other programmes of social development, while retaining its distinctive identity
7. a *'levelling up of opportunity and redressing of disadvantage'*
8. provision of *links between education, training and economic development*
9. *regional development* to achieve this
10. attention to *physical conditions for learning* – 'the current state of our school buildings stock is a national disgrace'.

(adapted from Sayer, 1993, p. 133)

These proposals remain at a high level of generalisation for the particular purposes of this present book. Yet they may be seen to offer an excellent broad framework for developing any aspect of school and college learning. Two further broad proposals might be added, each of which reflects concerns of language and imagination in learning:

11. acknowledgement that language and learning *belong to the individual, as a critical and a contributing member of the community*
12. provision for learners and teachers to make their *imaginative and creative contributions to learning and to knowledge*, since these are never fixed things.

The notion of a *critical* contribution to education, from all those involved in education, applies at all levels, from senior management (see, for example, Harrison, 1992a) to those who are in the first stages of access to learning. The seeds of such critical-creative powers in policy-making are, this chapter has argued, sown in the early stages of learning a language; they are nurtured through imaginative engagement, through language, with the lived world of the learner. The argument will move, now, to consider the actual place of imagination in language, learning and literacy.

Part I

DEVELOPING THE IMAGINATION

CHAPTER 2

Imagining in Learning

This chapter considers how imaginative engagement in language and learning, as proposed in the Introduction, may be better understood and better practised. In moving from some general reflections on imaginative thought to an account of teaching and learning processes, it considers:

- imagination as a *third realm* between thinking and feeling;
- the relevance of *Romantic* versions of the Imagination;
- debates on *'cultural heritage'*: teaching and reading imaginative texts, under National Curriculum constraints;
- *'relevance'* and *'engagement'* in A-level literary studies;
- a study by John Hodgson on a student's *imaginative encounter* with Wordsworth.

The naivete of these notes. Like maps of the world before they discovered it was round...before the magic of the word the clotted, choking reality of blank paper.

(Fugard, 1974, pp. xxxiii–xxiv)

The only way out of his writing impasse, Fugard knew, was to use his *imagination*; he was already trying his hardest to do just that. Yet he also knew that it would need more than just effort, in order to 'only connect', and to move his thinking forward. He needed, too, conditions to *relax*, and to *play*. How can teachers, then, help learners to develop their imaginative powers and to use them, in order to *realise* what they intend to disclose, of their feelings and thoughts?

Although we all may have an idea of what we mean by 'real', 'realising' and 'reality', there are problems in using these terms – not only in aesthetics, but also in all areas of our 'real' living. Acknowledging this, John Fowles suggested (1977, p. 139) that 'one cannot describe reality; only find metaphors that indicate it'. He continued:

All human modes of description (photographic, mathematical and the rest, as well as literary) are metaphorical. Even the most precise scientific description of an object or movement is a tissue of metaphors.

In the light of such a remark, the huge topic of metaphor will have its own chapter, to follow this. Meanwhile, to return to Fugard's reflection, the discomfort that can be experienced in imaginative thinking may not stop, when ideas do begin to flow. Peter Elbow, in *Embracing Contraries* (1986), described his experience of being at what he called the 'stuck-point' of *too many* ideas:

> All these ideas rolling around in my head...I can find words for them separately but I am going crazy spending tons of time because I can't write them down – can't figure out where to begin. It's like a tangled ball of string and I can't find the end. I can only find loops...I feel I'm in a terrible vacuum, in a sensory-deprivation room, trying to fight my way out of a wet paper-bag when there are endless folds of wet paper and though I fight through each fold, there's still more and more soggy, dank sodden, smelly paper hanging all over me.
>
> (p. 48)

Elbow's feelings are like those experienced in an anxiety dream; by contrast, Fugard counselled his mind, through his notebook, to *relax*, in order to move more effectively. When we are faced with dilemmas of imagination we confront, in fact, two broad choices – a Wordsworth-like openness to the world ('wise passiveness') or an allegiance to systems (philosophical or others), to rescue us from uncertainty. In the last part of his book, Elbow became suspicious of pitfalls in trying to express meaning through language, and came to refute what Fugard called the 'magic of the word'; he invoked Chaucer's *Nun's Priest's Tale*, to support his thesis on the limitations of language. Chaucer, he claimed, implies that we need some 'larger system or systems for trying to talk about individual agency and functioning when more than one individual is involved' (p. 244). It may be granted that Chaucer's Tale satirises the limitations in literary-academic rhetoric of those times, and its absurd pretensions to 'universalise' language and thought. Yet did not Chanticleer escape from the jaws of the fox – at the very last moment – by choosing the opposite path, and finding a local, 'right' language for the occasion, through using native, instinctive wit? For once in his life he rejected the vanity of 'universals'; he managed to live in the moment and to speak according to the particular needs of that time and place – and survived.

Similarly, teachers may need to be wary of 'universal' attempts to explain thinking and imagination. They may prefer to rely on their native wit, while continuing to try to make what sense they can of the mass of accumulated readings, from philosophical, through experiential to psychometric, on cognition in learning.

Many of these, admittedly, are likely to be of little direct value to the classroom teacher who genuinely seeks to understand the elusive activity that we call 'thinking'. There is also a smaller pile of literature on 'affective', 'feeling' or 'sense' aspects of learning. This second pile, which has tended to evolve its own separate theories and practice, may sometimes be more entertaining than the first (as is the case with Elbow's book). Yet the teacher has often been left with a dubious 'either-or', 'cognitive-affective' choice, sometimes shored up by a correspondingly dubious mythology about the separate functions of the two parts of the brain.

Thinking about thinking, like thinking about education itself, has involved a confusion of contributions from psychology, sociology, linguistics, philosophy and so on; meanwhile, teachers still wait for agreed clear definitions of such key terms as thinking, imagining, feeling, knowing and meaning. We still await a 'Newton of the Imagination'.

A later chapter in this book (Chapter 9) will focus on aspects of creative thinking. As for imagination, a text called *Imagination and Education* (Egan and Nadaner, 1988) had the brave aim to establish imagination as a third dimension to the debate about thinking and feeling; yet its contributors came to no clear conclusions about the role of the imagination in learning. Disappointingly, it even felt obliged to repeat somewhat worn criticisms made by Warnock (1976) and others, about the alleged 'disservice' done by the Romantic writers, in making too extravagant claims for the synoptic power of the imagination (p. 239). Yet Coleridge's classic distinction, between the 'esemplastic' power of imagination, and the 'parasitic' character of fancy, is of value, in resolving uncertainties about these terms, in language and learning.

In their plea for an extension of 're-enactive imagination' in the study of history and cultures, the editors acknowledged the work of the outstanding historian and aesthetic theorist Robin Collingwood as 'classic', although they disapproved of his 'rather dangerous metaphorical language' (p. 243). Collingwood was also blamed with other, unnamed enactment theorists, for saying 'remarkably little about the imagination' (p. 244). This was an astonishing charge against Collingwood who, as the author of a definitive study of imagination, *The Principles of Art* (1938), was not mentioned by any contributors to the Egan-Nadaner book (see Harrison, 1980, for an account of Collingwood on imagination). For these reasons, the serious investigator of imagination in learning would find more reward, not in focused educational texts, but in such writers as Romanyshyn (1982), Ricoeur (1977, 1991) or Macmurray (1962). One contribution to *Imagination and Education*, however, offered special relevance to this present chapter. This was a refreshing, shamelessly pro-Romantic, yet well-focused account of Wordsworth's achievement, by Jane Sturrock, whose fancifully entitled, anti-Gradgrind piece was called 'how the gramnivorous quadruped jumped over the moon: a romantic approach'. In a dessicated post-Warnock era, embarrassed by what it saw as Romantic excesses, Sturrock invoked Wordsworth's account (in *The Prelude*), of a child who is submitted to a totally structured, predictable curriculum. The child-victim is submitted to a system of daily improvement,

> where he must live
> Seeing that he grows wiser everyday
> Or else not live at all, and seeing too
> Each little drop wisdom as it falls
> Into the dimpling cistern of his heart;
> For this unnatural growth the trainer blame,
> Pity the tree.

(Book V, II, 323–9)

Freedom, unpredictability, a rich environment for play – all these are excised from the world of the child-victim, who is (as was J.S. Mill, under his father's 'enlightened' Benthamite principles) 'stringed like a poor man's heiffer at his feed' by educational theory.

Blake's capacity to see a world in a grain of sand; Coleridge's distinction between fancy and imagination; Goethe's view, that 'every attentive glance is an act of abstraction'; Wordsworth's notion of 'recollection in tranquillity; Keats' notion of negative capability: these, and other key Romantic terms, represent distillations of profound, poetic thought on the nature of imagination. Far from being derivative and muddled – which was Warnock's (1976) charge against Coleridge – they *ransacked* philosophy in order to illuminate what is, at first hand, *seen*. Their method was caught by Ruskin, who held that the greatest thing a human should ever do is to *see* something: 'the fact of truth, though it only be in the character of a single leaf earnestly studied'.

There are, let it be admitted, some pitfalls in Ruskin's aesthetic of particularity, which took a too restrictive view of Romantic versions of the imagination. It was one of Ruskin's contemporaries, Masson, who made the risible comment that Wordsworth's advice to be true to Nature had been interpreted, for the most part, as advice to study vegetation. Even so, the foundations laid down by the Romantics, consolidated by Victorian thinkers such as Ruskin and refined in the 20th century by Collingwood and others, provided an important bridge between the contributions of both creative art and of philosophy, to thought about imagination.

Imagination is a vast, complex topic, which can bring us uncomfortably near to 'effing' ineffable questions of meaning. Rather than take that direction, the rest of this chapter returns to issues in English teaching. It considers, first, the handling of works of imagination in the National Curriculum framework for English; it moves, then, to issues of imagination in the particular context of teaching A-level English literature.

Regenerating English A-level Literature: a dialogue

'this is so, isn't it?
yes, but....'

(John Hodgson, head of English studies at Bideford College, Devon, exchanges views with the author, on how imagination may be nurtured through the teaching of literature. He also provides a commentary on work by one of his sixth-form students on Wordsworth, as part of an A-level coursework syllabus, for which JH and BH collaborate as moderators).

JH: I agreed with much of your opening chapter – though I think you are unfair about the important contribution that Brian Cox made, in ensuring that the 1990 National Curriculum Order for English won the consent of so many English teachers at the time. Through his influence, the views of the National Association for the Teaching of English were given some respect; he deserves our thanks for that. And the Order, after all, *did* provide more scope for imaginative teaching than was the case with the proposed 1993 Order.

BH: For me, we seemed to face a choice between Cox's 'open' prison, and the 'closed' prison of the new proposals. Of course, an 'open' one is likely to be more comfortable; I wanted, however, to criticise the *principle* of government restrictions on the curriculum and, especially, to challenge the *principle* of the 'compliant learner'. In a way, that can be more easily done, where imprisonment is *obviously* damaging, as in the case of the 1993 proposals. Let me, though, accept your point – or accept, at least, that Cox was defending good things in the English curriculum. Can we consider, now, how we might go about teaching those works of imagination called literature.

JH: Right. Let me offer two starting points. *First*, that English studies have long held a position in the curriculum as the domain where imagination can be nurtured through the study of language. An influential view of the importance of literature teaching in schools, is that literature presents readers with a highly developed and subtle form of language, which has the power to both extend and refine their experience. This is the case with all the arts, but literature has, inevitably, a special place in English studies.

Second, that one of the more notorious aspects of the 1993 proposed Order for English was the provision of lists of approved books for students to read at each key stage of the National Curriculum. The reason for the publication of such lists was clear; it was related to the project implicit in the very choice of title for the Department for National Heritage. It expressed the fear of some members of government and of some educators, that students are not encountering the 'canon' of 'great' English literature, and that consequently they were being deprived of their cultural heritage.

The most extraordinary effect of this fear was the publication, by SEAC in 1993, of an Anthology of Literature, for all state-funded secondary schools. All year-nine pupils in these schools were required to study this collection of prose and drama extracts and short poems. It included Wordsworth's 'Daffodils', Browning's 'Home Thoughts from Abroad' and Edward Thomas's 'Adlestrop'...

BH: So, while you found no harm in any of these as individual choices, are you suggesting that, collectively, they were redolent of genteel rural prep-school life? Not surprisingly, I suppose, they were seen by many teachers in less-favoured parts, as representing an attempt by representatives of a favoured minority to restore their lost vision of an idyllic English past.

JH: Yes; reaction to the booklists and to the anthology itself was predictable. The majority of teachers saw them as irrelevant to the actual lives of contemporary pupils; others, however, applauded them as a means of returning to a time when English teachers fulfilled their duty of introducing their pupils to the richness of 'our literary heritage'.

BH: Meanwhile, debate about the actual *choice* of texts tended to obscure the far more serious question of whether government has the right to prescribe the curriculum, to the extent of publishing texts for compulsory study, and then testing them on their contents? Clearly, the anthology raised issues of freedom and society which go far beyond education itself.

JH: Yes. On the narrow issue, however, of 'which texts?', the polarised positions of teachers and others concerning the 1993 Anthology were based on principles that may, in crude form, be summarised as follows:

Either: the 'cultural heritage' view sees nothing problematic in what constitutes the 'heritage', nor in the ways that readers are expected to respond to it;

Or: the 'urban democracy' position would be that ordinary children, including those from working-class backgrounds and from many ethnic minorities, will find no relevance in texts from the 'heritage'.

BH: Yes, that certainly is to over-simplify – though I know what you mean. No thoughtful person would accept that particular 'either-or' choice; yet it may suit some politicians, to keep debate at that low level.

JH: Let's try to raise the level, then. Hostile critics have often linked the 'cultural heritage' position with the views of F.R. Leavis; Eagleton, for example, writing from a 'New Oxford Marxist' position, dismissed Leavis's work as just another 'illusion' of (Old Cambridge) liberal humanist criticism

(1983, p. 204). Yet Leavis actually offered a subtle account of the meaning of 'heritage' and of reading response, which can help to provide a meeting point between these either-or poles.

BH: Now you have introduced a formidable academic influence on English studies – in both schools and universities. And, to be fair, Leavis's achievement has been widely acknowledged, even by those who do not agree with all that he stood for. Andrew Goodwin's *English Teaching and Media Education* (1992), for example, drew attention to the 'force' of Leavis's and Thompson's *Culture and Environment* (1932), as a text which 'requires close attention' (p. 15); he noted the 'important, perhaps surprising point' – though you may not be surprised yourself, given your own views on media teaching (see Hodgson, in Harrison, 1983b) – that 'there is a real and living continuity between the ideas of *Culture and Environment* and present-day practice in the English class-room' (p. 16). Goodwin also recalled Masterman's point (1985, Chapter 3), that the challenge of Leavis and Thompson was disregarded by the literary establishment of that time. Leavis (author of the 'This is so, isn't it? Yes, but...' formula) received no answer from them. There is a Leavisian principle, too, behind Edwin Webb's claim (1992, p. 148) that 'Literature in education must be approached as an art' and that, as art, 'literature does *not* constitute a body of knowledge, but rather a means by which one comes to *know*' (original emphasis).

JH: We saw, in the early 1990s, how Masterman's point about a patronising establishment still holds true. The version of 'heritage' that was held by those who compiled the 1993 booklists – such as John Marenbon (who, until 1993, led the SEAC English Committee) – was *pre*-Leavisian. It assumed that 'great texts' are, unquestionably, great. They were to be traditionally hallowed as such because of their self-evident value, which needs no further justification. They need merely to be read accurately, for their meaning to be transmitted to the reader.

BH: So what we all thought was an old, dead quarrel, buried since the late 1960s under the new earth of post-structuralist deconstruction and feminist criticism, has been exhumed today by government policy. Marenbon is married to Sheila Lawlor, deputy director of the Conservative-led Centre for Policy Studies. He joined other government choices such as David Pascall (who was in Margaret Thatcher's policy unit) and Lord Griffiths of Fforestfach, in the campaign to press for more rigid standards of spelling, grammar and standard English. But Marenbon went further and campaigned for his own version of the 'tradition'. He listed Pope's *Epistle to Dr. Arbuthnot*, Milton's *Lycidas* and Dryden's *The Cock and the Fox* among the top ten books that children should read by the age of sixteen.

Certainly, those attacks in *Scrutiny* and elsewhere, on what Leavis then called the 'Oxford habit', carry fresh force now:

> the very conception of what a literature is, and of how as a living reality it exists is at issue...Everyone knows the reasons given...'the literatures are complete' – that is, finished; 'all the rules are known'.
>
> (F.R. Leavis, 1969, p. 17)

Q.D. Leavis, of course, matched this polemic in her own attacks on the academic establishment – as in her dry account of how the classicist George Gordon, through 'cannily directed industry', secured the Oxford Chair of English Literature, and who declared that to take literature seriously was 'an affront to life' (quoted in Q.D. Leavis, 1968, pp. 8-9).

JH: Yes; the *Scrutiny* team held notions about 'relevance' and 'engagement' in reading works of imagination that can contribute to the present debate. The issue is not *whether* we should read 'dead' or 'living' poets, but *how* we read them:

> It is only from the present, out of the present, in the present, that you can approach the literature of the past...it is only in the present that the past lives.
>
> (F.R. Leavis, 1969, p. 68)

BH: This was a principle that was carried into English teaching in secondary schools; many teachers saw no *essential* problem in matching Leavis's ideal of teaching with what they adopted as the best approach to, say, unstreamed classes in a London comprehensive school. They might, though, have shared two worries about Leavis, that Goodwin (1992) and others mentioned: his own adherence to an alleged past, pre-industrial 'organic community', and his stance on the 'elite minority'.

Webb, too, complained (1992, p. 42) about Leavis's 'partial and exclusive' selections for *The Great Tradition* (1948). It was not that Leavis subscribed to a cosy 'woodsy-birdsy' view of culture, nor that he was narrowly 'Cambridge-centred'. There is no doubt that his intention, in his slightly tongue-in-cheek reductions of choice for *The Great Tradition*, was to liberate students from sterile requirements to wade, uncritically, through masses of dead literature (which is quite different from literature by people who happen to be dead) and *belles-lettres*. And, if he was 'Cambridge-centred', he was certainly not narrowly anglocentric in his critical vision; he showed intelligent regard for crosscurrents in a whole range of writing – French, American, Russian and others. While a full account of the Scrutiny school would require investigation of these questions, they do not concern the essence of the *Scrutiny* challenge, which was to do with bringing a full heart, mind and body to engage with literature.

JH: *Scrutiny* argued that all the works of imagination in the literary tradition could not be taken for granted. Their critical search was, in the spirit of Matthew Arnold, for cultural expression as 'the best that has been thought and said'. They caused affront by *comparing* books, and finding that some within the 'canon' were better than others. Their school was characterised by challenge and incisive debate, since the claims of a text needed constantly to be 'scrutinised'. There was no shelf of 'safe' classics, on which 'right values' could be taken for granted.

For them, reading was not a matter of decoding the black marks on the page into fixed meanings; reading and analysis is a 'constructive or creative process' (Leavis, 1943). It involves interplay, and effort, between one's self and the world. In *The Living Principle* (1975) Leavis held that a poem is

> neither merely private, nor public in the sense that it can be brought into a laboratory, quantified, tripped over or even pointed to...it belongs to the 'Third Realm' – the realm of that which is neither public in the ordinary sense nor merely private.
>
> (p. 36)

This term, the 'third realm', has links with C.H. Waddington's definition (quoted in Bleich, 1978) of the 'third science', where scientists, like all observers of the world, recognise their place within their world. They therefore become 'incorporated into science'.

You have, yourself, discussed (Harrison, 1983a) how Leavis endorsed the phenomenological view of knowledge held by Michael Polanyi and Marjorie Grene. In rejecting a simple dichotomy between subjective and objective knowledge, Polanyi (1958, p. 59) wrote of knowing as 'in-dwelling'– of the mind-body lodging within the world, in order to realise it. Where imaginative works are concerned, this involves 'surrender' to works of art: 'this is neither to observe them nor handle them, but to live in them'.

BH: Yes; though that emphasis on being receptive does not, of course, imply that anything less than a full, critical intelligence is still at work. This point was made clear by David Best who showed, in *The Rationality of Feeling* (1992, p. 200) how, for Leavis, 'perceptive reasoning can give not just a richer understanding of feelings, but richer feelings. Without that rational understanding, one could not experience the feelings.'

You mentioned Waddington, and the world of science. Polanyi, of course, changed his academic Chair from mechanical engineering in order to investigate phenomenology. It is interesting, too, how theories from phenomenology have affected other areas of scientific thinking, such as psychology. Neil Bolton, for example, having written standard texts on cognition, moved beyond the framework of standard empirical psychology to write a phenomenological account of 'The Lived World' (1982).

John Teasdale and Philip Barnard combined clinical, experimental and theoretical approaches in their text on *Affect, Cognition and Change* (1993). Working at an interface between academic cognitive psychology and clinical therapy, they investigated patterns of feeling and thinking in depressive patients. They proposed a science-based version of holistic feeling processes, contrasting 'cold' (knowing in the head) and 'hot' (knowing in the heart) modes of thinking – all of which reflects, I suppose, what poets have claimed for many years about different modes of thinking.

JH: It is that *interrelation* between ('public') reason and ('private') feeling which is crucial, I think. To claim that reading books is an essentially personal, subjective and creative process (which it is) does not mean that it is a merely private activity, without responsibility or concern for other individuals, or for truth. For Polanyi, comprehension was neither arbitrary nor passive, but a responsible act. In his terms, the effort of knowing was guided by a 'sense of obligation to the truth'.

'Only connect...'– relevance and engagement in A-level English

BH: Let me build on what you are saying, about the need for students to be wholly involved in their own learning. We certainly agree about this, even though you are less suspicious than I, of the National Curriculum framework. We both work as moderators for the largest A-level English coursework syllabus in Britain. We saw this particular syllabus (AEB 660) flourish, as a direct result of its regard for both teachers and students, in the choosing and handling of texts. I was drawn into it in its early, experimental phase as long ago as the late 1970s (when I had almost given up hope that a really interesting English A-level syllabus could be devised).

Post-16 English studies were not restrained by the 1990 National Curriculum framework, and continued to develop in interesting ways. The scope and success of AEB 660, for example, were well documented in Buckroyd and Ogborn (1992). However, the Schools Curriculum Assessment Authority (SCAA) insisted that, from 1996, no A-level English literature syllabuses may contain more than 20 per cent coursework – a severe reduction from 50 per cent for this syllabus.

Inevitably, the very success of this and similar developments attracted criticism, notably from Tom Healy, Chair of the University Council for English, and Martin Dodsworth, Chair of the English Association, who wrote, in a letter in 1990 to all MPs and Heads of University English Departments, spelling out the dangers of this and other reformed syllabuses: 'If schoolchildren are not taught to read great books, the consequence will be an erosion of our national culture.'

We would say that he is right to want to defend the provision of books of quality in all stages of school/college learning, though he may have been misguided about the *means* by which students, even at A-level, may be led into independent reading. We should want students to feed their imagination on a wide diet of books, but not to be force-fed on an over-restricted diet of texts whose 'greatness' is not to be questioned. "SHOW me, don't tell me!', Brecht used to advise his players; similarly, students need to be shown, through sensitive teaching, the 'relevance' of literature and, in turn, need to show evidence of their own genuine 'engagement' with their chosen books. Having received a kind invitation from the Council for University English to give an account of new approaches to English literature A-level syllabuses, I explained that we aimed, above all, to involve students in full imaginative reflection on their literature course. I mentioned some innovations in the new syllabuses; for example, a greater emphasis on the work of women poets, dramatists and prose writers, and texts from the great body of English-speaking writers – Asian, Afro-Caribbean, Canadian, Australian, American – as well as key literary works in translation (what 19th-century writer in English, for example, was writing as Ibsen did?).

These were to be seen as *extending*, not replacing, more traditional choices of texts. We found that this fresh approach to choosing texts helped to achieve just the kind of wider reading among students that the Chair of the Council was recommending. This has been matched by fresh approaches to teaching; it is now fairly standard practice, for example, in a number of syllabuses for students to select their own texts – with advice from their teachers – for part, at least, of their coursework.

Such freedom fosters, above all, imaginative engagement, since students can at last take their own directions, informed by their experience of 'set' texts and by tutorial advice. Having, for example, discovered issues of importance in Doris Lessing's writing, they might pursue these further through a study of Nadine Gordimer's or Toni Morrison's fiction; or they might move from a study of Seamus Heaney's poetry (such as *North*) to consider how attitudes to language and culture in Brian Friel's play *Translations* might illuminate Heaney's own language, metaphors and perspective on Ireland.

The great majority of university English teachers with whom I discussed these approaches – at that meeting, and since then – welcomed them. There have been dissident voices, however: 'How can all this possibly dovetail into my first-year lectures?' complained one irritated don. There was also an occasion when, following inaccurate criticism of our syllabus in *The Sunday Telegraph, The Independent* and elsewhere, I was invited by the BBC *Today* programme to explain why there were no Shakespeare texts set on the syllabus. Having agreed that there was more Shakespeare, in fact, than in other A-level syllabuses, we moved on swiftly to a friendly discussion of Grace Nichols' poetry.

One of the most pleasing aspects of working with teachers on these approaches was to hear how they had, through renewed extensive reading of a much wider range of texts, regenerated their own imaginative thinking. 'It is a sad thing to admit', confessed an experienced teacher of English to me, 'That I had virtually given up reading for pleasure. It was either the treadmill of *Paradise Lost* Books 1 and 2 for the umpteenth time, or switching on the television'. This teacher, however, *still* continues to teach Milton, Chaucer and (sometimes) Spenser; the difference is, that she chooses these whenever she feels confident that there is something in them that will be *important* to young students, not because it is 'set' and must therefore be 'done'. Above all she has become skilled in seeking out what Edmund Wilson termed the 'shock of recognition' amongst her students, when their vital imagination has been quickened by what they read.

What we choose to call 'English' or 'British' culture is, of course, the product of an enormous variety of influences around the world. Therefore, there is every reason why the imaginative lives of people who live in Britain should be correspondingly worldwide. The awesome range of influences on Shakespeare's own imagination must surely explain his greatness. It should be no surprise, then, that *Hamlet* may come to life for students, not just by studying (or even acting out) the text, but by studying *beyond* the text. For example, a class that has been studying the appalling handling of Ophelia, by her family and by Hamlet himself (I'll loose my daughter to him', says Polonius, as though he were arranging for the siring of a brood mare) might be invited to compare her plight with that of the frail equestrienne in Franz Kafka's remarkable two-sentence short story, *Up in the Gallery* (which will be examined in a discussion on learning, in Chapter 4 of this book). Kafka's despairing portrayal of the passive equestrienne, first bullied by a ruthless whip-flourishing ringmaster, then (in the second sentence) more subtly manipulated by him as he 'comes towards her breathing animal devotion', can help to compel renewed engagement with Shakespeare's text, and his presentation, not only of Ophelia but of Gertrude too (see also Harrison, 'A Sense of Worth: Seven Days with *Hamlet*', 1984).

For a teacher in, say, a London tertiary college or a Birmingham comprehensive school, where many English A-level students may have a wide range of ethnic and cultural links, the students themselves may propose interesting links between apparently quite different kinds of texts. For example, one A-level student, studying Thomas Hardy's *Tess of the d'Urbervilles*, made her class sit up by introducing selections from Grace Nichols' poem 'i is a long memoried woman' (1989) into the context of 19th-century rural England:

We the women making
Something from this
Ache- and- pain-in -a -me
Back – o – hardness...
Who voices go unheard
Who deaths they sweep
Aside
As easy as dead leaves...

Gaps of distance and time between these texts are magically closed, as students revisualise their sense of Tess's plight at Flintcomb Ash, in the light of Nichols's poem of sorrow and social criticism on behalf of generations of women.

Issues of 'relevance' and 'engagement' in studying A-level literary texts were discussed by Harrison and Mountford (1992); this study included accounts of varying success in attracting the imaginative engagement of students, who were engaged on the coursework-based syllabus that we moderate. One of these concerned a class lesson on Trevor Griffiths' play *Comedians*, in a college which had developed interesting programmes in 'guided learning', rather than relying exclusively on traditional teacher-directed sessions. Students had been given a study guide to the text, twenty-five pages long, to support their independent studies (this was one of many such guides in current use in the department). In this particular lesson, however, the teacher's special task was to 'launch' the text.

After a five-minute introduction, the teacher engaged the class in discussion of what constitutes comedy; all students became intently involved in this. They listened to points made by other students, and there was much hilarity as examples of humour and kinds of comedy were exchanged. Students mentioned the recent ascendance of notable women comedians, absurd humour, 'black' comedy, situation comedy, unfunny humour and so on, all of which the teacher promised would be further examined in their study of the text. Satirical comedy was specially examined, as was the comedian Lenny Henry's view, that comedy should *challenge*. There was candid, sensitive examination of racist and sexist jokes, and other 'bad taste' areas. One Asian student spoke about the scarcity, in her view, of Asian humour, and about what she found to be sometimes offensive British-made examples that have been produced, even in texts approved by some 'liberals', such as *My Beautiful Launderette* and *My Mate Shofiq*. The teacher also introduced some classic versions of comedy – Aristophanes, Plautus, the Italian Commedia dell'Arte, and Shakespearian comedy – to provide a wider historical focus to the discussion. This lesson was a model of how to 'make connections' among the flow of imaginative contributions from both the teacher and her students. After the lesson, students declared that they had thoroughly enjoyed the hour; it had given them a rich range of ideas for thinking about comedy, and they were looking forward to studying the text. They said it was easy to talk and argue in this class; the opinions of all were felt to be valued, yet they could also be challenged. Students enjoyed the varying pace and activities of these lessons, which might involve a study of (say) a poem by Bertholt Brecht or Wole Soyinka on one day, or a passage by Brigitte Bardot about animal abuse on another occasion. The teacher was praised, especially, for her 'good ideas' and because she was 'interested in what we've got to say – even when it's a bit over the top.'

The modest-enough changes in choices of text and of teaching approach that quietly took place on many English literature A-level syllabuses in the 1980s did not change the essential *nature* of good English teaching at this level; they did, however, provide more *opportunities* for good teaching to happen. A teacher might, for example, choose the right moment to tell an A-level class about William Stafford's seven-line poem 'Vacation' (1963, pp. 105–6 – see end of this chapter), where he sits with an elegant companion in the dining car of a trans-American express train. While he pours the coffee, he looks out of the window, and sees a huddle of Navajo Indians burying one of their dead alongside the railtrack. The scene rushes by...he pours the cream.

This imperfect, second-hand recollecton of the poem led to a remarkable piece of collaborative work from two of my own A-level students, in pre-coursework days, who tracked the poem and the poet down, then moved on to 'discover' Carl Sandburg and Emily Dickinson, too.

At that time, this uncommon initiative could receive no credit on the A-level course that those students were following; it is entirely right that we have learned, now, to incorporate such enterprise into the syllabus.

As for the 'classics', Shakespeare, Pope and Austen *can* still speak for themselves, as long as their readers are genuinely engaged – attentive, agile, interrogating, above all, self-motivated – in their studies. They then become an imaginative, as well as literate generation, able to gain profit and pleasure from reading and from all the other arts.

Imaginative engagement with Wordsworth

I seemed to draw from a sense of inward joy, of sympathetic and imaginative pleasure, which could be shared with all human beings...Wordsworth taught me a greatly increased interest in the common feelings and common destiny of human beings.

(J.S. Mill quoted in Drabble, 1966, p. 148)

We know, from our work as moderators, that a student does not have to be an academic 'high-flier' in literary studies, in order to find enrichment in any classic that makes a *personal impact* on the student-reader. A whole-hearted *engagement* with the text, and inescapable sense of its *relevance* can raise the quality of response well beyond usual 'standards' of work.

Whether students choose to write about fiction and autobiography by Black American women writers; or 17th/18th-century satire; or the poetry of Emily Dickinson and of Emily Bronte; or the drama of Ibsen/ Chekhov/Brecht; or the poetry and prose of Grace Nichols; or Shakespeare's tragic heroes/heroines; or revenge/madness/homosexuality as literary themes; or comparing Athol Fugard and Gcina Mhlophe, as male and female voices in the theatre of South Africa; or two or three selected works of Dickens: all of these choices, when they reflected some genuine interest of the student, often produce work of unexpected high quality.

To turn to Wordsworth, and our earlier discussion of Leavis: I recall that, when he died in 1978, Q.D. Leavis kindly sent me an off-print of his paper on 'Wordsworth: The Creative Conditions' (published in America, 1971). She wrote, 'He was very productive in his old age, and I like best of all the [Wordsworth] lecture...one seems to get very close to him in this lecture, and to hear the sound of his unique voice.' The 'voice' here had none of the cut-and-thrust of some of his more famous critical battles; yet it *was* characteristic of him, in its sensitivity to Wordsworth's own poetic tone. Seeking to understand Wordsworth's creativity, and to explain its decline, Leavis took, as his starting point in this paper, Shelley's caricature of Wordsworth in 'Peter Bell the Third'. This, he suggested, was 'the criticism of Wordsworth that I have most use for', since it provides a dramatic contrast between Wordsworth's and Shelley's own, quite different kind of imagination –

> He had as much Imagination
> As a pint-pot

– claimed Shelley, following this with the crucial tribute,

> Yet his was individual mind

Leavis then moved to a study of 'The Ruined Cottage', where he was struck by its 'disturbing immediacy'; he provides a detailed and typically sophisticated examination of this 'poignant disturbingness', revealing at the same time a strongly personal engagement with these issues:

> But the trauma is there; even if it were possible in the country to escape the spectacle of the 'wretchedness' from which the Wanderer does *not* 'turn aside with coward fears', the 'painful pressure', the compulsion to 'feed on disquiet' is there.

> (p. 338)

The 'urgent personal problem' with which Wordsworth wrestles leads, Leavis suggested, to a decisive 'alteration of expression', which characterises his greatness as a poet. Leavis, as an eminent critic who must confront (and not over-simplify) that greatness, must find the art (and courage) to do so on *personal* terms – just as you show that your A-level student, at *her* level, had to do. Criticism can never be just a technical business; it involves the whole person. While Leavis held to some ideal of an 'organic community', he also confronted, in this study of Wordsworth, the understandable human temptation to seek for 'comforting' thoughts, in order to escape from pain. It might be recalled, after all, that he witnessed the full horrors of the First World War, as an ambulance attendant.

Sian's exploration of Wordsworth; by John Hodgson

The point made above, about engaging the personal life of the student, provides a focus for my account of Sian's encounter with Wordsworth.

What teaching should encourage, in the light of Polanyi's formulation about 'in-dwelling' (mentioned earlier), is a *subjective awareness* of the text. It is a response which is affective and individual, but which must also involve intelligence, and an attempt to contemplate the text in its full, unique form. The only response to a text that can be of value is a first-hand one; if the student is to experience 'relevance' and 'engagement' with the text, the student must be able to relate it to the living present.

This is what, in lived experience, the literary tradition means – the body of texts which, together, has meaning, in relation to one another and to the reader, *for* that reader. The 'tradition' cannot be *confined*, by Marenbon or his successors, to an established canon of texts; nor, at another extreme, can texts be *excluded* from the 'tradition', by those who may disagree with the 'establishment' view, through 'politically correct' allegations that they represent the views of (for example) dead or middle-aged white males. It is the reader, not even the teacher – and certainly not the government – who decides eventually on the 'relevance' or otherwise of a text.

I want, now, to illustrate this through reference to an A-level student's writing about Wordsworth. It would be hard to imagine a more 'canonical' author than Wordsworth, nor one who is more routinely castigated – even by A-level chief examiners – as having little to say to modern adolescents. Yet Wordsworth is surely our greatest thinker on the Imagination. He has, in my own experience, made a powerful impact on many students; in particular, *The Prelude* and some of his earlier poems came to mean a good deal to Sian.

I taught the first two books of *The Prelude* as a coursework text during the first year of a two-year A-level course, with a group of nine students (five male, four female). Within weeks of starting the course, I was made aware of a particular intensity in the atmosphere of the class, especially among those on one table occupied by female students. This hard-working group included Sian, who was already eighteen – two years older than the other students – when the course began; she had already completed a rather unsuccessful A-level course in modern languages. Eventually she gained a C grade in English.

Sian was clearly interested right from the start in Wordsworth. When the time came to discuss topics for the long essay (a literary enquiry, with the topic chosen by the student, of some 3,000 to 5,000 words, prepared as independent work by the student, under tutorial supervision) she chose to explore Wordsworth further. As with all the students, I discussed with her where her centre of interest lay. Was it in Wordsworth's philosophy? In his response to nature? In himself? The latter option seemed closest to her interest; she said that she had been struck by my remark, made by the way, that Wordsworth's later verse was generally regarded as inferior to his earlier, and that conjectures might be made about relating this to events in his life and changes in his feelings.

After further consultation over several weeks, she decided to try to trace Wordsworth's personal development through examining some of his poems. Her title was: 'The Development of William Wordsworth as Reflected in his Poetry'.

This title may appear to accentuate the 'life' rather than the 'work' of the poet. Yet it was the title that Sian and I agreed on, after much discussion on what she wanted to do, since her fundamental interest was, of course, in her own living. Her interest in Wordsworth was fuelled by this. Intuitively, she saw some parallels between Wordworth's experience and her own, which she wished to explore. The seriousness of this exploration would ensure that she paid close attention to the poetry.

I suggested that she should look at *Tintern Abbey, Resolution and Independence*, the *Immortality Ode* and the *Ode to Duty;* I also suggested Harold Bloom's *The Visionary Company* (1962), although she did not in fact consult this text.

The draft of Sian's essay was produced well ahead of schedule – half a term early. She had said nothing about her work while writing it, yet it was already well composed. Only the section on the *Ode to Duty* seemed weak, and I spent some minutes at the end of the lesson suggesting some aspects to this that I felt she might consider.

Her essay was ambitious; it aimed to explore, no less, Wordsworth's sense of the meaning of life, and the ways this changed between 1798 and 1805. She traced Wordsworth's personal development through commentaries on the poems, and dwelled on some ways in which the 'influence of natural objects' worked on and changed his feelings, between the writing of *Tintern Abbey* in 1798 and *The Ode to Duty* in 1805. Most striking was her close engagement with the subject; her writing conveyed an undeniable sense of personal urgency in her reading and writing, a need to comprehend what happened to Wordsworth – which was also a need to comprehend what has happened, is happening and will happen to her in *her own life*.

She began with *Tintern Abbey*, where she pointed out that the first lines of the poem, the 'long description of the scene around himself', emphasise:

> not the image of the scene, but what it means to him. It tells us what it meant to Wordsworth five years ago during his last visit when he was twenty-three, and what it means to him now; it is a projection of the poet's own mood.

Thus Sian established at the start of her essay that her interest is in Wordsworth's inner world. This was notable, since she had often communicated her own interest in nature as something 'out there'; she was an athlete, who had competed in the Dartmoor 'Ten Tors' competition, involving some tough walking and camping over several days in all kinds of weathers. However, Sian became immersed in the presence of nature in the *internal* world of the individual – of Wordsworth, and of herself:

> He does not try to describe the trees in the wood, the colour of the sky or the noise of the river; he is not painting a picture of the landscape...these elements are acting as a metaphor to describe the workings of his mind.

She recounts the way in which Wordsworth's recollections of the landscape 'seem to produce a somewhat therapeutic effect, as they bring "tranquil restoration" in "hours of weariness"'. She described his awareness, not of the nature around him, but of an inner force; reflecting that 'he seems more concerned for his inner feeling than for his bodily self', she quoted

> the breath of this corporeal frame
> And even the motion of our human blood
> Almost suspended, we are laid asleep
> In body, and become a living soul.

At this point, Sian introduced Wordsworth's sense of dilemma, that is central to the poem: his doubts about the powers of nature to reveal meaning. Quoting 'If this/Be but a vain belief...', she comments:

> Wordsworth may just mean by this that his visionary experiences do not derive from the Wye valley, but he may further mean that he is unsure of whether he is right, to think that these experiences really do allow him to 'see into the life of things'.

Sian reflects on this problem throughout her essay. Wordsworth's increasing doubts about the meaning he had derived from nature, and his attempts to overcome these. She comments on *Resolution and Independence*:

> 'As happy as a boy': Wordsworth contemplates spontaneous delight in nature, like that of a child. As he walks, he forgets all his troubles, and we witness the restorative power of nature at work, banishing the distresses of life...but he is suddenly hit by sadness and gloom for no apparent reason.

It is at this point that Wordsworth meets the leech-gatherer, on whose description Sian comments:

> Wordworth uses images, 'huge stone' and 'sea-beast crawled forth', which make this old man at once part of the landscape, a natural, almost inanimate object, yet at the same time an object alive with wonder and mystery.

The old man's appearance suggests great suffering, yet 'an exceptional strength somehow comes across, which has a great influence on Wordsworth himself'. As the poet studies the leech-gatherer, wrote Sian, he

> believes that he can adopt the human strength from the leech-gatherer...the insight into the old man's way of life which Wordsworth seeks comes, not from what the old man says about himself, but from Wordsworth's own *imagination*. He sees the leech-gatherer as having great strength of spirit and firmness of mind. The old man has become a symbol of human endurance. Wordsworth believes that his memory of the leech-gatherer will sustain him in future years, during times of depression and doubt.

Interwoven with this account of the development of a poet's imagination is Sian's consistent preoccupation with her own changing feelings, as in a revealing comment on the *Immortality Ode:* 'at first, the poem appears to be about childhood, but it is in fact about the death of childhood and the loss of joy'.

'In order to understand how to live'

When Sian had finished her A-level course, and before she went on to college (in the Lake District), I told her about my contribution to this book and asked her to write about her experience of A-level English. The long letter that she wrote some weeks later had a far stronger 'personal' than 'academic' preoccupation:

> Previous to studying Wordsworth, I had spent two holidays in the Lake District. One was an activity holiday and the other a sight-seeing tour. The sheer beauty of the total countryside could hardly be overlooked, but still they were just holidays. My third visit was last year, after having studied *The Prelude*.

At this point of the letter, Sian dwelled with might seem like simple effusion on the familiar tourist indulgences of Wordsworth devotees:

> During these short two weeks, I was in an ecstatic state of inspired appreciation of my whole surroundings...To walk around his home filled with his furniture, his clothes and even such personal items as toilet bags, pencil boxes and locks of hair was so very exciting. But the beautiful love letters beween himself and Mary Hutchinson and his own ice skates were my most memorable sight...I was filled with delight as *The Prelude* and other poems were brought to life.

Yet this disclosure suggests more than the simple enthusiasms of a Wordsworth admirer; the personal identification here is strong.

Later in her letter, Sian discloses more openly her latent feelings about the parent-like security which she found in 'natural objects', and the difficulty of accepting the separation of ourselves from the 'inanimate cold world' (to use Wordsworth's phrases). Both Wordsworth's parents had died by the time he reached his early teens; Sian's own father left home when she was a young child, and her mother became, as she put it, her 'whole world'. This sense of parental security was inevitably disrupted with the passage of time and adolescent growth. The rupture was sharpened when Sian found a boyfriend in her late teens, of whom her mother did not approve:

> we stayed at my grandparents one weekend, during which I shared a room with Mum. The hurt was already known to me – that she was wholly against my love for Rob. But these feelings were forced to remain cooped up inside myself; never did I feel allowed to show any signs of love and happiness, because they were externally unwelcome. My crying prompted much sympathetic care and love from Mum, until she found the reason... 'The World' was now angered; Mum means so much to me that she is my whole world.

While admitting her strong feelings of dependency upon her mother, Sian is equally aware of her growing need to express her sexuality in ways which her mother does not approve. Conflict is inevitable. Faced with a not dissimilar problem the loss of parents on whom he depended – Wordsworth turned to nature, and found that he could be sustained by a feeling transferred from his parents to natural objects:

> The props of my affection were removed,
> And yet the building stood, as if sustained
> By its own spirit!

In response to the difficulty with her mother, Sian found a similar sense of comfort in the natural world:

> I learned the way in which Wordsworth outlined his life and thoughts and feelings in relation to the natural world surrounding him. He acquired a precious comforting happiness through nature. I turned towards nature; I turned to this beauty, this tranquillity of the natural world around me, for nurturing and comfort.

At this point, her letter recorded a moving account of a Spring walk, where she reflects on the meanings she found in nature at that time:

> On one such occasion last Spring, my mood was solemn and self-pitying. One thing I despise is self-pity, and so I searched for comfort. Once again I was upset about Rob; all the ill-feeling shadowing our happiness. I went for a walk towards our water-well, along the backway, where an abundance of flowers covered either side of my walkway. There were single- and double-petalled flowers, and it soon became clear to see that this abundance of flowering beauties was not one huge mass of beauty, but a huge congregation of individual pleasures. If one were to see a crowd of people in front of them, one would certainly regard that crowd as a congregation of individual personalities; surely those snowdrops hold the same, unspoken request for individuality...I composed a short verse, while I spoke my sorrows to those uplifted, comforting faces:
>
> > Snowdrop, you prove with such gracious elegance
> > How pleasure and passion attribute to existence.
> > It is the same with a kiss;
> > Something absolute yet so simple,
> > Grows with an intention to disclose itself
> > As a passionate but most vulnerable desire: love.
>
> Perhaps some would see my beautification of a snowdrop as exaggerated, and even talking to them as madness; but my soul was comforted with a strange compassion. Surely that's all that really matters?

Sian's letter could hardly provide a more eloquent case for the value to her of having studied Wordsworth. Through him, she could explore her own separation and loss, the finding of compensatory objects in nature, and the confronting of fears of the future, when growth into maturity may bring a deeper, more permanent sense of aloneness. These are, I suggest, abiding themes in human life, and explain the powerful sense of connection that Sian felt with Wordsworth's poetry. It is the need to *understand how to live* that drove Sian's academic study. In order to manage her own life well, she educated her imagination, with Wordsworth as her chosen literary intermediary.

Concluding reflection

BH: Sian's identification with her world, expressed without sophisticated explanation yet wholeheartedly, reflects the philosophical standpoint of Hannah Arendt (1978), who wrote that 'living beings...are not just in the world, they are *of the world*, and this precisely because they are subjects and objects – perceiving and being perceived – at the same time' (p. 20). Arendt also goes on to comment, in a spirit that teachers – especially teachers of poetry – might commend:

> Nothing perhaps is more surprising in this world of ours than the almost infinite diversity of its appearances, the sheer entertainment value of its views, sounds, and smells, something that is hardly ever mentioned by the thinkers and philosophers.
>
> (p. 20)

– nor, it may be added, does this feature in unimaginative teaching. Clearly, John's own teaching approach *did* give room for this – which is why Sian thought she owed him the letter that she sent from college.

Her disclosure of how she finds her urgent personal need reflected in Wordsworth's own need for meaning – through relationship echoes, in a sense, the complex relationship that the poet had with his sister Dorothy. It was she, claimed Wordsworth, who 'gave him eyes and gave him ears'; as Drabble (1966), Clark (1960) and others have noted, she provided him with direct inspiration, both through her own life with him and (though less acknowledged by him), through the record of their lives that she kept in her own highly accomplished journals.

Some fascinating links between the personal journals and the published work of authors are discussed in Chapter 6. For the present, I simply comment on the remarkable literary symbiosis, between Dorothy and William. I can think of no other example, where a great writer's journal was virtually recorded by someone else – and written so well, as to be an art-form in its own right; and it does seem to be in the celebration of diversity and specific details that she was able to inspire her brother, as well as sharing his more abstract thinking.

The fact that hers is so emphatically *domestic* a journal indicates, perhaps, much of the nature of Wordsworth's need for her; the famous 'tranquillity' associated with their lives was not cheaply gained. He produced his great poetry at a cost – to himself, through his inner conflict and imaginative struggle; and to her, in his dependence on both her personal support and also her accompanying imaginative vision. He was, in short, less 'alone' in his search than he sometimes claimed – though (as with Sian, no doubt) he clearly *felt* alone.

Given our preoccupations here with poetry and the imagination, it is appropriate to close this chapter with a poem. In the lines that she composed for inclusion in her letter, Sian wrote of the eloquence she found in the simplicity of a snowdrop or a kiss, which 'grows with an intention to discover itself'. This commemorates the poignancy of realisation, at the moment where perception is shaped through metaphor, in what the painter Paul Klee experienced as 'the sap that flows through the artist and through his eye'. That 'sap' infuses William Stafford's art, in the poem referred to earlier in this chapter:

> One scene as I bow to pour her coffee:–
> Three Indians in the scouring drouth
> huddle at a grave scooped in the gravel.
> lean to the wind as our train goes by...
> ...I pour the cream.

> (from 'Vacation', by William Stafford, 1963, pp. 105–6)

CHAPTER 3

Using Metaphor

This chapter considers metaphor-making in language, imagination and learning. It considers:

- the learner's drive to *'connect'*;
- metaphor as reflecting a *living world*, which is still in the making;
- metaphor as *creative play;*
- distinctions between *literal, non-literal and metaphoric language;*
- the uses of metaphor in *connecting and contrasting;*
- *personal negotiation* in learning;
- metaphor and *good teaching*;
- metaphor and *wit*.

> The Secret of the Universe has been solved; it is made of small black holes.
> (News item, BBC Radio 4 *Today*, 18 November 1993)

An account of a dream is chosen to open this chapter on the place of metaphor and imagination in learning. The writer is an experienced art teacher, engaged in postgraduate educational studies; the writing was prepared as a 'term paper' for a course on The Teaching of Writing (directed by Lucy Calkins, University of Columbia, NY). The dream reflects this student's recent adventures into computing and word-processing, in ways which may illuminate the discussion to follow, on metaphor-making in language, imagination and learning.

Make Suns, by Muriel Rubin

Last night I had a dream – one of those exhausting dreams when every escape route turns into a 'cul de sac'. In my dream I was at a conference, a teachers' conference. I was standing in the middle of a vast, loft-like room and on my one side there were groups of teachers: some were writing, some were thinking, some were talking, some were reading aloud to others. They all had pens, pencils, papers, folders and piles of books and photocopies stapled together. Above the polite hum of voices I could make out a number of words and phrases: 'share', 'voice', 'audience', 'peer conference', 'error analysis'. Then a kind of chorus started, first soft and intermittent but then louder and louder as it drowned the general hum and humbug. 'Process... process... process... process... process... process... PROCESS... PROCESS.' The more the word was repeated the less sense it made, so I tried to escape to the other side of the loft where I could see a colourful group of people who seemed to be very busy. They were certainly a funny lot but, being a dream, the fact that some of them had arms growing out of their heads did not strike me as being at all odd.

Most of them were smiling as they worked, if you could call it work. They were printing and painting and sticking and cutting and all of them were making suns – suns of every shape and size, smiling, shining suns, sad suns, sulky suns, suns everywhere – even carved on the floor and suspended from the ceiling. As they finished they began to talk. What were they saying? I moved closer and to my surprise they were saying the same word, slower and softer and less insistent, but the same word, process. Well, if they were saying the same thing why not get the two groups together?

Now I knew what I had to do, why I was there. I rushed up to a rounded collage-like teacher, all texture and muted colours, I pulled her across to the other side towards an animated, trim teacher surrounded by papers and photocopies and videos. 'Lucy, this is Arlette. Guess what? She's also talking about process.' Then I grabbed a puzzled man and rushed him from the writing people to the painting people. The dream became more and more fantastic and confused as I tried to mix the smiling, colourful teachers with the talking, writing teachers. Then I had an idea. I picked up all the art materials, the chaos of colour and bits and pieces and shiny things and I dumped them in the middle of the writing group. 'Make suns,' I said. As they all rushed and pushed and scrambled to get to the pens and scissors and tape...I woke up.

Commenting on the dream, the writer suggested that it illustrates how, 'in an age of specialisation, I inhabit – or rather have temporary lodgings – in two worlds, the art world and the writing world'. Muriel wonders whether she is more 'fragmented' than her fellow students, but finds that her dream is, above all, about wanting to *connect*, to 'get across to both worlds, summed up in my dream by "Lucy, meet Arlette"'.

It would be clumsy to dismiss such a dream as an 'illusion', even though it may seem unclear and ambiguous. N. Wade, in *Visual Allusions* (1990, p.vii), distinguished between visual illusion ('when a genuine mistake is made; the moon appears to move when clouds pass by it') and visual allusion (which involves, as with a literary allusion, 'the perception of at least two aspects of the world simultaneously'). In his comprehensive account of the creative possibilities of visual allusions, Wade suggested that an essential aspect of allusion is that some degree of ambiguity should be embedded in the meaning.

Muriel's willingness to explore various worlds together, through narrating her dream, produces a kind of 'metafiction', where worlds become a book, or film, or other form of story. The term 'metafiction' was introduced by the critic-novelist William H. Gass (1970). It has, suggested Patricia Waugh (1984, p. 2), been widely applied since then, to address 'the problem of how human beings reflect, construct or mediate their experience of the world'. The role taken by Muriel in her dream allows her to explore her own subjectivity; her dream supplies imagery and language, for use in revising or reconstructing her personal 'reality', through fictional play.

This account reveals a close, 'con-fused' engagement between visual imagery (the writer was trained as a painter) and the language that she must use as a writer. She wants to represent, and re-present, her metafictive version of her world; but, in doing so, she risks entering the 'prison-house' (to use Waugh's term) of sedimented language, where metaphor is no longer in play, and which can only be analysed *through* language. Yet Muriel's account raises a fascinating possibility, that language may act as a direct, iconic reflection of the world (which would challenge Saussure's influential view of language as a system of arbitrary signs).

This would illustrate Landsberg's point, made in 'Iconic Aspects of Language: the Imitation of Nonlinguistic Reality' (1986, p. 321), that 'the linguistic symbols exchanged during the actual communicative event probably carry some deictic reference to their situational context' (that is, words may be less arbitrary signs than Saussure allowed). The interplay between sense experience and verbal reflection depends particularly on vision, since 'the information we gather about the world around us by our various senses reaches us in the following proportions: 12% by touch, smell and taste combined, 13% by hearing, and 75% by sight' (p. 321). This dependance on vision may, of course, be explained by the relentless cultural pressures, in what the poet Eugenio Montale (1976) criticised as 'our new, entirely visual civilisation' (p. 21); the possibility, in learning, of extending sense experiences to all senses will be explored in Chapter 9.

As Proust's famous madeleine cake revealed, much more than visual experience may be involved, of course, in the illumination of a dream, vision, memory or any experience. Rimbaud's words, used by Britton in his setting of *Les Illuminations* (1940), convey the complex mingling of many forms of experience, that make up the whole vision:

DÉPART. Assez vu. La vision s'est rencontrée à tous les airs.
Assez eu. Rumeurs des villes, le soir, at au soleil, et toujours.
Assez connu. Les arrêts de la vie – O Rumeurs et Visions!
Départ dans l'affection et le bruit neufs.

(DEPARTURE: Enough seen. The vision re-encountered in all its aspects.
Enough heard. Rumours from towns in the evening, in the sunlight, and at all
times.
Enough known. Life's decrees – what rumours, what visions!
Leaving amongst love and new sounds.)

Muriel's account of her dream nicely illustrates the many aspects –
including sense and memory – of dream-vision that Rimbaud includes. It
reveals, too, a number of key issues concerning metaphor in language,
imagination and learning, which will be the main focus for this chapter.
These include: metaphor as creative play; as the most 'concrete' means
we have of rendering the world in words; as a process of connecting and
contrasting; as a positive 'confusion' of feelings and ideas; as an aid in
personal negotiation in learning; and as 'truth-telling'.

Imagining – a childish phenomenon?

Please interpret the statement 'Children are snowflakes'.

(Gregory, 1993, p. 7)

Monica Gregory's study of metaphor comprehension attempted to
define, in scientific terms, whether metaphor comprehension requires
different thinking strategies from those involved in understanding 'literal
truth'. She reached no clear conclusion on this question; yet it is common to regard metaphoric activity as more elusive, original – and, perhaps, less 'trustworthy' – than more prosaic, 'truthful' accounts of experience. Definitive studies of the imagination – such as those, for example, by Ricoeur (1977) and Romanyshyn (1982) – emphasised that without the imaginal life, sometimes dismissed in the past as a childish or
'primitive' phenomenon that is confined in adult life 'only' to poets and
painters, there would be no truth, no reality, no meaning. The capacity
for imagination involves the power to create metaphor through which, to
recall a formulation by T.S. Eliot, we 'dislocate language into meaning'.

The displacement discerned by Eliot, from sedimented forms of language (where meanings are fixed) to new forms of expression, is crucial
in language and learning development. Ricoeur's book *La Métaphore
Vive* (1975) was translated with the not quite appropriate title, *The Rule
of Metaphor* (1978), since it showed how the metaphoric use of language
becomes attuned to a living world. In the life of this world, reality itself
is unfinished; it is continually in the making, shaped by all those who use
language as a living power. Ricoeur suggests elsewhere (1991, p. 462),
in a reflection on the creativity of language, that 'language in the making
celebrates reality in the making'.

Writing on these two versions of language in a study of 'Semantics and Ontology', Wheelwright (1972) defined 'block', 'steno' or 'literal' language as language that has no semantic fluidity, and which conforms to strict conventions of both expression and meaning. By contrast, 'fluid' language is capable of semantic variation, allowing interplay between meaning and expression, involving irony, humour and shifts of tonal qualities.

The difference between these two versions, is semantic, not ontological. It is to do with ways in which language relates to the world – as a predetermined, clichéd response, or else in a probing, wondering play of enquiry. Block language is, in fact, sedimented fluid language; and metaphor is to fluid language as the concept (a term from logic) is to block language. For daily living, of course, we need both versions. Without one, there would be no reliable framework for discourse; without the other, discourse – and life itself – would be a dreary series of repetitions.

Metaphor, then, is not just the 'virtual truth' that Suzanne Langer (1953) acknowledged; it is the only vehicle for new forms of meaning, or truth. Metaphor is thought, when we grant that thought covers an even wider field of activity than terms such as 'cognition' or 'reasoning' might imply. In an essay on 'Metaphor', Middleton-Murray (1972) invoked Nietzsche's view of (scientific) knowledge as the 'cemetery of perceptions'. This is not to be seen as a general rejection of science or knowledge; but it does require learners and teachers to distinguish between processes in learning (as the life being lived), compared to products of knowledge (as the life completed).

Consider, for example, this brief passage from the transcript of learning in process in a Birmingham classroom. Both children have 'special', but different needs in language development. Mazhar, a quiet, shy boy, has been asked to explain part of a lesson about gravity in the solar system to Adrian, whose command of English is limited, but who is determined to learn:

Mazhar: You see this little pathway?
Adrian: Yeah
Mazhar: Yeah... well... if there's no gravity to the sun... well... this planet should have gone Boom! Boom! Boom! An... and Earth would have gone crashing into Mercury... and Mercury should have gone Boom! Boom! into Venus..and Venus should have gone in... Boom!.. into Jupiter... if there was no gravity... and... and... that should have gone Boom! Boom! Boom! and all the planets should have gone like this... up in space.
Adrian [laughing]: Ah, No.

(quoted in Bakewell, 1986)

Mazhar's usual reserve vanishes, as he warms to the excitement of his topic. His dramatic account of planets colliding like ships in a fog is so effective that Adrian laughs in recognition of the power of gravity. Mazhar, the shy one, reveals rare qualities as teacher, and Adrian finds excitement and pleasure in learning.

Mazhar understands, indeed, what Norwottny (1962; quoted in Birch, 1989, p. 2) called the 'corporeality of words' and of the structures that connect them. Norwottny recognised how 'the various elements of poetic language interpenetrate one another with an intimacy which is of first importance in any consideration of how poetry "works"'. This, as Mazhar understood, also applies to the language of learning. Thus a classroom-based version of imagining demonstrates the principles that first, metaphor is an essential process by which the human mind discovers and confers meaning on the world, and second, since metaphor is a kind of 'play on words', conditions of play are essential within the structures of purposeful learning, if imaginative processes are to thrive.

The same is certainly true, too, of the need for a clear framework in learning. In the still recent wake, however, of a nationally imposed curriculum framework, it is the free and wayward flights of imagination that may need more space in learning, rather than even more emphasis on structures and 'quality control' through assessment.

The Czech research immunologist and poet Miroslav Holub is constantly preoccupied, in his poetry and prose reflections, by both the frailty and the power of the poetic imagination, in the face of 'official' versions of learning. In 'The Sick Primer' (1990, p. 45), he predicts that the 'primer' – which contains all the comfortable information about the world, but which 'isn't quite true' –

> may fall sick one day
> with what isn't quite true.

While 'wise men' may repair, 'bandage' and 'cover' the primer ('better a half-truth than nothing'), messages from information in the primer itself will eventually start a rebellion against its own clichés:

> but the primer
> will talk
> in its sleep,
>> don't believe in ghosts,
>> don't believe in plaster,
>> in eyes or in ears,
>> don't believe in words...
>> better a temporary nothing
>> than definitive half-truths...

When the 'wise men' repress the subversions of the primer (by translating it, for example, into a 'dead language'), the work of the pupils will once more become a comfortable, mindless routine:

> and children
> themselves
> will have to paint a dot,
> some will paint the sun
> some will draw a circle
> with compasses, for an alpha plus
> and the teacher will say
> I shall never get through
> testing and marking
> that lot.

Learners and teachers need the unpredictable, butterfly flight of metaphor in classroom discourse. Middleton-Murry (1972, p. 28) quoted Aristotle's ancient view, that metaphor consists of giving something a name that belongs to something else, and that it is the greatest achievement to be expert in its use:

> It is the one thing that cannot be learned from others, and it is also a sign of original genius, since a good metaphor implies the intuitive perception of similarity in dissimilars.

Metaphor and play in learning

In 'What is Poetry?' (1973), J.S. Mill distinguished between the imagery of poetry and that of rhetoric. He identified an essentially *'confessional'* quality in poetry, which embodies itself 'in symbols which are the nearest possible representative of the feeling in the exact shape in which it exists in the poet's mind'.

That is so, and it helps to explain why metaphor has the great power to move us; yet Mill's earnest emphasis on confession lacks the element of *play* that characterises original poetry, in even its most serious forms. The verses of King Lear's Fool may come to mind; or Donne's conceits; or Emily Dickinson's verbal conjuring; or the spare appreciation of life in Ezra Pound's haiku, 'In a station in the Metro':

> The apparition of these faces in the crowd,
> Petals on a wet, black bough.

(Collected Poems, 1968)

Hannah Arendt recognised, in *The Life of the Mind* (1978, Volume 1, pp. 104–6) that, while philosophy depends just as greatly as poetry on the 'frozen analogies' of metaphor, it is poetry that is most in tune with the essential dynamic function of metaphor; the poet requires metaphor to be *in play*.

The haiku by Ezra Pound commemorates a broad definition proposed by Evelyn Richards (1992, p. 2), that metaphor is:

an implicit comparison between things, including actions;

or

an implicit acknowledgement of similarity between them.

The word 'metaphor' is from the Greek *metaphora*, which is derived from *meta* (meaning 'over') and *pherein* (to carry). While there are various kinds of metaphor (including simile, synecdoche and metonymy, with further rhetorical refinements available), the essence of metaphor is to carry over, or transfer the qualities of one thing to another to another thing, in order to illuminate it in a new way. Metaphor is figurative, not literal language. The review that follows, of the value of verbal play, makes substantial reference to Eve Richards' interesting study (1992), of metaphor in learning and teaching.

Her work examined a range of theories on metaphor, from philosophy, language studies and psychology. While there were many uncertainties and disagreements among these, she identified six points of basic agreement, that:

- language can be used either literally or metaphorically and that we can generally tell which is which;
- metaphor is a more complex mode of speech than literal language;
- metaphor, in identifying one thing with another, implicitly brings out certain aspects of experience and plays down other aspects;
- metaphor says things which literal language may not be able to say and, what is more, says them succinctly, vividly and elegantly;
- because of its brevity and therefore its elliptical nature, a metaphor stays in our minds for some time; and the longer it stays the more we can see in it;
- for these and other reasons – see, for example, Verbrugge's account of the power of 'fantasy' (1980) – metaphor allows us to speculate about unknown things in new, often valuable ways.

Richards' own fieldwork study of metaphor in action, which examined how primary school teachers use metaphor in their classroom talk, led her to modify the first of these points. She found a third language category, 'not purely metaphorical, but not exactly literal either, which I call non-literal language' (p. 2). Since metaphor is a kind of irony, in which what is said is not to be taken at face-value, this third category of non-literal language is of use in describing a wide area of discourse, where we 'lift language above the one-to-one correspondence of word to thing, when we want to communicate something different from, yet necessary to, the statements that we are making' (p. 140).

When we use metaphor, Richards suggests,

> We are saying more and at the same time less than we do in literal speech: more, in that metaphor is always ironic, with a literal interpretation that is not true and a series of metaphorical interpretations that are true in different ways; less, because of what Black (in Johnson, 1981, p. 173) calls the 'filter effect'. This 'filter effect' means that, if we describe human life as a *pilgrimage*, we lessen the possibility of seeing it as, say, a prelude, an interlude, a struggle or a bed of roses; we are emphasising life as a journey and a search for the transcendent. (p. 97)

The relationship between literal and metaphoric language was, however, seen more as a unity by Rummelhart (1979), particularly as revealed in the speech of children. Rummelhart argued that when children choose a word from their wordstock to apply to a new experience, they follow a metaphoric process of transferring concepts from one domain, in order to illuminate another. In this way, language development and learning are integrated with metaphoric process. All parents and teachers would be able to add their own examples of this to the one provided by my own son, at age four; when a sudden shower of hail fell during a hillside walk, he began to cry. Then he summed up the feelings of us all by shaking a small fist to the sky and saying, 'They're like bloody marbles...'. Rummelhart's view, that the language of children shows a continuous play of new, imaginative connections between words and experiences, endorsed Gardner's finding (1974) that the spontaneous discourse of children shows metaphoric activity, and anticipated later evidence (in Gardner and Winner, 1986) of their competence in metaphoric operation. This capacity to handle metaphor through language play should not be seen as 'category error', or as misapplied logic, but as a crucial element in language and learning development.

While Gardner accepted that the capacity to create new metaphor, which is strong in young children, then declines in later childhood to re-emerge sporadically in adolescence, it might be wondered whether this is an entirely natural process, or whether it may be unduly influenced by the requirements of formal education.

Richards goes on to suggest that this experimental game, of making a metaphor by looking at a thing (or person) not as it appears to us at first glance, but in terms of something else, is like a girl in a hat shop playing the game of 'trying on hats' – to see what she might look like if she were in fact a bridesmaid, a vicar's wife or an actress – partly in order to pretend and partly, perhaps, to learn something about herself. But all the time, while trying on hats, she knows too that they belong to the shop and that she came in bareheaded – 'everything is what it is and not another thing'. She is playing a game and the main condition of the game is the trying on, the impermanence... In the same way we make a metaphor because we are intrigued and sometimes enlightened by a glimpse – it need be no more than that of what A looks like in terms of B; and this quality of impermanence seems to be the essence of metaphor.

(p. 98)

Recalling Verbrugge's view (1980, p. 96) that metaphor is of particular value in describing things which are in the process of becoming other things, Richards suggests that metaphor is especially effective when applied to people. Metaphor has unique virtues, in being able to record not only the flux ('impermanence') of change in people and events, but also to retain a flexible link ('elasticity') between static and changing versions:

Since by definition we meet other people only when they are changing from 'themselves' to the role they assume when they are with us, we need metaphor constantly to evoke and describe them. More fundamentally, if most things – including people – are in the process of change, metaphor would be more effective than literal language in describing them. This leads to the possibility that, while literal language is a device for enabling people to think of the world as static, metaphor is a way of representing the world as it is, in all its impermanence.

If a metaphor were to lose the property of impermanence it would also lose another equally important property, which may be called elasticity. 'Elasticity' describes the power a metaphor has of seeming both true and untrue at the same time. Although the words in a metaphor are exactly the same words that are used in ordinary language – metaphor has no special vocabulary of its own – the metaphor conveyed by the words appears at one moment to stretch the language, so as to allow a new concept to be expressed, and immediately to shrink language back again.

(p. 100)

These qualities of impermanence and of elasticity are characterised by the essential element of *play* in language. It is these qualities which distinguish the fresh from the old, sedimented metaphors that abound in every-day speech, where meanings have become static. The case for encouraging initiative in learning, through fun and creativity in language use, was put with wit by David Allen (1981, p. 17); he records an exchange, as a teacher-parent, with his daughter on her homework:

'As cold as ice is a ......?'
Cliché? – suggests Allen.
Wrong; the answer is a simile.
Collective nouns: 'a ...... of arrows.
Why not a fizz of arrows?
A ...... of hounds.
Why can't it be a bark of hounds?

Elasticity in metaphor

Richards explains that she prefers the term 'elasticity' to Ortony's version (1980, p. 73) of 'a sense of tension', with its implied sense of strain and of no subsequent 'sense of release and of springing back, nor of vibration and of resonance':

> Not tension alone, then, but tension followed by release... characterises metaphor as we use it. The combination of these qualities gives the sense of buoyancy and ease that I feel is typical of metaphor. This sense of buoyancy and ease – of the certainty of coming up again if one goes down – must, I think, result from our knowing that, after a metaphor, language returns to its normal unstretched state, and this in turn depends on our knowing that a metaphor is an impermanent thing.

> (p. 102)

Metaphor is, as many have recognised, as important to the frontiers of knowledge as it is to normal learning. Quine (1981), for example, cited the molecular theory of gases, perceived as a swarm of insects, to illustrate how new concepts may be outlined. Popper (1992), writing on 'The magic of myths', declared that poetry and science – and music, too – are blood relations, each representing 'a naive attempt, inspired by imagination, at explaining our world to ourselves' (p. 15). The continuous review of poetic and scientific metaphors, to test their power and appropriateness, is an act of ruthless self-criticism, which advances understanding.

Popper quotes from Kepler, whose quest in the 17th century to discover the source of the heavenly music of the spheres led to his great theory of the elliptical movement of space bodies. Kepler concluded his thesis with a hymn of praise that draws entirely on a musical metaphor:

> Thus the heavenly motions are nothing but a kind of perennial concert, rational rather than audible or vocal. They move through the tension of dissonances which are like syncopations or suspensions with their resolutions (by which men imitate the corresponding dissonances of nature), reaching secure and

determined closures, each containing six terms like a chord of six voices. And by these marks they distinguish and articulate the immensity of time.

(in Popper, 1992, p. 18)

It is usual to suggest that Newtonian physics introduced notions of a dead, mechanical universe to science, and produced an irrevocable split between 'sober rationality' in the sciences and the 'play of feeling' in the arts. Yet Popper's testament to a partnership in scientific and artistic enquiry is echoed throughout the history of science. When Kekule presented his discovery of the complex structure of the benzine molecule to the Royal Society, he described how its structure was presented to him in a dream about snakes, that twisted into the shape that he sought. 'Let us learn to dream', he declared; though he added, with a scientist's caution, that we should also 'be wary of our dreams'.

A further, remarkable illustration of affinities between 'poetic' imagination and scientific enquiry is provided in a letter written by Humphry Davy, when at the height of his fame at the Royal Institution, to the poet Coleridge, on his departure abroad. He pays tribute to Coleridge, whose intellect he greatly admired, 'as a recollection possessed of creative energy, as an Imagination winged with fire inspiriting and rejoicing' (quoted in Holmes, 1989, p. 360). Coleridge, on his part, whose own writing is suffused with his sense of the 'esemplastic' powers of the imagination, saw his own work as a poet-metaphysician, in terms that echo Kepler's scientific enquiry into the spheres:

he looked into his own Soul with a Telescope: what seemed all irregular, he saw and showed to be beautiful constellations and he added to the Consciousness hidden worlds within worlds.

(Notebooks, quoted in Holmes, 1989, p. 358)

'Only a metaphor'

Metaphor provides space for further experiment and adjustment, since what is 'only a metaphor' may easily be changed. Eve Richards uses her own metaphor for this, which recalls the 'process' theme of the dream account, at the beginning of this chapter:

When we use language we are perhaps treating language as if it were on the screen of a word-processor. What we say is not permanent and is capable of change, sometimes beyond all likeness to the original; nothing has yet taken the permanence of print. Playing and using metaphor are alike in being able to protect us from our mistakes and misjudgements...

...Metaphor is particularly useful in helping us build up bit by bit the details of complex and contradictory notions which cannot be properly be covered by literal language. Metaphor invites us, half-seriously, to 'think of A as B', but in the same moment to remember that A is still A, and that it may also be thought of as C. Still, the playing of the game has taught us something: a way of thinking about A, about the speaker, the context, the language or about ourselves. The definition of play as 'the establishment and exploration of relationships' (Bateson, 1979, p. 137) is a useful one here. The relationships Bateson has in mind may be those between persons, but in other contexts I think we could say that users of metaphor establish and explore cognitive relations between the self and object in the world and can, of course, play with the relationships within language.

(pp. 104–6)

Richards concludes her account of the playful and creative qualities of metaphor with an illuminating analogy:

I suggest that literal language can be thought of as a *simple piece of string*, such as anyone could use to tie up a parcel. This piece of string can be measured to find out its length, its thickness, its weight and so on. It is inert.

But take this piece of string, and make it part of a yo-yo, and its character changes, in exactly the same way as language changes when we use it in metaphor. Instead of having only one consistent set of qualities, it now has two mutually contradictory ones it both is and is not the piece of string described above; just as language in a metaphor is seen as simultaneously true and untrue, permissible and impermissible. Although we know it is the same piece of string it seems no longer inert but alive, just as the words in a metaphor may separately be defined as they have always been, yet together making a meaning which is different for everyone and at the same time understandable by everyone, and more than the sum of its parts, so to speak.

Instead of being fixed and predictable, the string in a yo-yo can do all sorts of apparently magical things, stretching and shrinking, becoming longer and shorter in quick succession, like the experimental and elastic things that can be done with a word in a metaphor. Instead of being inert, the string seems alive; like the words in a metaphor, it no longer corresponds exactly with what we remember about it from elsewhere (the dimensions in the case of the string; the definitions in the case of the words). Where we used to be able to measure the string when it was inert, now, in play, we cannot. But when we stop playing with it the string reverts to what it was before; the speaker reverts to literal language, and words to their normal meanings. In the meantime, playing with the yo-yo has given pleasure.

(pp. 107–8)

Not only that: through the play of metaphor the learner may have developed language and understanding; for the advanced thinker, it may have opened up new areas of knowing.

Metaphor and good teaching

Metaphor, claimed Wallace Stevens in his poem 'The Motive for Metaphor' (1955), has a life-force of its own; its expression may not always be well-mannered. The 'ABC of being' involves

> Steel against intimation – the sharp flesh,
> The vital, arrogant, fatal, dominant...

When we make new meanings through new metaphors, we operate what Kant called 'the blind but indispensible faculty' which links sensation to understanding, through giving verbal shape to our imagined forms. This is the essence of metaphorical thought. Moreover, the new metaphor can never simply be 'implanted' into those who share the discourse; for listening, too, requires attention, active thinking, and – at moments of new discovery – a capacity for creative response, in order to understand the new insight offered.

The imaginative life that good teaching generates in the learner provides essential conditions for original metpahoric thought. Other aspects of thought (rational, analogic, lateral, and so on) are at its service. Without it, thought is incomplete in form and in essential bearings. The learner can only 'think' along lines prescribed by the teacher or the curriculum (just as characters in a work of fiction may never come to life when manipulated by an intrusive novelist, who will only let them do what the ringmaster-artist decrees).

The term 'organic' teaching comes from the work of Sylvia Ashton-Warner who declared, in an affrontingly simple metaphor, that 'when I teach people I marry them'. Her autobiographical novel *Spinster* (1980a), followed by her direct account of teaching (*Teacher*, 1980b) and her autobiography (*I Passed This Way*, 1980c), were all fuelled by powers that were generated by her 'marriage' with teaching. This passion for teaching was ruthlessly concentrated on her chosen object – the learning of the learner. Teaching involved, for her, much pain and even resentment at so impossible a marriage, as well as the 'returns of fine delight' from the harvest of her remarkable career.

Ashton-Warner made high claims for teaching as a rare art – for organic teaching, that is, where teacher and learner explore in co-labour from the 'deep hidden' places of being, working in a 'gracious movement' towards discovery. For her, teaching and learning involved the body, including gesture, dance, the plastic and visual arts, as well as 'passionate interchange of talk', in order to give creative direction to the flux of her classroom. Rather than strive to suppress inadmissible feelings among the children, she worked subtly to harness these, as energy sources in the organic process.

It may, sometimes, seem absurd to her readers, that teaching – or, indeed, any career – should absorb so much of one's brief life-span. Ashton-Warner justified it by declaring that teaching is an art, requiring nothing less than the full commitment of the maker, while new forms are being realised. Here, though, she recognised that the teacher cannot expect to have the full reward of completed work, after her efforts; since only pernicious versions of teaching would regard the learner as a 'product' of the teacher's vision. The rarer art is to *meet the otherness* of the learner, which involves both empathy and renunciation. This is what it means, to 'marry' them.

As the thinly disguised autobiographical element in the fiction of *Spinster* recorded, her own work with Maori children in rural New Zealand made sometimes extreme demands on her 'marriage to – teaching' ideal. Yet this, and her accounts in *Teacher*, placed her work among that eminent minority of dissidents (some of whom held influential positions in education – such as Alec Clegg, Marjorie Hourd, George Sampson, David Holbrook or Sybil Marshall) who declared throughout their careers that teaching and learning are best understood as a creative relationship, in a 'crèche of living where people can still be changed'.

In practical terms, her accounts showed how she provided creative space for learners, which became the centre for her 'organic' teaching. In developing the reading and writing of her pupils stressed the importance of 'key' words – such as 'kiss' or 'ghost' – in engaging children's imagination she disregarded exercises in calligraphy and copy-writing, and stressed that the writing of learners must be genuinely *theirs*: even her five-year-old beginners 'have a most distinctive style' (1980b, p. 51), and 'their self-chosen vocabulary remains with them' as they move through the school grades, and develop their own organic view of the world, through metaphoric connection. Her concern for the 'developing idea' of the learner within the 'grand design' of a whole personal vision is, of course, the metaphoric quest and the overall design of the learner, not the teacher. For many of Ashton-Warner's learners, that was likely to involve a future within a culture that was not hers. Her concern, though, was to lead out (educate) the learner, not to impose the fixed images of an inflexible curriculum.

Metaphor and wit

The fixed images of a fixed curriculum are a deathblow to metaphoric play, to wonder, to imaginative reflection, and to wit.

With humorous irony, Mark Twain showed in *Pudd'nhead Wilson*, how wit depends on a witty audience, for survival. In the opening chapter of the novel young Wilson, on his first day in town as the new lawyer, complains to some fellow citizens about a tiresome dog that will not stop barking:

"I wish I owned half of that dog."
"Why?" somebody asked.
"Because I would kill my half."
The group searched his face with curiosity, with anxiety even, but found no light there, no expression that they could read. They fell away from him as something uncanny, and went into privacy to discuss him. One said:
"'Pears to be a fool."
"'Pears?" said another, "Is, I reckon you better say."
"Said he wished he owned *half* of that dog, the idiot," said a third. "What did he reckon would become of the other half if he killed his half? Do you reckon he thought it would live?"

After further discussion the citizens decide that Wilson is a 'pudd'nhead', a verdict which 'made him a fool, and he was not able to get it set aside, or even modified'. An unusual statement or fresh viewpoint may seem naive, even foolish to those who are not attuned to elements of wit or irony. Yet it is the willingness to reveal an individual feeling or view, that gives metaphor its truth-telling quality. To perceive relations in the world is to make metaphors; it is thought in its most original form.

Intuitive insight is not, of course, always a comfortable experience; while we may not be able to choose the feelings that lead to new insights, we may choose either to suppress them, or to admit them further. Intuitive insights are, to use a term from Collingwood (1938), like wild animals, which may prove friendly or dangerous to our conscious selves. Thus Macbeth forces away the potentially moral, healing vision of a dagger which reveals the blood on its blade, that would follow his plan to murder to Duncan. The 'wild' element in metaphor is the element which defeats Pudd'nhead Wilson's citizens, and which is wilfully ignored by Macbeth.

Intuitive insight is also the element that is most often resisted among the more determinist structure-and-function linguisticians and literary structuralists. Firth (1930), for example, whose work exerted a decades-long influence in language studies, doubted whether 'there could be such a thing as individual speech behaviour'. For him, speech was the 'telephone network of our society'. The teacher's task was to condition in the pupil the range of prescribed roles available in society. This he viewed as 'sense', unlike the 'nonsense' of poetry. Changing his metaphor, he declared that 'more plumbing, less poetry, is the motto for modern education' (1937).

The plumbing analogy dominates structuralist poetics, such as those of Culler (1975), who defined metaphoric activity as though it were a kind of sealed hot-and-cold water system. He described metaphor as a 'combination of two synecdoches', which 'moves from a whole to one of its parts to another whole which contains that part', and back again, in a predictable flow. This consigning of fluid metaphor to a system of psychic pipelines avoids the unexpected *transformation* of ideas that metaphor achieves. The effect on fixed ideas of a powerful metaphor may, in fact, have more of the qualities of nuclear fission, than of separate pipe systems. Even so, the merging of hot and cold water is effective in conveying Romanyshyn's persuasive view (1982) that metaphor produces a positive confusion (with its root sense of 'pouring together') of ideas. The truth-telling power of metaphor can make its impact, then, through destroying with violence or reshaping with stealth, the old forms of old truth.

To conclude: metaphor in daily living and in the curriculum

Allow me to conclude in a way which would be consistent with a theory of interpretation which lays the stress on opening up a world.

Ricoeur (1991, p. 318)

While good poetry may be a particularly powerful distilling of metaphor-making, let it be conceded that ordinary discourse rarely shows the intensity or cliché-breaking powers of fresh ideas. Much of our talk includes phatic exchanges, routine messages of information, request, instruction and so on, or contains 'encapsulated' wisdom such as proverbs, theorems and slogans. Yet while such acts of language provide essential maintenance and repair of cells in the body of language and culture, they are not part of the quest-to-meaning that learning crucially involves. If the learner is not engaged, to some degree, in creating new possibilities for living, then little significance can be claimed for what is being learned.

Throughout the curriculum there needs to be a regard for the power of metaphor. This is most obviously so, perhaps, in the area of language development where, through skill in the use of metaphor, learners may discover personal meaning in what is being learned. All knowledge is, after all, eventually negotiable; this may be less obvious in physics than in poetry, say, and may not be easy to apply until it becomes a cornerstone principle for the National Curriculum. Yet we have noted that it is not unusual for scientists themselves to acknowledge the place of metaphor in scientific discovery. This acknowledgement should be present, now, throughout the curriculum. We need, in short, an *open* curriculum, which provides space for learners and their teachers to genuinely re-examine their world. 'To understand oneself before, in front of, a world', declared Ricoeur, 'is the contrary of projecting oneself and one's belief and prejudices; it is to let the work and its world enlarge the horizon of my own understanding' (1991, p. 315).

Just as there are countless individual differences of physiognomy, or finger prints, or character, there are countless different *kinds* of intelligence, and modes of thinking. Subtle mathematicians may be naive moralists; research engineers may find it impossibly challenging to organise an outing for a group of colleagues; captains of industry or psychologists may be hopeless as parents – unless they can shift from the tramlines of their habitual modes of thought, through using their imagination. This involves personal suppleness in and adventurousness in metaphoric thought.

The complex interrelation between person and world was conveyed by the eminent chemist and writer Primo Levi, through the beautiful metaphor that concludes *The Periodic Table* (1984). In order to investigate the 'micro-history' of his own life, Levi worked through Mendeleyev's periodic table of elements, seeking metaphoric connections to illuminate his experience. His book, which deals with his own direct experiences of the Nazi Holocaust, celebrates the serious game of metaphoric thinking. Levi's handling of this, though, is in complete contrast to the insensitive metaphoric games about war and violence that may be played by those who have not been directly involved (see, for example, Marvin Ching's account of 'Games and Play: Pervasive Metaphors in American Life', 1993).

In a final serious – playful chapter, Levi investigates carbon which, since it can bind itself into long stable chains, is the 'key element of living substance' (p. 227). Yet the process of its translation from the inorganic to the organic world is highly complex. To follow this process, Levi traces the history of one particular atom, from its form over hundreds of millions of years in limestone, through to the milk that he drinks, which then becomes part of his own act of writing:

> It is swallowed...the chain is meticulously broken apart, and the fragments, one by one, are accepted or rejected. One, the one that concerns us, crosses the intestinal threshold and enters the bloodstream; it migrates, knocks at the door of a nerve cell, enters, and supplants the carbon which was part of it. This cell belongs to a brain, and it is my brain, the brain of *me* who is writing;

and the cell in question, and within it the atom in question, is in charge of my writing, in a gigantic miniscule game which nobody has yet described. It is that which at this instant, issuing out of a labyrinthine tangle of yeses and nos, makes my hand run a long a certain path on the paper, mark it with these volutes that are signs: a double snap, up and down, between two levels of energy, guides this hand of mine to impress on the paper this dot, here, this one.

(pp. 232–3)

In order to understand processes of learning and writing – a 'game which nobody has yet described' – Levi must move beyond the efforts of physiology, or biology, or psychology, or his own chemistry, into metaphor – or into a biology of the imagination. He makes plain the benefit to education, and indeed to evolution, of this metaphoric 'I-Thou' play, in order to understand what cannot yet be scientifically explained.

Metaphor helps learners, within a lifetime, to comprehend the complexity of carbon chains, or the still inexplicable intricacy of a wren's song; with life so short, and with so much to learn, they cannot wait for ever, for empirical confirmation of what is at once illuminated by metaphor. 'When I see the peacock's tail I really feel sick', admitted Darwin.

The case for metaphor in learning rests here. The argument moves, now, to address learners themselves, their readiness to learn, and the need to find their own language, to name the world on their terms.

CHAPTER 4

Learning Through Language

This chapter proposes the learner as an active and creative agent in learning. It considers:

- *self-determination* in learning; the learner as freedom-fighter;
- the *'dangers'* of learning, for those with learning difficulties;
- learning from a *'sense of marginality'*;
- some literary views of learning – *for conformity? or for choice?* (Dickens, Morrison, Dickinson, Kakfa);
- learning to *name*; making the language one's own;
- the *self versus the system* – a personal history by Kath Green, whose contribution here is acknowledged with gratitude.

The essence of learning

This chapter takes, as a text for realising through learning, Frank Smith's view (Smith *et al.*, 1984) that *'creativity is the essence of learning itself'*. Smith argued that:

> the current metaphor for the brain as an information processing device is inadequate and misleading. It would be far more appropriate and productive to regard the brain as a creative artist, except that it is entire worlds that are created. The actual world around us, if it exists in the mind at all (let alone as any kind of objective reality), exists only as one among a number of possible worlds the brain continually creates...Creative imagination is not a by-product of our interactions with the world but the basis of them.
>
> (p. 151)

The mind is too inventive and interesting to be seen merely as a recording/retrieval system for the 'facts' of the world. And, as acknowledged in the last chapter, reality itself is elusive and protean; it cannot be reduced to a collection of 'facts'. Yet, while the nature of reality may remain a problem for philosophers, it is no problem for most young learners, who *know* that reality is what *they* make of it. Citing many familiar examples of ways in which children *actively* engage with early literacy and learning – through invented spelling, mock writing, 'creative' errors in grammar, and complex role-playing in their games and response to stories Smith demonstrated the powerful drive in young learners to 'create worlds' (p. 156).

This is not to say that they are blindly willing to learn anything presented to them; on the contrary, healthy patterns of learning involve self-determination and choice, not simple compliance. 'Literacy', claimed Smith, 'is more than utility and understanding for children, it is power...' (p. 156). This view of an active, self-determining learner is reflected in, for example, the epistemology of philosophers such as Michael Polanyi (who was discussed in Chapter 2) or of Bernard Lonergan, who saw learning as a unified, dynamic activity which involves experience, understanding and judging. This activity presses the enquirer to discover knowledge – 'what Lonergan has called the 'eros of the mind', the free, unrestricted desire to know' (Fitzpatrick, 1982, p. 219).

Such views of learning will also be investigated in this chapter – and in those that follow – on reading, writing and talking in learning.

The learner as freedom-fighter

If, then, it is perfectly 'natural' to learn, to create and to imagine, why do things go wrong in learning, for many children and students? And what lessons may be learned here, for *all* learners, since there can be few people for whom learning, in some way or another, has never been a problem? Writing on Lonergan's version of knowing as a conscious, *intending* activity, Jo Fitzpatrick reflected on the dilemma facing the would-be active learner, who must look for coherence in whatever data the world happens to present. The coherence that the learner seeks is *not* necessarily logical coherence, but 'the coherence involved in the suggested explanation or interpretation *fitting the data*, cohering with the data' (1982, p. 221). The learner, he suggested, is like a prisoner who plans an escape route from the gaol, but who must investigate all the 'givens' that may provide a chance to escape:

> There is the plank of wood, but is it strong enough, propped against the wall, to support the prisoner's weight? Are the loose bricks removable and at the right height to allow the prisoner to scale within a few feet of the top? Finally,

is the piece of rope long enough and strong enough for the prisoner to loop it round the spikes surmounting the wall and haul himself to the top? These are the conditions that have to be fulfilled before a secure judgement, 'There *is* an escape route', can be made.

(p. 221)

No matter how rich the inner imaginative life of the individual may be, the 'facts' of the world are *there*, and are irreducible; they must be understood and surmounted, if the world is to be claimed. The prisoner knows only too well that, while freedom may be preferred to imprisonment, there are dangers to overcome in order to be free. It is not surprising, then, that some of those who are imprisoned in a learning dilemma of one kind or another may lose the confidence to believe that escape is possible.

When learning seems 'dangerous'

In creating new worlds through learning, we can clarify experience, overcome problem problems and move towards understanding. When, however, learning itself is felt to be a problem, this usual view of learning cannot apply. It will be argued in Chapter 8 that, even when specific special needs in language and learning may be identified, the labelling of disabilities can be unhelpful; on the other hand, right kinds of support need to be based on right kinds of diagnosis. The focus now, however, will be on how disabling problems of *attitude* to learning may be handled.

The importance of sensitive detection of particular problems in learning was emphasised in Karen Zelan's *The Risks of Knowing* (1991). Her clinical accounts, of children who have 'made a decision to fail' or 'to renounce learning', showed how youngsters of various ages can become active partners again, in coming to understand the nature of their problem, and to overcome it. Zelan believed that, although it may be common for parents and teaches to respect differences in the ways that children, adolescents and adults achieve understanding, it is less common to allow appropriate degrees of *self-determination* among the young.

Simply to announce to children with learning problems that they have a disability may be to conspire in their abdicating of self-responsibility; it denies their autonomy. Zelan cited studies by Tuma (1989), which revealed that about a sixth of all US children suffer from emotional disturbances that may affect learning; and by Chalfant (1989), that 4 per cent (over two million) were classified as learning-disabled – which, she noted with 'surprise', showed a doubling of such numbers over a period of ten years.

Commenting on these, she declared that a therapeutic approach to children with learning difficulties should aim at *intellectual* as well as affective development; it is 'not enough to restore a fuller emotional life to these children...Their abilities to investigate and make constructive use of knowledge needed our attention as well' (p. 11). Zelan's findings – that 'to investigate the world, the child must feel moderately independant' (p. 64), and that even those 4 per cent of young learners with classified learning problems are 'capable of inquiry about the risks of knowing' (p. 299) – provide useful directions for supporting autonomy in learning, for *all* learners. On 'normal' patterns of learning, she suggested:

> The unknown attracts the youngster from his very first attempts whether he is walking, talking, learning the alphabet, or endeavouring to understand literature and the sciences. Exploring his world in bits and pieces, he is much like the scholar who seeks knowledge on a larger scale and in a more organised fashion. Whatever is not immediately comprehensive to the child and to the scholar holds compelling fascination. For the scholar, repeated attempts to explore the unknown result in increasingly comprehensive versions of what is true and real. Children, too, must learn to replace earlier, immature 'theories' with more accurate thought construction, accounting for additional, sometimes unexpected reality features.
>
> (p. 29)

While Zelan's view of 'accurate thought construction' and of 'reality features' may be thought to be altogether less flexible than Frank Smith's notion of many worlds and of multiple realities, she placed an equally strong emphasis on personal ownership and power in learning. She drew on Piaget (1973, 1978, for example), as well as her own experience as a clinical therapist, to show that, while refusing to learn is complicated, there is no reason why learning itself need not be natural, straightforward and pleasurable. Learners often require simply their own space and non-interfence, in order to develop their own 'energetic, inquiring atttitude' (p. 490). Too much testing, for example – and children are notoriously over-tested, in her view – creates a 'disability expectation' in both young learner and parents; and non-learners without specific problems risk the danger of being wrongly labelled, or over-labelled. She endorsed Furth's (1987) emphasis on the *activity* of young learners in overcoming their own transitory 'knowledge disturbances', and also Elkind's view (1987) that it may be the curriculum, not the learner that is disabled (although a mismatch may, of course, also be within an individual learner).

In a notably interesting chapter called 'Perceptions and Realities' Zelan categorised three main types of learning disorders: underachievers, overachievers and school phobics. She then investigated 'family myths' that may conspire to create any of these categories and, in doing so, to harm the 'living root' of learning (Miller, 1981, p. 75). Miller's work, on the 'narcissistic' parents of children whom they claim to be gifted, elucidated ways in which pressures that are epiphenomenal to the actual learning task may injure progress in learning. Children who must strive to demonstrate 'gifts' that they do not possess are no less fortunate than children who have been inappropriately categorised as 'slow' (or, more oddly, as 'only average', given that 'average' implies the ordinary normality for which parents typically pray on behalf of their offspring at birth).

The confusions caused by a natural tendency in all young learners to 'associate knowing with a myriad of other activities, such as placating, confounding, remembering, feeling and even denying' (Zelan, pp. 36–7), may result in the learner with problems having to use considerable powers of ingenious thought to avoid acquiring knowledge which, for one reason or another, is felt to be 'dangerous'. Just as Coles, in *The Learning Mystique* (1987) identifed socio-political factors which explain such attitudes as 'learning disablity', Zelan's case studies reveal unexpected causes for learning problems. A child may have – in her own view – excellent reasons for refusing to learn ('won't'), while pretending that she is unable ('can't'). Such was the case of Sonja, who was thought by both her mother and teacher to be unready to move to her next grade in school:

> At the first appointment her mother explained that she believed Sonja was 'just incapable of third grade work'. As soon as her mother left, Sonja wrote on the blackboard the words *couldn't, don't and doesn't*. I praised her for her correct spelling of these contractions (many second grade children have difficulty spelling them). When she heard her teacher and mother repeatedly say, 'She's not ready', Sonja assumed that *don't* (her decision not to learn) was equivalent to *couldn't*. But as she thought about it, she knew better – it was more like she *does not* do schoolwork. As she later told me, 'Not ready means you can't!'...Not wishing to contradict her mother's opinion, nor to reveal that it was her choice when she did not spell in school, Sonja erased the words just before her mother returned to pick her up.
>
> (p. 43)

Zelan shows how Sonja has learned to use considerable ingenuity, in trying to overcome her confusion about what her mother and teacher 'meant', which has affected her normal motivation to learn. In exercising their choice of whether or not to learn, children may often reach a decision that the adults who must care for them would rather not hear (some readers may themselves recall announcing as a child, soon after first going to school, that they would not be going again, and also recalling a parent's equally firm reply that indeed they *would* be going...). Even so, there is a world of difference between having good reasons to over-rule children, and actually confusing them (and one's self, too) in their grasp of language and their understanding of 'reality'.

Sonja was one of sixty young learners who were included in Zelan's study. While they all had serious learning problems, Zelan also emphasised the considerable positive talents that they revealed in their school lives. All of them, she claimed, excelled in at least one school subject, and more than half of them showed exceptional talent in that area, at least. While individuals may not be linguistically or mathematically proficient, they may excel in sports, crafts, technology or other curriculum areas.

Sadly, Zelan disclosed, they are not *perceived* this way. When their particular talents are ignored or underrated, this provides learners who are at risk with a further reason for not learning, since what they can do is so little appreciated.

The uses of life histories for research into learning

The Winter 1993 issue of the *British Educational Research Journal* highlighted an interesting revaluation of aims and methods in educational research which has, among some researchers at least, grown steadily in recent years. The three opening papers in this issue were concerned with the uses of life histories in educational enquiry, and were interlinked in their argument. In the first of these, Peter Woods wrote on 'Managing Marginality'. He examined the life history of a teacher who had sought to base his own teaching on:

> the importance of freedom, space, latitude, flexibility. Education, he believes, is for the child, and not for a pre-ordained order of society into which they should be socialised. The teacher is a facilitator, catalytic agent, midwife, novice, as well as guru, for the teacher also is always learning. Teaching...should capitalise on children's natural curiosity and inventiveness. It should not seek to shut them down.

(p. 448)

This life history shows how enlightened views about learning and teaching grew from the teacher's own sense of 'marginality', at earlier stages in his life. As with the students in Zelan's case studies, this 'marginality' was caused by a refusal to conform to arbitrary demands from school or society. In physical education, for example, he 'detested the preliminaries – the pointless "drill" and even worse the apparatus sessions' (p.

70

454). He became used to failure in these school sessions, and was judged as incompetent when teachers wrote his reports – yet, during weekends spent by himself, he had 'cycled 25 miles in a single day to get to a new birds' nesting area and had, on arrival, climbed some 40 feet up a difficult fir tree to get at a clutch of crow's eggs' (p. 454).

This is, of course, both a familiar view of teaching and also a familiar story; less familiar, yet welcome, is the stamp of respectability that was granted by BERA, through this journal issue, to grounded life histories as a valid instrument for educational research.

Similarly, a long-standing mistrust of imaginative discourse in the social sciences has given some ground, in recognising how poetry, fiction and drama may be appropriate sources for enquiry. In a special issue of *The Journal of Educational Administration* (1990) called 'The Preparation of Educational Leaders', for example, William Simpkins argued that 'in fiction, as in social research, the internal logic of a work draws on both rationality and imagination, to help sustain a cumulative presentation'. He addded that the arts depend on the 'complete and personal presentation' of the artist, and that artistic success derives from the 'internal logic' of the work.

Reflection, rationality and creative imagination combine in a person's whole act of thinking, instead of being separate, even contradictory activities. This constitutes an essential hermeneutic approach, requiring the educational researcher to be a whole person, engaged in all three dimensions of educational activity – ratiocination, open reflection and metaphoric-creative imagination.

Simpkins addressed his argument, in a journal devoted to studies in educational management, to the heart of the educational research and administrative establishment, in order to reclaim the place of the expressive arts in educational enquiry. It was a liberating argument, that offered benefits to the arts curriculum, as well as to educational research; the questions faced by 'serious' literature are often precisely those that must be faced by policy-makers and managers in education. In my attempt, for example, to equate values in English studies with values in educational management (Harrison, 1992b), meanings and contexts of power, leadership and responsibility were explored through a range of literary and political texts. These included Stewart Ransom's argument (1992) that the economic, social and political transformations of the 1980s 'raise deep questions for the government of education and for the polity in general about: what is it to be a person? Is a person a passive being possessed by powers that define his or her essential agency?'

Unlike the serious poet, novelist or dramatist, Ransom did not feel obliged to seek an answer to these questions; rather than dwell on them, he moved straight to 'strategies for reconstruction', with that confident eye to the future that characterises much writing on education. Yet he did, at least, open them up on behalf of all learners – who must share the obligation of serious writers, to seek answers for themselves.

Learning for conformity? Or for choice? Some literary insights

Encouraged by these new directions in educational enquiry, our argument moves from clinical or empirical evidence, to some imaginative insights by creative writers into what it means to learn, in order to pursue Smith's claim that 'creativity is the essence of learning'.

Dickens and the 'natural bent' of the learner

Charles Dickens, whose own formal education was terminated at a tender age by his father's bankruptcy, filled his novels with studies of people who are trapped into the conformities of their class, or education, or occupation, and have no powers to imagine alternative ways of living. In *Bleak House*, (Chapter 13) for example, Jarndyce is understandably irritated by Richard's 'indecision of character'. Richard had learned, in his eight years at public school, to compose Latin verses in skilful imitation of classic writers – 'but I never heard that it had been anybody's business to find out what his natural bent was, or where his failings lay, or to adapt any kind of knowledge to him'.

We are, though, told that Richard had, at least, 'enlarged his education by forgetting how to do it'. That game of composing imitative Latin verses may have gone out of fashion long ago; yet how much of the present school curriculum seeks genuinely to follow the 'natural bent' of the learner, or to 'adapt any kind of knowledge to him'?

When reading Dickens it is tempting to draw an analogy between the teacher-learner and the author-character relationship. This is not to suggest that the teacher should manipulate the learner, any more than the novelist should manipulate characters; it is, rather, to recognise the *independence* of new life that is inspired, in each case. Dickens' son, Charles, for example, reported that he often heard his father 'complain that he could *not* get the people of his imagination to do what he wanted and that they would insist on working at histories in *their* way, and not his (in Ackroyd, 1990, pp. 400–1). If the 'author' (novelist or teacher) acknowledges the separate, demonic nature of newly quickened life, then anything might happen. Dickens himself recorded his discomfort when *'the character took possession of me* and made me do exactly the contrary to what I had originally intended'; in this way, he became the observer, who 'heard' and recorded, rather than directed them (Ackroyd, 1990, p. 401).

Yet, perhaps inevitably, institutions of learning – schools, colleges, universities – have developed their own defences against originality of thought, independence of action or other signs of the demonic individual. Reflecting on the labours of 'deconstructionist' critics and scholars, for example, to dismiss the originality of Dickens' own work, by explaining how it was all determined by this-or-that source, Ackroyd suggested that 'it is one of the sins of scholarship to assume, however unconsciously, that there is nothing original in the world' (p. 193).

In a famous, tongue-in-cheek comparison, Terry Eagleton once suggested that a bus-ticket could provide rich sociological evidence, just as *King Lear* could, about a culture or community. Just as scholarly deconstruction of texts may reveal useful evidence of cultural/historical/social components, yet may absurdly diminish the whole quality of a text through the exercise, so may conventional pedagogical 'analysis' through testing and assessment be of some specific use, yet evade crucial, distinctively original elements in teaching and learning. Who would doubt that, while the human body itself can be 'analysed' and reduced to so much water, carbon and other chemical residues, it amounts to considerably more than that?

Toni Morrison and the need to 'speak his name'

Learners and their teachers must, of course, work within some obvious conventions – lexical, semantic, cultural, grammatical and so on – in order to find freedom for wider *individual* choices in language and learning. Yet freedom (as Zelan showed) eludes many learners, who may feel imprisoned by labels and values that are imposed through the same language that they need for their own growth in learning. Paradoxically, the only way out of such imprisonment is to learn to 'name' – to be as skilful with language as those who operate the labelling or restrictions on them.

This skill, at the highest level, is arguably what makes fiction of writers such as Dickens 'serious'. Dwelling on 'my own unrealised possibilities' Milan Kundera suggested, in *The Unbearable Lightness of Being* (1984) that, in fiction,

> characters are not born, like people, of women; they are born of a situation, a sentence, a metaphor containing in a nutshell a basic human possibility that the author thinks no-one else has discovered or said anything about.

In this way, valid *alternative* worlds are built by the imaginative thinker.

The identity of actual people, too, may be born of a 'metaphor' – and may also be harmed by a refusal to 'imagine'. In Toni Morrison's *Jazz* (1992) the narrator confesses:

> what was I thinking of? How could I have imagined him so poorly? Not noticed the hurt that was not linked to the color of his skin, or the blood that beat beneath it. But to some other thing that longed for authenticity, for a right to be in this place, effortlessly without needing to acquire a false face, a laughless grin, a talking posture...I want to be the language that wished him well, speaks his name, wakes him when his eyes need to be open.
>
> (pp. 160–1)

Morrison's books are about the experience of black Americans, in taking personal possession of life through 'naming' it on their own terms. In her story *Song of Solomon* (1989), Guitar rejects the name given to him as part of a former tagging system for slaves, and asserts his own choice of name: 'I don't give a shit what white people know or even think...Guitar is my name. Bains is the Slave Master's name and I'm all of that.'

Literacy itself, when misused, easily becomes an instrument of oppression. Macon Dead, in *Song of Solomon*, explains to his son about how his own father came by his name; he recalls how, when emancipation came, all the coloured people in the state had to register with the Freedman's Bureau. The man behind the desk, who was drunk, asked papa where he was born. Papa said Macon. Then he asked him who his father was. Papa replied, 'He's dead.' The drunk wrote down this information in wrong spaces on the form and, for his name, the fool wrote, 'Dead, Macon'.

In the same book, Pilate thinks secretly that

> he and his sister had some ancestor, some lithe young man with onyx skin...who had a name that was real. A name given to him with love and seriousness. A name that was not a joke, nor a disguise, nor a brand name.

Their own name is among the very first 'names' that children claim for their own, along with 'mum' and/or 'dad', and is virtually always the first word that they will learn to write.

The 'love and seriousness' with which the name was first given becomes, then, crucial to the growth of confidence in learning. As with all aspects of language, literacy is not enough in itself to guarantee that naming also bestows identity and free relation in learning. Literacy must be directed to self-determination and a knowledge that the learner's own choices count in the world. The responsible uses of learning, language and literacy involve *taking* responsibility: 'to exist, humanly is to name the world, to change it', claimed Freire (1970, p. 76), adding that we 'are not built in silence, but in a word, a work, in action-reflection'.

Emily Dickinson's refusal to be invisible

There are, suggested Ralph Ellison, in *Invisible Man* (1965), a vast number of invisible people in the world, 'simply because people refuse to see them'. When, however, the 'invisible' of the world do choose an individual voice they are unlikely, initially at least, to find a ready audience. The more original and radical the viewpoint, the more sharply will this be experienced, as with Emily Dickinson, who wrote that her poetry

> Is my letter to the world
> That never wrote to me

Dickinson recalled her own imprisonment in forms of language that she did not feel to be her own:

> They shut me up in Prose –
> As when a little Girl
> They put me in the Closet –
> Because they liked me 'still'

In her case, of course – as with that of Blake and other poets of outstanding originality – she applied her genius to find undiscovered freedoms of poetic expression. Her daring, imaginative adventures in poetry involved plays of wit, parody, irony, experiments with syntax and diction, and original metaphoric flights which subverted conventional meanings. She recorded her own, original vision of the world by 'naming' what it contains with her own, unique terms. Her variation, for example of 'In the Name of the Father –

> in the name of the Bee --
> And of the Butterfly --
> And of the Breeze --
> Amen!

– encapsulates her sense of a living universe that inspires all religions; it also confirms, tacitly, her stubborn refusal to submit to an externally imposed (Christian, or whatever) set of values.

In realising her own, personal voice and refusing to accept being 'shut up' in the 'prose' of other people, Dickinson had to struggle against pressures on her courage and will, to achieve knowledge on her own terms. The privilege – and cost – of winning that struggle was to gain freedom and independence of spirit. This, Dickinson acknowledged with sadness, involved not just the pleasure of seeing the familiar with fresh insight, but also the pain of isolation:

> 'Tis the Majority
> In this as All, prevail –

Assent – and you are sane –
Demur – you're straightway dangerous –
And handled with a Chain –

All school learners and students will resent, at some point, the treadmill
of having to conform to the curriculum and to the learning patterns of the
'system'. Yet that experience of resentment, when we recognise our
imprisoned state, may itself mark a point of potential personal growth.
Where school learning is concerned, the risks of expressing dissent as a
learner were throughly explored by the fifteen-year-old 'Sarah', in
Sarah's Letters (Harrison, 1986a):

'I enjoy schoolwork but I want to do it because it means something to
me...This seems a terrible time to feel so rebellious towards homework and
exams...I am not against work. I need to keep my mind in action but I just
detest the *way* we are expected to work'

(p. 38)

In letters that convey a schoolgirl's version of the anguish felt by
Dickinson, Sarah acknowledged the pain of finding her individual
voice. Yet she understands, too, that it will be a kind of death to 'conform' – to endure the treadmill only because her teachers and society
require it, rather than using her ingenuity to find freedom through
learning on her terms.

The energies released through a learner's rebellion against learning
must, somehow, be invested on behalf of the learner; this is the extremely demanding task that faces all teachers – especially, perhaps, those who
teach adolescents. The teacher must provide conditions to support personal learning, and cannot abdicate from that; it then becomes the
responsibility of learners themselves, using all their native courage and
ingenuity, to ensure that they do not remain 'invisible' to the world.

Kafka and the loss of autonomy

In Kafka's unfinished novel *Wedding Preparations in the Country* (1954)
the main character, Raban, is paralysed by anxieties about plans being
made for his life that seem to be out of his own control. Brooding on the
prospect of going into the country with his future wife, he finds some
dubious comfort in the possibility of 'separating' his body from his 'real'
self, as he did when he was a child, in order to avoid being 'really there':
'And, besides, can't I do what I always used to do as a child in matters
that were dangerous? I don't even need to go to the country myself, it
isn't necessary. I'll send my clothed body.' (p. 11).
Raban is, of course, yet another fictional projection by Kafka, of his

own fears about encountering the world. Kafka's personal *Diaries* (1948–9) recorded both his powerful inner life, and the great dangers which he was convinced that he would risk, if he made the attempt to live on his own free terms in the world: 'The tremendous world I have in my head. But how to free myself and free it without being torn to pieces?' (Volume 1, p. 288). There are few more eloquent testaments to the dangers of the world that are experienced by those who – for whatever reason – have lost the courage to face it, than in Kafka's diaries and stories.

One of Kafka's most remarkable short stories – composed of just two sentences in two separate paragraphs – explores the theme of loss of autonomy:

UP IN THE GALLERY

If some frail, consumptive equestrienne in the circus were to be urged round and round on an undulating horse for months on end without respite by a ruthless whip-flourishing ringmaster, before an insatiable public whizzing along on her horse, throwing kisses, swaying from the waist, and if this performance were likely to continue in the infinite perspective of a drab future to the unceasing roar of the orchestra and hum of the ventilators, accompanied by ebbing and renewed swelling bursts of applause which are really steamhammers – then, perhaps, a young visitor to the gallery might race down the long stairs through all the circles, rush into the ring, and yell, 'Stop!' against the fanfares of the orchestra still playing the appropriate music.

But since this is not so; a lovely lady, pink and white, floats in between the curtains, which proud lackeys open before her; the ring-master, deferentially catching her eye, comes towards her, breathing animal devotion; tenderly lifts her up on the dapple-grey, as if she were his own most precious grand-daughter about to start on a dangerous journey; cannot make up his mind whether to give the signal with his whip; finally masters himself enough to crack the whip loudly; runs along beside the horse, open-mouthed; follows with a sharp eye the leaps taken by its rider; finds her artistic skill almost beyond belief; calls to her with English shouts of warning; angrily exhorts the grooms who hold the hoops to be most attentive; before the great somersault lifts up his arms and implores the orchestra to be silent; finally lifts the little one down from her trembling horse, kisses her on both cheeks and finds that all the ovation she gets from the audience is barely sufficient; while she herself, supported by him, right up on the tips of her toes, in a cloud of dust, with outstretched arms and small head thrown back, invites the whole circus to share her triumph – since that is so, the visitor to the gallery lays his face on the rail before him and, sinking into the closing march as in a heavy dream, weeps without knowing it.

While it seems easy, in the first sentence, to see what is wrong with the treatment of the equestrienne, the second is more elusive. Here, the lady appears to be well treated by the ringmaster, who is attentive to her 'as if she were his own most precious grand-daughter'. He encourages her, demands silence for her, orchestrates her ovation, invites 'the whole circus to share her triumph'. The onlooker in the gallery does not protest this time; yet he seems to experience an even greater weight of distress and, 'as in a heavy dream, weeps without knowing it' (from Kafka, 1949).

Within the economy of just two sentences, Kafka shows that there is more than one way of imprisoning the 'lovely lady'. She may become a metaphor for the social constraints on girls and women in education, over many generations. More likely, however, would be Kafka's own identification with her plight, in revealing the cost of his own solitary artistic achievement – a cost which would not be alleviated by an appreciative public, even if he had one (Kafka, we recall, gave strict instructions that all his writing should be destroyed after his death). I would suggest, too, that the equestrienne may symbolise all vulnerable learners, who must negotiate the 'dangers' of parents, school and society, in the arduous journey towards genuine individuality and confident relation with the world.

Kafka's writing reveals courage in its willingness to confront his inner life; his personal tragedy, it seems, may be explained by a failure to risk bringing his whole, 'real' self into the world. Writing in his diary on his likely fate as a writer, he confessed: 'My talent for portraying my dreamlike inner life has thrust all other matters into the background; my life has dwindled dreadfully, nor will it cease to dwindle'(Volume 2, p. 77).

This experience of a spirit imprisoned from the world is in utter contrast to, say, the art of Albert Camus. When Camus accepted the Nobel Prize for Literature, he attempted to explain the sources of artistic courage of many writers who sacificed personal freedoms in the service of a larger truth and freedom. He suggested (1961) that his own art, however austere its expression, had its origins in 'the sunlight, the delight in life, the freedom in which I grew up'. It was this that gave him a sense of solidarity with all the writers who were silenced throughout the world, and 'who endure the life that has been made for them only because they remember or fleetingly experience free moments of happiness' (p. 198). Applying this to young learners, childhood is not a rehearsal for life; it *is* life, which must thrive on free conditions for learning.

The self versus the system: a personal history by Kath Green

To draw together the issues raised in this chapter, about autonomy in learning and 'risks' of learning, a teacher gives her account, first of teaching and then of fostering a boy who, although he had no diagnosed disabilities, had experienced a number of severe setbacks in his learning progress. The teacher, Kath, highlights some important issues about encouraging literacy, in her reflections on her son's progress in learning:

Earlier years: I became the foster mother of James when he was eight; by then he already had a history of behaviour and learning difficulties. The experience of living with him throughout his years of schooling from that age provided me with a quite different view of education from the one I had formed as a teacher; the new insights that I formed were a major influence on my own professional development. At the same time, it also aroused in me considerable feelings of anger and frustration. I was often shocked to find that professional teachers can, perhaps unwittingly, behave in uncaring ways to the least fortunate of their pupils. In writing this personal account of my experiences I hope to be able to share with you a parent's thoughts and feelings, where the learning needs of a particular child were concerned. I first met James when I visited his feeder infant school, just before he joined my class of first-year juniors. He had a history of extreme neglect and ill-treatment; at that time he was living in a nearby children's home where he was reported to be deeply unhappy. In school James was a difficult child to handle, as he was subject to wild swings of mood; he could neither read nor write.

As an experienced primary school teacher I thought I was quite expert in the teaching of reading. During the year James spent in my class, I used all the skill I knew in a determined effort to teach him to read, yet he made virtually no progress. It was towards the end of that school year, that we decided to apply to foster James.

When he finally came to live us, I learned to adjust roles from teacher to parent. I abandoned attempts to 'teach' him to read but instead, like many parents, I spent many hours reading and telling bedtimes stories to him. Three months later, to my amazement, James was reading. This seemed to run counter to the evidence of all the in-service courses I had attended – namely, that children with learning difficulties need more 'structure' than other children, and that a carefully graded reading scheme was an essential prerequisite for them in learning to read.

James' success refuted these claims. For nearly four years he had been subjected to a variety of tightly structured reading schemes, yet he *chose* to read from a range of *real* stories, all of which would have been classified as unsuitable for nonreaders. Indeed, *Umpty Elephant* (a treasured possession, with an uncontrolled vocabulary of words, given to him by a newly acquired grandmother) was one of the first books he ever read by himself. I was left to ponder whether the methods parents use in teaching children to talk – namely, involving them in rich contexts of meaningful language – would also be appropriate for the teaching of reading.

At the age of nine James moved to a local junior school, and I began to experience his schooling through the restricted role of a parent. Perhaps the most frustrating aspect of this has been the number of times when

James has been expected to 'try hard' at tasks that were quite inappropriate for his needs.

For example, in his last year at junior school James was given a 50-word spelling test every Monday morning. Throughout that school year he never scored more than 3 marks; yet his teacher seemed unable to grasp that this was a disastrous way for James to start each week. As a parent, the weekly spelling test had a fairly dramatic effect on the start of my week, too, for James was always reluctant to go to school on a Monday morning. After much encouragement he would set off for his weekly dose of negative reinforcement – leaving me with a sense of guilt that I had somehow conspired with the school to act against his best interests. My confusion could only be resolved by seeing it from his point of view: why should a child be expected to try when he knows that, no matter how hard he tries, he is going to fail?

Why should he be tested on totally inappropriate material? Why should he suffer the ridicule of both teachers and pupils on being placed yet again at the bottom of the pecking order?

Secondary school: When James moved to the local comprehensive school much of his first year was to be spent in a first year base on 'resource-based learning'. Broadly, this meant that pupils used work cards on individually chosen topics. I felt hopeful that this system would at least allow James to work at his own level, and to avoid the problems caused by inappropriate tasks. But I was alerted when he mentioned that one of his first tasks was to write about 'the effect of World War II on world trade'. He had been told to 'look it up in the library', but he had no idea where to start. On further investigation I discovered that, although covering a wide variety of topics, the work sheets were not graded in any way. Each work sheet included 15–20 questions; whereas the 'brighter' children were expected to answer all the questions, the 'less able' were expected to try only a few. When I asked why there were no work sheets suited to James' level of attainment I was told that staff had not had time to make them yet. Would teachers, I wondered, admit so freely to the parents of 'bright' children that they had not had time to prepare suitable work for them yet?

Homework: As a parent I have been made to realise the deeply disruptive effect that homework for someone with James' learning needs can have on family life. While we were keen to cooperate with the school by seeing to it that James attempted any homework he had been set, and while we were also prepared to spend a good deal of time helping him, in practice this proved to be almost impossible. In so many instances James had grasped so little about the work in progress that he was in no position to 'finish it off for homework'.

How, for example, could he – or we – finish writing up an experiment if he – or we – had no idea what it was that was measured in class to decimal places?

And then there were exams...I can well remember James' intense feelings of anxiety at the prospect of his first set of examinations. For several weeks beforehand he was told to spend his homework time 'revising'. This presented him (and us) with two major difficulties. First, James had no idea of what was meant by 'revision'. Second, it was virtually impossible to do any meaningful revision, even with family support, when all that he had at his disposal was a set of exercise books containing a vast number of incomplete pieces of work. At times like this the child with learning problems and his/her parents are doubly disadvantaged.

All in all, the mammoth task of supervising James' homework was as frustrating for his parents as it was for James himself. Were we justified, we wondered, in giving up so much of our evenings to this activity, when as a family we could have been involved in more interesting things together?

Parents' evenings: Over a period of more than ten years we attended all parents' evenings at James' schools. The cumulative effect of these visits was to leave me with a profound sense of shame about the attitudes of many teachers towards those with learning problems. I listened to endless monologues about my son's lack of ability and lack of effort, all within easy ear-shot of friends and neighbours waiting 'in the queue'. These have left me with intense feelings of guilt and embarrassment, not to mention large dents in my own self-esteem. No wonder that parents of children with problems at school are tempted not to keep going back for more criticism. Indeed, one could argue that if doctors decided to conduct their consultations in the waiting room there might be a similar fall-off of patients attending the surgery.

Why did we keep going? Our main reason was to provide information, as well as seek it, since James' teachers knew little about his background and problems. Even the most sympathetic and committed form tutor would have found it difficult to keep all his teachers fully informed about his needs. Parents' evenings gave us the opportunity of making that personal contact with each of them.

The after-effects were often dramatic. One week after the first parents' evening at the comprehensive school, when we had complained about the enormous amount of negative feedback he had received, James proudly announced that he had been awarded the highest number of 'merit marks' in his house for that week. Teachers had responded to our visit by taking notice of him, and making the effort to see him in a better light. As a result, merit marks flowed in all directions. Not only did his work show obvious signs of improvement but, perhaps more significantly, James' relations with other children also improved dramatically. He became, overnight, a child with some status who was valued – if only for the merit marks he had gained for the team.

Sadly, this change was temporary; gradually, teachers slipped back into emphasising what James could not do, and ignoring what he could do. However, the one thing that we learned from this experience was that James benefited when we made contact with his teachers. We therefore resolved to make regular requests to discuss his progress with the teachers who actually taught him. We did this throughout his secondary school career, and James always benefited. As a teacher I know that many parents of children with learning difficulties either lack the confidence or feel too alienated to make this sort of regular contact. As a parent I cannot over-emphasise the value of such contact, which schools should seek to make in all possible ways.

Marking work: Towards the end of James' secondary career I went to a parents' evening, when a succession of teachers told me that James was capable of much better work than he normally produced, and that his major problem was 'lack of effort'. I felt irritated by this attitude, as I had been looking through James' school books the previous night, and had been appalled by teachers' comments on his written work; these had regressed yet again to negative, condemning remarks. After the parents' evening I compiled a list of all teachers' comments on James' written work during that term.

The 58 comments I listed made depressing reading; none of them was encouraging, and advice was mainly limited to the use of margins and rulers. Their cumulative effect is powerful:

This is not a good start to a new book.
Why have you left all this space? Do not waste space.
You are still wasting a lot of space.
You are *still* wasting space. Untidy. Underline.
This should be at the back of your book.
This work should have been done in your rough book.
What is this? This is a mess. If there is not a big improvement in your presentation, action will have to be taken. Very careless work. Very untidy. Rule off.
Spelling still needs care. You must try to *copy* correctly.
Finish off this question. Please use ink. Watch your spelling. Underline.
Why have you not used this page?
An untidy piece of work. Very untidy. Very untidy. Careless untidy work.
How many times do I need to tell you about using a ruler for *all* work.
Very careless. Rule off.
USE A RULER. Why is this not complete? A careless piece of work. Why have you not used a RULER? You are still not using a ruler.
James, you must learn to set your work out in better fashion. Use a ruler.
This should have been in your rough book. You must make more effort to set your work out in a more presentable manner.
Copy up the rest and also conclusions. Notes missing.
FINISH. You can write better than this, James.
Copy up. Very poor effort James. Finish tests. FINISH.
You can write better than this James. COPY UP.
Very poor effort James. Finish tests. FINISH. Answers to questions?
Cannot read your labels James.
I told you that you were to do this again.
Careless work. Use a RULER ALL THE TIME. Margin?
Use a ruler. FINISH. Diagrams should be in pencil.
FINISH. See me. Untidy. I cannot read some of this.
Care needed with writing up some of the results.

Could none of his teachers break the pattern, to end this litany of criticism? Apart from the complete lack of positive comment, none of these remarks was about the actual *content* of James' work. Given that this is often the only aspect of teachers' work seen by parents, they may be tempted to wonder about a system that results in such useless repetition of criticism, instead of constructive support given to do better.

Were the teachers concerned really surprised that James tackled each succeeding piece of work with diminishing enthusiasm? Among his various pieces of work there were considerable variations of standard. In some he had clearly tried hard; in others he had clearly given up hope. Yet there was little variation in the markers' comments. One piece of work which showed marked improvement still received a totally negative comment. Whatever pressures exist in schools to conspire against adequate marking time, the all-round lapses of professional or of *collaborative* concern, that are revealed in these comments, make useless the whole process of marking James' work.

A poor deal for those with learning problems? One of the most striking features of the teaching James received throughout his secondary schooling was the policy of attempting to 'remedy' James' lack of attainment in written work by concentrating on what he could *not* do, and giving him more of the same. I was appalled to find that he had been withdrawn from mainstream English lessons in order to spend his time working through the most boring English comprehension texts, in an attempt (it was explained) to build up his writing skills. Where, I wondered, was he to gain the sort of rich variety of learning experiences that would make him *want* to write?

Inevitably, having been withdrawn from several mainstream lessons, he experienced additional difficulties in the lessons that he missed. How can a child with learning difficulties make sense of three-fifths only of an English course? Any ideas about the importance of continuity of experience had seemed to vanish.

I recall vividly a time halfway through a school year, when James' attitude to English suddenly changed. He came home talking about the books and poems he had been reading until late into the night. He even brought a poetry book home and read one or two out loud to us all. I remember lengthy family discussions about *Animal Farm*, in which my husband was astonished by James' ability to discuss issues arising in the story. We both wondered what had brought on this sudden change in attitude and, at a parents' evening shortly afterwards, we discovered that James had simply had a change of teacher. This new teacher believed that his first priority was to get children interested in reading, by providing a range of literature that would be meaningful, and that would promote lively discussion. Judging by the the improved quality of our evening discussions, his success had been remarkable.

James at sixteen-plus: When James was fifteen, proposals to set up a sixth form in the school were discussed. I remember attending an open evening at which parents were invited to question a panel of local dignitaries about the proposal. Numerous questions were raised about the relative merits of this or that A-level syllabus, and about entry requirements for various universities.

When I got up to ask what non-examination courses would be on offer in the sixth-form, I was greeted as if I'd just arrived from Mars. Was this a political question? – enquired the Director of Education. When I explained that I felt my son had as much right to another two years of schooling as anyone else, experts looked genuinely taken aback. So unused were they to questions from parents of children with learning problems, that they all assumed my question to be a political plant. It was clear that the provision of non-examination sixth-form courses was not even on the agenda for discussion in the foreseeable future. Again, I felt angry and dejected, that at sixteen-plus the pupils with fewest learning problems could continue their education uninterrupted, while the least able were forced to journey across the city in search of further education. Is it not strange that those who most need the security of familiar surroundings are forced into strange, intimidatingly large institutions where they know neither the teachers nor their peers?

Realising that the school had nothing further to offer, we eventually found a college of further education on the other side of the city, which had a special course for students with disabilities, called 'Towards Employment'. Although James did not normally fall into a 'disability' category, we were impressed by the emphasis in the course outline on individual development of students. After detailed discussions, he was eventually admitted to the course in the category of 'social disability', in view of the appalling circumstances of his earlier years.

We did, of course, wonder whether this was the best course for James; yet the only alternative was to enrol as a 'general studies' student, where he would not have the same individual attention to his needs as on the special course.

Once James started the course, a striking feature was that of the attitudes of staff towards him. The tutors seemed to concentrate on telling him what he *could* do, rather than what he could not. James came home with comments such as, 'Mr X says I'm really good at maths.' Needless to say, this produced a notable difference in James' own attitude to his work.

The staff tried to treat their students as young adults rather than as children. It would be easy to argue that James' attitude improved so radically because he had moved up the pecking order. He was now one of the more successful members of this new group; could he, perhaps, be benefiting at someone else's expense? I think that one major influence was that staff were clearly involved in trying to build up patterns of *mutual support* in the group. The use of competition as a motivational ploy – so rife throughout James' earlier schooling – did not feature much here. Students were constantly encouraged to view success as a new step forward for themselves, which did not require beating someone else. It was most noticeable, how quickly this attitude resulted in individuals being pleased about the success of friends. James often spoke of friends who had achieved something for the first time, and it was a pleasure to see this mutual concern and support building up. At last, he was building foundations of confidence, and enjoying learning.

Issues to be faced

Kath's account dwells on:

- the value of *real* books and real things to learn;
- the *uselessness of mechanical tasks*, in developing reading and writing;
- the need for *individual attention* by teachers to individual needs;
- the *pointlessness of repetitive, negative criticism* of 'poor performance';
- the beneficial difference that *imaginative teaching* can make to a learner's progress;
- the benefits to be gained by *matching appropriate courses* to individual learning needs;
- the fundamental importance of *good relationships and support* in learning/teaching groups.

These issues will be explored in the chapters to follow – on reading, writing and talking/listening in learning, and on the quality of teaching needed to meet the special learning requirements of some pupils.

Part II

DEVELOPING LITERACY

CHAPTER 5

Realising Through Reading

This chapter examines reading in a wider context of literacy needs for learners, and also within the school. It considers:

- the need for *univeral access* to literacy;
- some *international comparisons* of attitude and achievement in the *transforming powers* of reading;
- *making meaning* in reading;
- *assessing reading* – a cautionary tale of SATs: by Denise Aitken;
- reading as a *creative and recreative* process;
- reading to *think, converse and argue*;
- *the communicative power of a good story*: by Alan Thornsby.

I faintly remember her teaching me the alphabet; and when I look upon the fat black letters in the primer, the puzzling novelty of their shapes, the easy good nature of O and S always seem to present themselves before me as they used to do.

(Dickens, quoted in Ackroyd, 1990, p. 47)

Following this childhood recollection by Dickens of his mother as teacher, his biographer Ackroyd noted how, in this 'first entry into that world of words that so enthralled him...it is clear how the words satisfy him, how he finds peace in the letters' (p. 47). The emphasis here on the alphabet letters as friends is worth keeping in mind, even though issues of literacy often can involve considerable distress to those who have not yet found confidence, access or pleasure in reading. As with 'natural' skills such as walking and running, or swimming, or riding a bicycle, reading may quickly lose its mystery, once we can do it. Conversely, failure can involve anxiety and shame for both learners and teachers –

and, indeed for a whole community. Few British people, for example, would have enjoyed the news report of a survey by the Adult Literacy and Basic Skills Unit in 1993 ('Literacy of College Students Criticised', *Independent*, 1993), which found that more than a third of 10,000 students in further education, aged 16–19, had reading skills below those of an average fourteen year old. While the validity of the 20-minute written test that was used for this survey needed to be challenged, our reaction is to wish that the students had been able to perform better. Reflecting on the shame that accompanies illiteracy, Berel Lang (1991) warned:

> Certainly *illiterate* is a pejorative term, often used as an insult – and even *non-literate* and *pre-literate* carry with them a sense of the primitive, the undeveloped...Not to be taken to be literate is often to imply that one has nothing worth reading or writing about.

> (p. 19)

Yet, Lang added, it is important not to assume that being literate necessarily makes someone a better person. This point was made with force in an anecdote retold by James Axtell (1988, from an account by Alexander Long in 1725):

> When the evangelizing Alexander Long told the Cherokees that their religious beliefs were all false, the Indians replied that the fault was not theirs because they did not have the ability to learn from reading and writing. 'If we had', their spokesman said, with a hint of sarcasm, 'we should be as wise as you...and could do and make all things you do: such as making guns and powder and bullets and cloth...and peradventure the great god of the English would cause us to turn white as you are.

> (p. 306)

There are also educational reasons why anxiety and shame should not be the driving force in any programme of reading development; as the last chapter argued, when the focus is only on 'problems', 'deficit' or 'substandard attainment', there will be no space for the *enjoyment* that learning to read must involve – even if (as in the case of many adult groups of would-be readers as well as children), the enjoyment must closely reflect other serious life games.

All people who can read may carry their own library round in their minds, full of all the books and print they have ever read. That internal library makes an indelible impact on all their thinking and discourse, spoken or written. While it cannot, of itself, guarantee power in intellect, breadth in knowledge, wisdom in judgement or freedom in political life, it provides some essential conditions in the modern world, for these qualities to grow.

The conditions for such growth require that, unlike public libraries, our personal internal library should not be a silent place. Its domain is shared with the busy world of what is termed, after Vygotsky (1962), 'inner' speech, or all internalised spoken discourse. Through this combined inner discourse we declare ourselves in speech and writing to other worlds, personal and public. The needs of young children in this respect, as identified by Whitehead (1990, p. 176), apply as well to all readers: 'Children need opportunities for *conversations* about books and stories and time to...sort out their feelings and response to them'. These are the beginnings of acquiring the power to declare one's view to a potentially universal audience; it is empowerment through literacy.

Reading: a universal concern

Concluding a report on reading education in Brazil, Gomes de Matos (Hladczuk and Eller, 1992, p. 42) acknowledged the importance of a universal sharing of experience in literacy studies:

> Let's paraphrase Cicero: 'A country without fluent readers is a country without a soul'. Accordingly, let's exchange our results and experiences and promote reading as a universally uniting power.

His plea, published in the *International Handbook of Reading Education* (Hladczuk and Eller, 1992) was echoed by other contributors, whose reports from various countries are placed in alphabetical order. Two of these, placed sequentially, offer compelling points for comparison. Both of these countries have two official languages, and both are former British colonies; they have, however, little else in common.

In the first of these Reports, Lesotho is described by Roshan Fitter as a mountainous country, landlocked within the Republic of South Africa. Its official languages are Sesotho and English; most children there receive only seven years of full-time schooling. While there have been no recent studies to determine levels of literacy among its mainly rural population, a 1976 report found that about a third of the men and three-fifths of the women could meet a basic UNESCO definition of elementary literacy. Their need for higher levels is urgent:

> We have many adults in Lesotho who are not able to participate fully in Lesotho's society because they cannot read and write and cannot count. For example, if a farmer cannot read and count, how can he calculate the amount of food and fertilizer plus costs that he will need for a year's supply of crops grown on his land?

(pp. 215–16)

The report that follows this, by Warwick Elley, is from New Zealand, where the official languages are English and (since 1987) Maori. Here, the Department of Education 'normally reports literacy levels to international bodies at approximately 99 per cent'– though it also discloses that 'a few pupils do emerge from their primary years with serious reading difficulties' (pp. 228–9), in being unable to read independently. New Zealand's achievements in literacy have, of course, won much international attention.

National provision in New Zealand has included: a vigorous Central Schools Publications Branch of the Education Department; the Reading Recovery Programme pioneered by Marie Clay (1982, 1988); special provision for the development of the Maori language and culture, such as the pre-school movement Te Kohanga Reo (the Language Nest); and the development of bilingual classrooms (although English is still the medium of instruction in over 99 per cent of all classrooms).

The gross contrast between these two reports hardly requires, in a sense, any comment. The Lesotho report reminds us – though few will need to be reminded – of the urgent need to invest in literacy so that literacy may, in turn, bring investment to the economy. The New Zealand case demonstrates just what *can* be done, where investment is adequate and enlightened policies are carried through.

Yet there are significant lessons to be drawn, on further reading of these reports, for a country such as Britain.

The Lesotho report draws attention, for example, to its overall pupil-teacher average of 55-1, and to an important disparity in provision, and in literacy levels, between urban and rural schools. In urban areas there are 'better learning resources, including audio-visual equipment', whereas a scarcity of provision in rural areas forces the teachers to emphasise counting, reading and writing 'in the form of repetitive and monotonous drills' (p. 217). In contrast to the better resourced urban schools, rural teachers 'stress rote teaching such as counting and saying the letters of the alphabet' (p. 217).

The rural teachers in Lesotho are forced 'back to basics' by simple lack of funds and of training – unlike, for example, teachers in British infant and primary schools who were pressed by government advisers on the National Curriculum Council in 1993 to drop their enlightened (or 'trendy', as hostile politicians and journalists would paraphrase) methods, and to adopt 'basic' methods in teaching the first stages of reading, including rote learning of the alphabet. In Lesotho, children outside the capital of Maseru do not have access to libraries, or other opportunities to read for pleasure. There is, moreover, a discrepancy between resourcing for the English and Sesotho languages, where the prescribed texts for Sesotho are far less attractively produced than those for English.

The inevitable inference made by Fitter – that better resourcing needs also to be accompanied by more enlightened teaching approaches and materials – is endorsed by the New Zealand report. There, Elley points out that the New Zealand Department of Education, while retaining centralised powers, encouraged teachers to use their own initiative and to exercise autonomy in developing their own methods and resources for the teaching of reading and, especially, to adapt their teaching approach to the observed needs of their children. Indeed, a key principle in the underlying philosophy of teaching reading in New Zealand is that it should be 'child-centred, with the individual pupil's interests at the heart of the process' (p. 227). Teachers have always played a 'major role in preparing materials and formulating policies, as the Department involves them heavily in the development process'. (My own visits in recent years to New Zealand schools would confirm this; I found that levels of debate among teachers about research and national educational policy, as well as about particulars of curiculum provision within an individual school, are remarkably high and well informed.)

Reading goals

Elley provides a summary of *reading goals*, devised by the New Zealand Department of Education, which encapsulate national policies on the teaching of reading:

1. To make reading an enjoyable and purposeful task;
2. To develop a permanent interest in reading;
3. To develop an attitude of demanding meaning – that which is read makes sense;
4. To develop independence in reading – that is, to help the child become self-sufficient in monitoring his or her own reading, and overcoming difficulties met in extracting a message from a given text;
5. To enable the child to select reading materials appropriate to his or her interests and experience;
6. To help the child become a critical reader;
7. To develop flexibility in adapting the rate of reading to the purpose;
8. To bring each child into contact with a variety of books that will enrich or extend his or her experiences;
9. To increase the child's resourcefulness in using reading to meet everyday needs;
10. To develop the skills of reading aloud and effectively.

(pp. 227–8)

While these government-inspired aims to do not highlight the fostering of imagination (to be looked at later in this chapter), they include many essential conditions for this, such as 'enjoyable and purposeful', 'engagement', 'demanding meaning', 'independence', 'critical', 'flexibility', 'variety of books' and 'resourcefulness'.

That first emphasis, on the enjoyment of reading, reflects world-wide views on the importance of the pleasure principle in literacy. It was stressed long ago in the Newbolt Report (BoE, 1921), for example, which recommended the 'communication of zest' in classroom reading. Teacher-commentary, declared George Sampson (who was undoubtedly the author of that enlightened Report – see Gordon and Harrison, 1991), should be used as a means of heightening the pleasure of books, and pupils should 'be encouraged to read widely for their own pleasure'.

Marie Clay, a New Zealander whose work on reading development and recovery has had a world-wide impact, emphasised (1991) that pleasure goes hand-in-hand with finding personal meaning in reading. Teachers, she suggested, should ask, 'What evidence can I find that the child relates his other language and real world experience to this reading task?' (p. 312). Life experiences, story experiences, familiarity with the story being read, and all the learner's previous successes in reading will contribute to confident possession of a text. She made a 'special plea', too, that 'some children need extra resources and many more supportive interactions with teachers' (p. 345), to get them through all the stages of reading development that they require to become confident adult readers (a similar case for confidence in talking will be made by Janet Collins, in Chapter 7 of this book).

The New Zealand reading goals reveal an official programme in reading development which reflects many of Marie Clay's ideals for universal confidence in literacy. The programme remains unusually enlightened (although Elley mentioned, also, that there is still a 'significant lack of Maori language books'). Yet, in spite of their evident success and their wide acceptance among parents and teachers, there are still periodic calls even in New Zealand for a 'return to basics' in the teaching of reading. As Marie Clay showed, a genuinely fundamental programme for developing literacy needs to be well resourced – especially for those who have difficulties in reading.

Both the New Zealand report and the contrasting report from Lesotho provide powerful confirmation of the case for adequate provision of good books, provided within a framework of coherent, enlightened policies, in the teaching of reading. Each of them sets the teaching of reading in schools in a larger context, of literacy in the community, since reading is too important to be left only to the schools. Children need to see their parents reading, and need to share reading with them. Reading at home, claimed Waterland (1985), 'is the root system that feeds the apprentice reader; if the people at home understand and support what we are doing, everything at school will be made so much easier. If we cannot carry the parents with us, we are diminished.' In this important area of parental support for reading – and of the great field of literacy that may surround children, apart from schools themselves – Peter Hannon and co-workers have provided illuminating studies (see, for example, Hannon and Weinberger, 1990).

An international focus on reading must take whole communities into account and cannot, of course, ignore the *politics* of literacy. Whole communities require, just as do individual readers, to be able to feel that books and print really do offer a world for them to inherit. In his accounts of working on literacy programmes with Brazilian peasants, Paulo Freire described how he and his co-workers sought to identify key words and phrases that carried the greatest emotional force and meaning for the students, and how the tutors then proceeded to build a literacy programme round these. Freire claimed (1973) that literacy makes sense when people begin to reflect on their relation with the world, and their power to transform their world. In this way, literacy becomes a part of their empowerment, rather than something imposed on them by government decree. Literacy, Freire concluded, is valid only where people have come to 'understand words in their true significance: as a force to transform the world'. His view echoes countless examples from literature itself, of the liberating powers of literacy, such as the personal testament of the poet Frances Harper who, as the daughter of free Negro parents, campaigned throughout her life against slavery and white injustice to blacks:

Our masters always tried to hide
Book learning from our eyes;
Knowledge didn't agree with slavery –
'Twould make us all too wise.

But some of us would try to steal
A little from the book,
And put the words together,
And learn by hook or crook.

I remember Uncle Caldwell,
Who took pot liquor fat
And greased the pages of his book,
And hid it in his hat.

And had his master ever seen
The leaves upon his head,
He'd have called them greasy papers,
But nothing to be read.

(from 'Learning to Read', 1872)

Harper's account of 'Learning to Read', like Freire's, celebrates the reader's growth into critical independence; it remains surprising, how those in authority can react so fearfully to this sturdy off-shoot of literacy. To take an example from 1990s Britain: following some vague recommendations in the Kingman Report on the teaching of English (DES, 1988) that student-teachers should be trained in knowledge of language, the Language in the National Curriculum (LINC) Project produced a training manual in 1991 (see Carter, 1990). To the astonishment of many, the Secretary of State for Education not only rejected the manual but also suppressed its publication. This zeal to censor led swiftly, however, to a copy of the materials being made available in virtually every school in the country, leaving many heads and teachers confused about the reasons for suppressing such harmless-looking material.

Was it that the materials invited mildly critical investigations of language in use? In Section Two of the 'Reading Repertoire', on 'Reading the World' there was, for example, a quite useful framework for looking at texts, which dared to invite readers to raise questions about values and about the cultural contexts of what they read. It asked,

1. Who speaks this text?
2. Who is being spoken to?
3. Where does this text come from?
4. What kind of text is this?
5. What does the text want?
6. What does this text mean to me?

Perhaps, as will be argued later, these will not be the *first* responses of a reader, who may be too directly, naively involved in 'what happens' to be ready for any questioning of this kind; but they summarised reasonable steps towards critical reading. They hardly represented the red-blooded left-wing stance of, say, Charles Sarland, whose text on *Young People Reading: Culture and Response* (1991) argued with some ferocity for recognition of alternative cultures in classrooms.

Making meaning through reading

The needs of Freire's Brazilian students are reflected in all people who are emerging into literacy. In urging the importance of finding texts to suit readers, Margaret Meek (1980) challenged the facile assumption that suitable 'standard' reading materials can be universally distributed alongside standardised reading tests, with a telling anecdote:

> When a middle-aged Irish woman who had never read anything began to have reading lessons, her teacher read with her the novels of Edna O'Brien. To the teacher's astonishment she began to read fluently, passionately, and explained, 'Everyone in Ireland knows these stories, but I didn't know they wrote them in books...'
>
> (p. 36)

It is, suggested Meek, through the power of the reader to make personal connections, to create an 'interior fiction', that literacy flourishes. She offered, too, a health warning to teachers, on behalf of learner-readers, not to intervene too much on the personal engagement between reader, or listener, and text: when reading stories with children, 'I know that in order to hand down the magic that is literature I have to disappear and let the tale speak for itself' (p. 38).

Readers, suggested Beard (1987), need to be creative makers of meaning; he concluded that reading is not just a matter of message reception, 'for at the heart of developing reading is the generation of meaning' (p. 282). To demonstrate that it is what words *point* to, rather than what they are supposed to denote, he cited a point by Fries (1962), that five hundred of the most common words in English share between them over fourteen thousand meanings. The word 'form', for example, carries at least twenty different denotations, while the Shorter Oxford Dictionary of 1983 covered nearly three columns working through 'image' to 'imagist'; such a wealth of 'definition' ceases, eventually, to be helpful, in contrast to the *context* in which we find a word, where we can seek out its associations, in making sense of it.

Reading, then, is essentially active, purposeful and selective. It follows, for example, that provision should be made in every classroom for the best classroom library possible, to meet particular needs and interests in the class; investment in real books (including picture books, of course), at all stages, supported by sensitive teacher support, is far more beneficial than standard reading schemes whose very existence assumes a kind of teacher intervention which is likely to interfere with 'meaning-making' as it is understood here. A reading approach based on the linguistic strengths that learners, including young children, bring to the classroom, enables learners and teachers to build on their 'repertoire', rather than supposed 'deficit' of language.

The view of an *emergent literacy*, which is replacing assumptions about reading readiness, was noted by Hall (1987, p. 10): 'development takes place from *within*...emergence is a gradual process...things usually only emerge if the conditions are right' (p. 10). Inevitably, the quality of those conditions will vary from classroom to classroom, and from school to school. Yet what about the quality of advice on reading development that is aimed at the teachers?

Enquiries into reading and texts on reading for teachers have reflected a long-standing confrontation between two main groups, that has taken place over the whole field of education. One of these may be identified as the self-styled 'makers of meaning', who see education as an unfolding, creative/critical process. The second group has been caricatured by its opponents as the 'pedagogic dieticians' who 'with their will-to-domination operating on our propensity to guilt' (Sanders, 1986, p. 229), follow the line that programmes of education must be strictly prescribed and measured.

It is left to teachers to mediate between these entrenched positions as well as they can.

Standardised assessment tests (SATs) in reading: a cautionary tale

Understandably, teachers have expressed frustration, when assessment demands become unreasonable, as in the case of requirements to carry out summative standardised assessment tests in reading. Such tests, supposed to be fully standardised in order to give all children an equal opportunity in them, have been found to betray cultural bias, to the disadvantage of ethnic minorities. Birmingham City Council, for example, reported (1992, p. 10) that reading accuracy grades were criticised by teachers because there was 'evidence that the grade fluctuated according to the texts used'– a finding that would surprise few teachers in classrooms which include ethnic groups.

The attempt in 1993 to impose reading and writing tests at key stage 3, despite the enormous criticism that they had received, led directly to the review by Dearing of the whole National Curriculum. Denise Aitken (1993), who conducted interviews with heads of secondary school English departments during the Spring and Summer of 1993, recorded the strength of antagonism among her interviewees. One department head had strong misgivings about the time to be spent on bureaucratic procedures, and the need for teachers to be trained to recognise and standardise levels; 'these misgivings were nothing, however, compared to her feelings of disappointment and cynicism' (p. 78) when she realised what kind of impact the tests would make on the curriculum. The worst aspect of the tests, for her, was their academic (and thus social) divisiveness, since they were prepared in ways which required pupils to be placed in ability/attainment sets:

> Although she restricted SATs preparation to one lesson each week she reported an immediate reaction from the pupils to being divided in this way; the reactions ranged from disgruntled to openly hostile. She even resorted to writing home to parents of the bottom set who misbehaved, threatening extra lessons after school if the poor behaviour resulted in their not covering the required preparation for the tests in lesson time – a course of action which, she agreed, would hardly promote in her pupils a lifelong love of literature. The same gender pattern emerged as in school A, with a top set of passive girls and a bottom set of demotivated boys.
>
> She felt that the tests only test how to take a test, and was particularly anxious about the reductive nature of the questions, only requiring very brief replies and inhibiting the pupils from developing their responses and demonstrating what they know. She admitted that this has had a definite effect on her teaching: instead of encouraging her pupils to think for themselves, teaching them to expand on and discuss themes and issues from the texts, she gets the pupils to prepare for the SATs by doing quick comprehension-type exercises
>
> (pp. 78–79)

This view came from a teacher who had been prepared to offer qualified support for the National Curriculum provisions in English. Other interviewees were more forthright in their condemnation of 'horrific' sample SATs papers and their 'destructive' impact on teaching and reading progress. Those heads of department who had resisted setting in ability/attainment groups were simply faced with different dilemmas:

> The heads of department who insisted on mixed ability were faced with the problems of preparing some pupils in the group for a Shakespeare paper, and others for a paper on an alternative test, and the prospect of teaching a minimum of seven pieces from the prescribed anthology. Taking into consideration the fact that these texts had to be taught with a SAT in mind, it is easy to see why an interviewee described the effect of the SATs as 'devastating, without any doubt whatever'.
>
> (p. 90)

Following the widespread and successful boycott of the tests (which was upheld in Court only on the workload issue), Aitken acknowledged that the part of her study which addressed SATs became, in a sense, out of date even before it was completed. Even so, it highlighted key concerns about standardised testing of reading; similar mistakes must not be allowed to be made again.

Where research into reading has been concerned, government itself has often been ambivalent about which side to support, when it came to funding projects for *developing* reading, or programmes for *assessing* reading. A succession of National Reports have emphasised enjoyment and pleasure in reading, and acknowledged that sound reading programmes should be linked with a concern for self-directed learning (for example Newbolt (BoE, 1921); Hadow (BoE, 1927); Bullock (DES, 1975). Yet one area of reading research which has attracted almost automatic funding over recent decades has been the psychometric 'standards and assessment' industry. An explanation for this is suggested by Taverner (1990); recalling that, in the Newcastle Commission era of payment by results for teachers, a teacher was fined 2s. 8d. for every scholar's failure to satisfy the Inspector for reading, he commented:

> it conditioned thinking towards the quantitative evaluation of children's work with the implication that what could be measured was important and, conversely, what could be tested was peripheral.

(p. 1)

The industry continued to flourish in the 1980s, despite a range of evidence from the 1970s that even those who were in favour of standard assessment procedures became pessimistic about their worth. Vincent (1979), for example, reported on a range of research in the field of measuring reading comprehension, with the meagre finding that 'in experimental studies, differences in both the qualitative and quantitative outcomes of a "read" appear to depend very much on the reader's perception of the purpose of a reading task' (p. 148).

How much-funded research, qualitative or quantitative, has been spent since then, one wonders, to re-discover the striking obviousness of this finding? Vincent acknowledged, too, that many studies which set out to identify discrete skills or sub-skills in comprehension have only tended to 'show comprehension as more of a unitary and indivisible trait' (p. 141). Yet, in the face of his own evidence on the unreliability of research into standardised testing, Vincent concluded, inexplicably, that 'standardised testing will continue to be more of a liability in schools than an asset' *unless teachers are 'trained' to be proficient in using them* (p. 154). Since the tests are of such dubious value, teachers could clearly use scarce time resources more effectively than this. The bankruptcy of the psychometric tradition in research into reading reflects, I think, a more general failure in education to link the notion of a learner's intelligence with actual processes of understanding. This larger point was investigated by Robin Barrow, in *Language, Intelligence and Thought* (1993), who argued that intelligence is a dynamic quality, which may only be developed by developing understanding. Our first obsession should be to teach, not to assess.

By the 1990s, those who joined the debate had to confront the fact that test methods which had been found inadequate as long ago as the Bullock Report (DES, 1975) had still changed little in design or concept since then. This was despite deep changes in modes of educational research during that period, towards holistic, hermeneutics-based methods of enquiry. In a brave attempt to take account of newer approaches, Pamela Owen (1992, p. 107) proposed a framework for assessment which, she claimed, offered a 'view of assessment which is teacher-controlled, theoretically principled, standardised, but flexible', and which would 'meet the needs of the individual child'. Owen rejected, on statistical grounds, Perera's advice (1980, p. 151) about the advantages of 'informed judgements by a thoughtful teacher' over a defined formula in the assessment of reading. However, while her own framework of nine generic traits (based on audience, purpose and organisation) may represent an updating of earlier principles for assessment that she rejected, it seems still to be too distanced from what actually happens when someone is reading, and someone is – in one way or another – 'listening' to what is read.

It might be thought that, rather than training teachers to apply tests whose only known use is to keep standardisers (whether psychometric or heuristic-based) in business, it would be better for teachers themselves to become engaged in alternative forms of research and development – for example, in classroom-linked enquiries into what makes reading meaningful, and what methods bring success in particular contexts. Since we are still, as Margaret Meek declared (1982), far from understanding how children read, we need to draw on as much successful experience as possible, in the practice of teaching reading. Above all, though, it should be as *natural* a process as possible, taking its cue from the (painless) ways in which children learn to talk. For Jerome Bruner, the starting-point is the child's talk:

> My suggestion is that we begin by making reading an instrument for entering possible worlds of human experience as drama, story, or tale – in order to bring it as close as possible to the forms in which children already know spoken language best.
>
> (in Smith *et al.*, 1984, p. 200)

Reading as a creative and recreative process

There was, included in the same text as the report by Vincent (1979), an account of teaching literature in the secondary school which suggested:

A book that offers the chance of a living relationship with its reader offers support and release; and this may be as true of the reluctant readers' comics as it is of work by Solzhenitsyn or Shakespeare...the learner will develop 'standards' of enjoyment and meaningfulness according to personal needs and intimations.

(Harrison, 1979, p. 92)

Such a view is, of course, open to debate; and questions about 'standards', in terms of the intrinsic value of reading material, rather than on measurable 'performance', continue to produce regular fierce arguments among teachers (such as, for example, issues of 'quality' in children's books, and who decides these).

There have in this century been only two full national enquiries in Britain into children's reading interests – by Jenkinson (1940) and Whitehead et al. (1977). However, there have been many local and international studies in the wider area of enjoyment and personal profit in children's reading; there has also been a wealth of good books and of advice in the professional English journals, on enhancing the experience of reading. These share a recognition with Meek (1982), of ways in which authors themselves may, subtly, have crucial effects on teaching reading.

One of the most influential advocates of reading as a natural process, requiring support but not interference, is Herbert Kohl. The subtitle to his revised edition of *Reading, How to* (1988) contained an obvious challenge to British readers, published as it was in the same year that The Education Reform Act laid down the foundations for National Curriculum requirements in reading *'a people's guide to alternatives to learning and testing'*; Kohl had in mind, of course, *imposed* learning. When the first edition of this book appeared in 1973, it won wide attention; yet by the time of its reissue, its impact was largely forgotten. The revised version had, I noted, been borrowed from my own university library only four times in a period of four years since its publication, and many recent books on reading include no mention of his work.

Yet the incisiveness with which Kohl challenged 'myths' about the teaching of reading – 'there is no reading problem. There are problem teachers and problem schools' – is based on sound experience and research. While accepting, for example, that a knowledge of phonics may be useful for a teacher of reading, he describes in the introductory chapter how phonics-based reading programmes can become 'crippling' for the learner-reader. In laying down his Ten Conditions for reading development, Kohl advocated the 'open class room'; he criticised 'racist, competitive and authoritarian tendencies' in a culture which over-values individualism at the expense of cooperation:

people who cannot share knowledge, experience and things are not open to each other. They hold back, hoard...Consider learning to read. In a collective situation students would naturally help each other, would read stories to each other, ask each other for help, share insights. They would need to look to the adult for help as a last resort. A sensible balance between the individual and collective aspects of learning is hard to achieve. However, it can be developed in a context where people respect and trust each other.

(pp. 136-7)

The need also to provide supportive relationships for readers, in the form of rich books, was well recognised by Robert Protherough (1983), who recorded accounts by children of their experience of reading. He cited a fifteen-year-old boy who shared his sense that, while reading, 'the characters are part of you and you of them, and as you are reading you want to help them and live for real the life the character has' (p. 25). The importance of conversation in realising texts, and John Dixon's view (1994) on 'voices and bodies' in learning, is also discussed in Chapter 7.

It is the 'real-ness' of books, and of characters in books, that explains their power to educate. Muriel Rubin (1988), working in a London girls' comprehensive school on Jamaica Kinkaid's work of autobiographical fiction, *Annie John*, reported:

To what extent is the narrator/character, Annie John, identified with the writer Jamaica Kincaid? My pupils, a class of twelve year old girls, were at first convinced that they were reading a book about Annie John by Annie John. Or that if Jamaica Kincaid does exist she is really Annie John with a pseudonym. Annie John was that real to them – and the notion of autobiographical fiction relatively difficult to grasp. In some strange and complex way, fiction can be truer and more real than life itself; for some of these girls Annie must have have seemed more real than any pen-pal – and, after all, why not?

(p. 11)

In his classic work on reading response, *Experience into Words* (1963), Denys Harding suggested that such a complete absorption in the text characterises all real response, from the most naive to the most sophisticated readers. While it is an inner, highly personal experience it is a response that we need to share, so that other kinds of response – reflective, analytical, speculative – may follow and also be shared. Indeed, Carol Fox (1989), writing on the 'Divine Dialogues' of five-year-old story-tellers, suggested that thinking and argument are implicit in the actual recounting of a story. The 'yarning-on' of young story-tellers can reveal, through their story-metaphors 'cool and serious minds at work, weighing up the pros and cons of imaginary problems, problems posed by themselves as narrators, and solved in satisfying and elegant ways' (p. 42).

Some remarkable examples of the value of conversations about books and reading were provided in Donald Fry's *Children Talk About Books* (1985). In this case, the conversations were with an adult teacher-researcher, as well as with fellow-readers; but they are genuine conversations, not just formal interviews. In one of the transcripts, Joanne reflects on imagining herself inside a book she is reading; this prompts a question from the interviewer, which leads in turn to a gradual disclosure by Sharon of an important moment in her reading of *Jane Eyre*. This brief passage from the transcript provides a vivid illustration of Kohl's general point about 'blending individual and collective aspects' in the sharing of reading experience:

Joanne: You can, um, imagine...Going back, in that time
Interviewer: ...what was your phrase, you can imagine yourself..?
Sharon: ...The book is in your mind, you can imagine that you're somewhere else.
Interviewer: Yes. Can we get at that a little more precisely, and see if you're both saying the same thing. Are you, are you simply saying that you can picture it?
Sharon: No, you can really *feel* that you're there. Um, um, I'm trying to think of something I can use as an example. (6 seconds pause). Like with, um, the first scene in *Jane Eyre* where she's sitting in the window seat with the rain outside, you can actually feel the cold window panes and the rain beating against them, and how lonely she is, you know...You really feel sorry for her, feel it yourself, I mean, you imagine yourself being there, being a little girl sitting in the window seat.

(p. 124)

Sharon's account, as revealed here and in the whole chapter that Fry devotes to her conversations, demonstrates both Meek's remark (quoted earlier) about reading as an 'interior fiction', and also a later suggestion by Meek (1991), about 'experimental and developmental' qualities of reading. Sharon's reflections on how the 'reader becomes the book' point to the remarkable completeness of experience that reading may provide; yet a full reading remains, paradoxically, incomplete, just as a living relationship must remain unfinished. Moreover, Sharon admitted to feeling an experience of death when she finished reading a book; the second reading of a book was never quite the same experience.

It might be presumed that teachers who have experienced this entire taking possession of a text should be more likely to encourage their classes to form their own response; yet even the most expert and sensitive teachers can forget, as this experienced college teacher confessed:

While reading a short story at home, I became excited at the possibility of linking it to some poetry being studied in my A-level class. At the next lesson I began reading it aloud, ignoring some building-site noise outside. I had not been able to produce enough copies for each student to have one, the story was too long, and my voice became tired of reading. When I reached the end, with relief, I found I had totally lost the attention of the students, and although one or two made efforts to give comments, it was more to please me than because they cared about the text...The session with them had been teacher-centred, both story and poetry were well and truly mine – a perfect recipe for how not to teach.

The next lesson saw us all back in the usual small groups, preparing poems for presentation, collecting cuttings from newpapers, role-playing...I was relegated to the sidelines, exactly where I should be – supporting, ready to help, arbitrating, handling questions, suggesting new lines, but not instructing.

It is so important to hand the material over to the students, even without introduction, so that they feel *their* reading really matters. Once the teacher has expressed her opinion, it is so hard for the student to make a fresh or differing contribution. One student this year complained about a class: 'We want it to be our class not hers.'

(Marina, with acknowledgements)

To sense the complexity of reading and of all learning is, in short, to sense the complexity of human relations; good teaching is about good relationships in learning. Would-be 'scientific' accounts of the experience of reading must, inevitably, be inadequate by comparison to the insights revealed by this teacher into how to relate to reading, or the kinds of insights that Sharon provided (above). Helen Gardner's *In Defence of the Imagination* (1982) dwelled on the 'immense complexity' of the mental processes that reading involves. The power to understand what is said or what is read 'takes place in time, the process by which the past incessantly moves into the future' (p. 88), so that ultimate meanings must always lie beyond the reader's power. This, for Gardner, is the immense reward of living with a text, that the relationship is never finished.

The communicative power of a well-imagined story

Children cannot be taught to read. A teacher's responsibility is not to teach children to read but to make it possible for them to learn to read.

(Smith, 1978)

The final section of this chapter on reading is intended to link with the next chapter, on writing, in dwelling on how teachers may help to establish learners in (to use Frank Smith's phrase) the 'literacy club'. It offers some glimpses of how teachers themselves may themselves be alerted, for various reasons, to write their own stories as reading material for children, or for fellow-teachers. In doing so, they may succeed in communicating complex feelings and ideas, that would be weaker or even inaccessible in other (discursive) forms.

Betty Rosen suggested, in her account of teachers as story-tellers (1991), that 'the more a child is entertained by tales of surmountable fearful fantasies, the less that child is oppressed by the phantoms that form within his or her personal darkness'. In an account of his own handling of children's books as a primary classroom teacher, Alan Thornsby (1994) provides some illustrations of how writers have been prompted, through disturbance and even fear, into imaginative writing. He cites, for example, Bernard Ashley's story about bullying, *Terry on the Fence* (1986). In a televised interview, Ashley linked his discovery of a runaway boy huddled in a doorway, late at night, with a childhood memory of fearing to go to a certain area of a common, which was 'owned' by children from another school, and with the recollection of a burglary at his own school (where he was headteacher).

In another case based partly on teaching experience, Philippa Pearce derived the title story in her supernatural short story collection, *The Shadow Cage* (1977), from a classroom incident. The story grew as a strategy to quell some phantom whistlers at the back of the room who could be heard when she, as a supply teacher, read a story to the class. Through wittily enlisting her audience to help her find an answer to the unanswerable question, 'who are the whistlers?' she invited them to share her teacher's discomfort, even fear, when meeting something unidentified and hostile. Thus the familiar school playground becomes menacing at nightfall for young Kevin, when

> He saw the bars of shadow as he approached; he actually hesitated; and then, like a fool, he stepped inside the cage of shadows...

Other stories in this book reveal, less directly, further teacher experiences – such as 'Guess', where the ghostly Tess Oakes moves disconcertingly between two identities, first as an unkempt, smelly schoolgirl and eventually as a tree-spirit. These stories depend, for their success, on Philippa Pearce's gift for depicting an outlandish sense of place and of character, while keeping one foot firmly in the ground of commonsense living (see, for example, Harrison, 1983c, for a further account of her work).

The uses of good pictures to accompany reading material are well documented (see, for example, Graham, 1990). To demonstrate how they add a valuable extra dimension of visual 'language' – which is especially valuable to inexperienced readers, but also attracts readers of all ages – Alan Thornsby decided to write his own story, with accompanying illustrations. The story and the pictures are an imaginative transformation of a problem encountered in his own teaching, in order to appeal to an audience 'of all ages'. Each 'verse' of his brief text was illustrated; he also provided a general reflection on the composition of his story about an encounter with a difficult child. While space does not allow inclusion of the large-scale illustrations, the story text is given on page 106, with the accompanying commentary alongside it.

This teacher's story provides persuasive evidence of the power of a well- told tale to convey, as a fully imagined picture, essentials of the general professional points raised in his accompanying commentary, with far more vivid impact than the general statement could achieve, and in a way that communicates as effectively to a seven year old as to an adult.

Which might, perhaps, suggest that this present chapter, or even the whole book, should be re-cast as a work of fiction.

The argument turns, now, to writing processes in learning.

106

I'm Not Bothered
The Text

– Richard had a computer, a television and video, a stereo, a snooker table and lots of toys and games. They were all in his bedroom.
– 'I'm not bothered,' said Richard.

– At school, Richard spoilt the games of other children. He pulled their hair. He stole their crisps. Even his friends were afraid of him.
– 'I'm not bothered,' said Richard.

– In the classroom Richard could work hard, but he never listened to the teacher.
– He only said 'I'm not bothered.'

– Even when the teacher got very angry Richard muttered 'I'm not bothered.'

– When he got home, his Mum and Dad were still at work.
'I'm not bothered,' said Richard and got his tea ready.
– He went out to play. He didn't care about the time.

– He went back home very late. His dad was cross and made him go to bed.
'I'm not bothered,' said Richard.

– 'I've bought you some new clothes,' said his mother.
'I'm not bothered,' said Richard.

– But the next day Richard wore his new clothes. When he got them dirty, he just said 'I'm not bothered.'

I'm Not Bothered
Commentary

Having been involved with picture books, and the concern that there should be an appeal within a book for all ages, I felt obliged to attempt to create a book of my own.

The general subject matter choice was simple, children and school were obvious starting points. The more focused point was more difficult. I finally decided that I would like to base a story on one child, who throughout his years at school had proved to be a difficult child. He was physically and verbally aggressive and generally took very little interest in his work. However, on a 'good' day, especially in a one-to-one situation, he would show great interest and display a keen knowledge. Too often, in discussion about his work and behaviour his comment was 'I'm Not Bothered.'

In writing this story, I have tried to make some attempt to understand and explain the behaviour of a child, and make him respond in a positive way, to the care and concern given to him by people around him.

The early part of the story was simple, as was the ending, where the child responds, and is able to relate to the people around him (and conform?). It was the 'transformation scene' that proved difficult. What event could precipitate the realisation that other people, especially families do care and do matter? I finally decided that being lost in unfamiliar surroundings would solve the problem.

The story introduces Richard, a child who has everything materially. He accepts this as normal, with no gratitude and at school continues to 'take' what he wants from other children. He sees no reason to make any effort to develop himself or his work, and although unconcerned about friends within his peer group, still by his behaviour and attitude needs to be noticed, despite the constant 'I'm Not Bothered'.

– Look at your new clothes,'said his Mum. You are a naughty boy! Richard only said 'I'm not bothered.' Richard went straight to bed.

'We're going on a picnic tomorrow,' said Dad. 'I'm not bothered,' said Richard.

– 'Hurry up or we will go without you,' said his Mum. 'I'm not bothered,' said Richard.

– When they got to the countryside Richard ate crisps and sweets and chocolate biscuits. He drank lots of fizzy pop. 'You'll be sick' said his Dad. 'I'm not bothered,' said Richard.

– I'm going for a walk,' said Richard. 'Don't go too far,' said his Mum, 'it will be dark soon.' 'I'm not bothered,' said Richard.

Richard walked over the hill. Stars began to twinkle in the sky. It got dark. 'I'm not bothered,' said Richard, in a quiet voice.

– An owl hooted. A twig snapped. 'I'm not bbothered.' said Richard, but he was beginning to feel alone and frightened. He turned to go back to his Mum and Dad.

– He could not see at all. He was lost. He started to run. He slipped on some mud. Thorns tore his clothes. He was bothered.

– He shouted at the top of his voice 'MUM I'M HERE'

On his return home, both parents are still out at work. Richard feeds himself, goes out to play, only returning home when he is ready, and is unconcerned about any anxiety he may have caused.

Despite Richard's behaviour and lack of remorse, his mother gives him new clothes, which he wears and spoils the next day. As ever, he still shows no regret or sorrow about his behaviour, or reaction to his punishment.

His parents take him on a picnic, and Richard, as independent as ever wanders off, gets lost and finally becomes terrified by the dark, the noises, the surroundings and his imagination. He is alone, but finally has to cry out 'MUM I'M HERE!'

It is the final shout from Richard that is the focus of the story. It is not simply a cry for help from a lost boy. It is a statement of fact relating to that situation, and a cry for acceptance in life and most of all for love, not just material possessions.

Like many families, both Richard's parents need to work, and have little time to share with him. They shower Richard with material things, to make up for their lack of attention while at the same time Richard readily knows that any demand by him will be met for the same reason. For these reasons they are shown in the book as shadowy figures who are there, but not playing a full role in the life of Richard.

As a counter to the situation, Richard has built a self defence mechanism around him; arrogance, greed, and apparent lack of concern for other people, their feelings or possessions. His unhappy life continues, accepted by Richard and his parents, until the plea comes from him for acceptance, and a full part in family life.

There are many social issues and comments in this book, which need to be examined, explored and discussed, to help children understand other people and themselves and as with many books, to sow some seeds for better lives in the future.

CHAPTER 6

Realising Through Writing

This chapter dwells on writing in learning, especially on the importance of *personal writing* in learning development. Looking at *'what'* learners write, rather than *'how'* they write, it considers;

- phases of *learning through writing*, in developing the literate imagination;
- making writing, as with all language, *one's* own;
- the uses of *personal and journal-writing* – for professional writers, and for school students;
- personal writing for *student-teachers*, to support their professional development.

Write OE *writan*, connected with Icel. *rita*, to tear, cut, scratch out...

Brewer's Dictionary of Phrase and Fable

The inventors of writing doubtless discovered that it could be a difficult business. It is understandable, then, that the 'how' of writing should have been given all the weight of attention that was directed to it in the 1980s, not least through National Curriculum Orders and guidelines. Advice proliferated on pre-writing, planning, drafting, re-drafting, composing, re-reading, write-reading and read-writing, contemplating, conferencing, polishing and post-writing. Much of this work is reflected in a text such as *Writing Policy in Action* (Bearne and Farrow, 1991), which drew on a wide range of work from the National Writing project of the 1980s, to provide a compendium of advice for teachers.

Now, in the light of a suggestion by Washe (1990), that 'writers, young or old, need to give undivided attention...to the discovery of *ideas*' (p. 36) it may be timely to focus on *what writers write about*, and *why* they write, rather than just how they do it. This is, of course, simply to reiterate what has been long claimed – that even very young writers can be genuinely interesting, when given the chance. This was demonstrated by Tolstoy (1862), in his classic account of working with children in his free school at Yasnaya Polanya. More recently, Murray (1984) and Smith (1982) provided influential accounts of how to generate motivation for learners to write. Steedman (1982) showed how the collaborative account of 'The Tidy House' by a group of eight-year-old girls provided 'valuable evidence of the fact that children are not the passive subjects of their socialisation but active, thoughtful and frequently resentful participants in the process' (p. 32). Like Sarah (in Harrison, 1986) these children sought and found a 'voice' in their writing which did not only reflect, but also critically investigated their world. Accounts in *The Development of Children's Imaginative Writing* (Cowie, 1982) and Dyson (1989) also included persuasive accounts of achievements by the youngest writers in schools, in original writing.

In an account of research into *Learning Through Writing* (Harrison, 1983a) I proposed a sequence of phases in writing processes, which served the learner in gaining personal ownership of learning. Writing, I argued, grows with reading, out of the first language arts of speaking and listening. While the vitality of writing depends intimately on living speech, it requires a more self-conscious sifting of expression than is the case in speech:

> For one thing, writing is a much more gradual process and, because we cannot rely on sheer verbal fluency, we may find it less easy to rely on clichéd expression. This prompted Denis Harding to suggest (in *Experience into Words*, 1963) that 'some people...speak so fluently that thought processes apart from words hardly seem to occur...A subtler use of language often consists of breaking and reshaping the familiar moulds'. At best, writing gives us opportunities of time and space that are less available in talking. The learner can explore emerging representations of experience, as perhaps only the most intimate conversations allow.
>
> (p. 20)

Five interrelated aspects of developing writing were identified in *Learning Through Writing*, each of them in answer to an enquiry about lived experience:

1. Q: What do I sense, feel, do, in this world?
   A: Through my writing I can TELL what has happened.
2. Q: What effect does my experience have on me; how do I respond, adjust, change?
   A: Through my writing I can REFLECT on what has happened.
3. Q: What do I know; what can I now clearly understand, as the 'truth' about things?

A: Through my writing I can *IDENTIFY* my world.
4. Q: How may I live in effective relationship with my world?
A: Through my writing I can *ORGANISE* my world.
5. Q. What patterns of meaning can I discern in this new learning; what is my vision of living?
A. Through my writing I can *INTEGRATE* my learning into a whole world view.

Each of these phases was examined in detail, accompanied by examples of writing by a whole class of school students who were followed through three years, from years ten to twelve (14–16 years old). Together, these phases of learning through writing might be seen in diagrammatic 'tree-model' form:

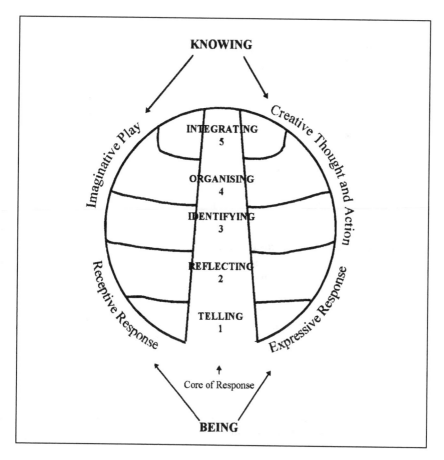

Figure 6.1 Five phases in learning through writing
Source: derived from Harrison, 1983a

The model in Figure 6.1, derived partly from Polanyi's account of *Knowing and Being* (1969), highlighted the holistic relationship of the phases. However, it disguised the untidy, piecemeal actual process of learning, to which Polanyi himself drew attention. It is, I suggested, because we *are* learning, that writing may become confused, or repetitive, or meandering, in the search for threads of meaning:

> the first phases of writing, as concepts begin shadowily to emerge, can involve all kinds of loose ends and jottings around that ought to be included, since they are felt to be potentially part of the pattern, yet they seem irreducible to any kind of order.
>
> (p. 19)

This area of writing – which may include jottings, notes, journal keeping and personal reflections, with or without an intended audience – will be the special focus of the present chapter. These versions of writing may be found in all phases of learning through writing; indeed, it would be hard to imagine any of the phases happening without them. In the domain of personal writing it is obvious that writers are more inclined to claim *personal ownership* of what they write. Moreover, and to qualify an emphasis in my earlier text, personal writing may involve highly complex forms of thinking and writing.

'Myself my own experiment'

Learning, and learning through writing, can be an uncomfortable business, even without the intrusion of teachers:

> A wakeful, changeless touchstone in my brain,
> receiving, noting, testing all the while
> These passing curious, new phenomena,
> Painful, and yet not not painful unto it,
> Though tortured in the crucible I lie,
> Myself my own experiment.
>
> (Arthur H. Clough, Adam and Eve, Sc. II, 34–39)

Through the search to put new learning into the right focus – with one's self, and with the world – we can, suggests Clough, put our very identity at risk. The act of learning, like any release of energy, involves risk; furthermore, the *language* of learning may involve particular risk, in exposing the learner to conflicting versions of experience.

In 'Among Schoolchildren' (1986, p. 3) Seamus Heaney reflects, in an essay which is 'more autobiography than argument', on the teaching of children as 'a matter of sympathetic recognition'. As a Catholic

Ulsterman who became steeped in English studies, his own experience of Clough's 'crucible' of self-inspection amongst the flux of the world was sharper than most. He felt, especially, the force of cultural contradictions in his upbringing – 'Was I two persons or one? Was I extending myself or breaking myself apart?'

Heaney acknowledged that his experience could be paralleled by many others who did not share his background (such as Larkin's experience as a provincial student among the higher wealth and pretensions of an Oxford College). He showed, too, how 'Irishness' has its own powerful language and viewpoint, making its own sense of the world. Long after Stephen Dedalus, the linguistically self-conscious hero of Joyce's *Portrait of the Artist as a Young Man*, was made to feel by the Dean that his own Drumcondra word 'tundish' was inferior to the standard English 'funnel', Stephen records in his diary at the end of the *Portrait*:

> That tundish has been on my mind a long time. I looked it up and found it in English and good old blunt English too. Damn the Dean of studies and his funnel! What did he come here for? To teach us our own language or to learn it from us? Damn him one way or another.

To speak the dialect of Ireland, Heaney concludes, need not mean exclusion from the world's banquet, since

> that banquet is eaten at the table of one's own life, savoured by the tongue one speaks. Stephen now trusts what he calls 'our own language', and in that trust he will go to encounter what he calls 'the reality of experience'
>
> (pp. 10–11)

Issues of talk in learning are the focus of the next chapter. For now, in applying Stephen's experience of speech to writing, we need not dispute the commonsense argument, that to insist on standardised speech is less justifiable than to require a grasp of standard conventions in writing. Yet Stephen's assertion, that *he* will choose his language for *his* use, points to an important principle for personal writing in schools, which is: since the world of the learner must count in learning, some respect is required for all the personal hallmarks that an individual learner may reveal in writing, just as in any discourse. Stephen's assertion of selfhood is echoed in the words of a school student, Jameela Musaid (Earl Marshall School, 1992):

> Speak up, speak up, don't be scared!
> Shout loud don't be sad!
> Be proud.
> This is your language.
> Make them hear and feel and fear.
> Make them feel what you are feeling,
> Don't be afraid, I am here!

Don't feel what they are feeling,
Shout loud, don't be afraid, this is your language.
That is why you are here.

('My Arabic Language', p. 21)

Reflecting on the autonomy of the writer, Ruth Townsley (1993) suggested that writing 'embodies the individual and social meanings which contribute to human existence. When we scrawl our signature across a page, we are not just signing our name, we are signing our identity' (p. 23). She cited, too, Lucy Calkins' account (1983, p. 12) of a six year old's writing: 'In large, splashy letters, Jen had left her mark. Her writing reflects her style, her life-force. Jen was saying "I am".'

What the beginner-writer proclaims through her name, the more experienced learner may use as a means of higher persuasion. Reeve and Peel (1993) revealed, for example, the self-assertive elements in rhetoric which students can exploit in their own writing; they defined expository prose as

prose writing in which a sense of authorial self and statement of being is paramount. The self may be mediated through a persona, as in Swift's *Modest Proposal*...it may be inscribed more overtly, as in Alice Walker's *In Search of our Mother's Garden*, or it may be all but effaced, as in Mayhew's *London Labour and the London Poor*, in order to expand and support the promulgation of an argument.

(pp. 37–8)

Such writing would come, in the scheme of phases in writing outlined earlier, into the organising phase, though its roots must surely be in that first 'I am', announced by Jen. In the light of this we should, perhaps, review the inevitable power relationship that exists between teacher and learner. Berel Lang's point (1991, p. 8) that writing involves ethics, since 'someone (the writer) *does* something to someone else (the reader)' should be extended to include *response* to writing: whatever we say or write about has the power to enhance, or to damage confidence in future writing. This may be especially true in that broad area of writing known as 'personal' writing, whether or not it is intended for an audience; and where the audience is a teacher it may need, crucially, to be a *listening*, non-intervening audience (which is not to imply that teacher-criticism will be absent).

Personal journal-keeping

When looking for clues about the nature of the writing process, the note-

books and journals of writers reveal rich evidence of points of disturbance, emerging metaphors and moments of connection that generate
imaginative writing. These have important implications for good classroom practice in handling personal writing, where the teacher aims to
ensure that the power relationship between teacher and learner is placed
at an effective distance. School learning is, inevitably, in the public
domain; yet it must also contain space for the private reflection and private discourse that personal writing involves. In *Diaries and Journals of
Literary Women* (1990) Judy Simons argues, indeed, that private writing,
which claims its own space for retirement in order to contemplate, can be
regarded as a full art-form; she certainly demonstrates how personal
journals may provide conditions for writing that breeds independence,
and subverts conventions. Fanny Burney, for example, disclosed the need
of many diarists and journal-keepers for a 'nobody' audience: 'to
Nobody can I be wholly unreserved to Nobody can I reveal every
thought, every wish of my heart, with the most unlimited confidence' (in
Simons, 1990, p. 2).

Even the most sociable of people, as Edith Wharton confessed, need
their escape routes to self-containment: 'I love to be with my friends; with
four or five of them I feel my wings but, oh, when I'm alone how good
the talk is!' (in Simons, p. 2). Similarly reflective 'talk' in classroom
learning can be with the 'other' in one's self, as identified by Heaney, not
always with other people. The painter Ivy Jacquier wrote that her diary
helped her to understand 'the fluctuations of self. One never is, one has
been or is becoming' (in Simons, p. 12). A diary, suggests Simons, can
act as 'therapy, consolation and a means of expression of...divided sensi-
bility' (p. 15). One of the most powerful justifications of space for the
individual's viewpoint is provided in Burney's account of her operation
for breast cancer in 1811, which she underwent without anaesthetic; this
rare account of the perception of the patient in surgery highlights the
'awareness and responsiveness of the central character in the drama' (p.
36), rather than dwelling on the technical skills of the surgeons.

Virginia Woolf, who doubted sometimes whether she had an 'inner
life' (Simons, p. 169), provided an intriguing view of what sense a diary
might make of the 'loose, drifting material' of her life. It should

> resemble some deep old desk, or capacious hold-all, in which one flings a
> mass of odds and ends, without looking them through. I should like to come
> back after a year or two, & find that the collection had sorted itself & refined
> itself & coalesced, as such deposits mysteriously do, into a mould, transparent
> enough to reflect the light of our life, & yet steady, tranquil, composed with
> the aloofness of a work of art.

> (Woolf, April 1919, in Simons, p. 176)

She acknowledged, too, that diary writing would need some real effort, lest the writing should become 'slick and untidy'.

Various uses of personal writing

Simons identified four main critical aspects of diary/journal writing:

1. The nature of the *relationship* between private writing and writing for a wider audience;
2. Ways in which private writing may support enquiry into *modes of production* of finished, formal writing;
3. How private writing may be a form of *autobiographical* writing in its own right – but as a daily, rather than 'overview' record of experience;
4. How diaries and journals may be seen as a fully fledged literary text, as a 'highly self-conscious piece of writing' and *art-form* in their own right.

Each of these aspects has implications for classroom writing. The first draws attention to natural processes of *development* in writing (which were discussed earlier in this chapter); the second draws attention to the value of a personal journal as a valid source of *evidence for evaluating* coursework, or project and research work; the third highlights the uses of *day-to-day particulars of experience*, for possible incorporation into later work (which may or may not be autobiographical); and the fourth celebrates such writing *for its own sake*. In the words of Anais Nin, 'The core of us is an artist, a writer...it is in our work, by our work, that we reassemble the fragments, recreate wholeness' (in Simons, p. 204). This view of the artist in all of us helps to explain how quite pedestrian journals are sometimes illuminated with passages which have the inevitability of fully worked art, as in the Diary of Thomas Ward (1909), sometime master Cutler of Sheffield. Ward, who kept a diary from early manhood until his death at the age of ninety, recorded both small rewards and small pains of living, with some perfectly visualised moments:

A tall honeysuckle is nailed against the house and mounts higher than the windows. Birds dart up and down searching for food...If this honeysuckle were taken from me, I should lament its loss as Jonah his gourd but not I hope like him, be angry.
...More solitary hours with little but my own thoughts to divert me. These become stale and I resort to murmuring a tune and singing a song or psalm, not loudly articulating or whispering but silently in my own mind which is significant for the purpose.

Perhaps these recorded moments could be worked into a haiku, though they hardly need to be. In a quite different context (though with a Sheffield link) the remarkable writing skills of ordinary people, when given opportunities to reflect on their lives in writing, are movingly recorded in an anthology of personal writing called *Lives of Love and Hope* (Earl Marshall School, 1993). Among a world-wide range of accounts of 'dramatic and difficult' lives from schoolgirls and their families in this multi-ethnic community school is a chapter by 'Amala', who prefaces her story of family loves and conflicts (which includes unflinching details of murder, fatal illness, riots and divorce) with a glimpse of rural Bangladesh. This contradicts orientalist or standard 'third world' images of that country:

> The village where I was born was a fine and beautiful place...extremely clean, with no litter lying around. Most of the people who lived in the village cared about it very much, and did their best to keep it looking remarkably well and tidy. To me the people were environmentalists. When one came to the village, one could see and smell the green grass, also smell the perfume from the different types of flowers...The pond was extremely pretty with the water lilies, and white pebbles down beneath the bottom, which appeared to look like pearls. Probably that was why the village was called Suna Pur (Village of Gold).
>
> (p. 41)

In her Introduction to this book the writer and playwright Rukhsana Ahmed noted that, in the widely diverse accounts of personal lives provided by the writers,

> it is interesting to see the patterns emerge as women's lives, virtually across continents, echo similarities and join together to form a crisscross of both constraints and oppressions as well as courage and resourcefulness.
>
> (p. v)

The cumulative record of personal experience gains, in short, a political impact.

The journal as a work-aid

At other times, the writing of a journal is very much a working document, recording incidents that may need to be thoroughly re-worked in later writing. Athol Fugard, for example, recorded in his notebook that the genesis of his play *Boesman and Lena* was 'in an image from over ten years ago – Coloured man and woman, burdened with all their belongings, whom I passed somewhere on the road near Laingsburg' (1974, p. xx). This memory became linked with that of another woman who also gave weight to his image of Lena:

> Sense of terrible physical and spiritual destitution, of servility. Did the house-work without a sound, without the slightest flicker of 'self'...After telling the woman we had no work she left to try a few other houses. Last sight of her about two hours later. Heat even more fierce...trudging up the hill on her way back to the Glenmore bush.
>
> That hill, that sun, that walk! Possibly even a walk that my Lena has not yet, but *will* one day...A walk into the final ignominy of silence, burdened at that moment as never before by those unanswerable little words, Why? How? Who? What?

(p. xxi)

Fugard recorded, then, his frustration when trying to write Lena's first, long soliloquy in the play – 'very clear on the function and "feel" of this moment, but can't get it down on paper'. He recalls how, when writing his play *Hello and Goodbye*, he noted in his diary that he was 'skating on a hard surface reality, waiting for it to break somewhere, somehow, so that I could fall in and be forced to survive in "depth"', and comments:

> I'm sure the Zen precept is right – the harder you try the more it will elude you. (Beating a drum while hunting the fugitive.) Spontaneity. Must rediscover this in my writing. Without it there will be no 'happy accidents'. Will leave the first act for the moment and sketch in, wherever I feel I want to, the second act. So often the paradox in writing discover your beginning when you reach the end.

(p. xxii)

(This view of writing, incidentally, highlights the virtues of the word-processor, for all writers who work in Fugard's pattern; the freedom that the word-processor gives to move around, when composing a text, should be available to all learners and writers.)

Fugard, of course, had to endure not only the discomforts familiar to many writers, but also the ever-present threat of an aggressive censorship – 'one of the most inhibiting factors in the South African artistic scene' (pp. xxiv–xxv). This crude pressure to put writers on their guard needed, though, to be resisted by him, if meaning was to be shaped through writing. He had to become expert in understanding how censorship itself could be used as an *instrument* in conveying meaning; he learned the lesson that 'silence and repression – the gaps in and around writing – are themselves part of the text' (Lang, 1991, p. 8). As for his paradox, that the beginnings of writing may be discovered in its ends, this was echoed in Tom Stoppard's reflection (1993), that 'you can't write anything until you know where it's going, and you don't know where it's going until you write it'.

The labour of composing sense in writing is clearly, for many writers, a gradual, piecemeal business, which may often involve frustration. Even so, as was argued in 'The Pleasure of Writing' (Harrison, 1986b), there can be enjoyment in the task. Citing Craig Raine's reflection on a morning walk – relaxed in tone, not rigidly tidy in content –

> when I went for a walk with my daughter earlier today I saw two cricket sidescreens as a couple reading newspapers; that's the way it struck me...I find that my thinking is fluid, and I'm often out of phase with it. I'll start to write something and then discover what I've been writing about.
>
> (in Haffenden, 1981, p. 184)

– I suggested that this lies 'somewhere between talking and writing. Its easy, conversational style conveys a sense that writing, like talking, can be an unforced, quite natural activity' (p. 60). The pleasure to be found in writing may, however, be elusive. Not only are there spelling, punctuation, syntax, grammar and motor skills to be learned, but writing – even personal, informal writing – demands particular skills in the organising of ideas:

> While writing involves, in part, a compressing, distilling and reshaping of talk, it also provides scope for a particular kind of ideas-making that does not happen so readily in spoken discourse; it prompts a kind of echo-sounding in the mind, seeking (in Raine's phrase) to 'discover what I'd been thinking about'. Some of the discomfort of writing may be explained by this, in that we sit before a blank screen or sheet of paper, rather like a radar operator waiting for blips on the screen blips which may or may not prove to be of significance.
>
> (Harrison, 1986b, p. 61)

All who have tried their hand at original writing will feel some measure of sympathy with the would-be writer Grand, depicted by Camus in *La Peste*, who 'doomed himself to polishing and perfecting the opening sentence of his never-to-finished novel each day of his life, never progressing beyond that sentence'.

Yet, in noting how established writers draw on their informal notes and journals when preparing for an audience, school pupils too can be encouraged to draw on swift writing 'sketches' which have distilled a particular idea or experience. My own 'teaching log' records work with a group of ten year olds, in a school near to the Sheffield Wednesday football ground; they were working on John Gordon's story *Giant under the Snow*. This story was chosen for its interesting intermingling of 'ordinary' school characters with an exciting plot involving myth and fantasy, around a mysterious 'Green Man' figure.

The children, lying and sitting in small groups around a (pleasantly carpeted) room, were nearly all fluent readers (their regular teacher was enthusiastic and highly resourceful in the uses of fiction for many aspects of the primary curriculum), and had all read the book for themselves. They still, however, thoroughly enjoyed having parts of the book read aloud by the teacher. After a teacher-led reading session, the pupils themselves talked together about the book – about buried treasure, and dreams about this...about caves, and dreams of caves...about demon animals...memories of being very young, when you can't understand what adults are saying, even though you can remember them talking fast and loud (this came up as an example from them of groping around in your imagination to make sense of some strange experience, as the children in the book had to do)...about the flying in the book (which several readers disapproved of, as not being possible; an interesting distinction, here, between fantasy and myth, since nobody objected to the myth elements in the story)...about differences between dreaming (which you can't help) and day-dreaming (which you can 'programme')...about the nature of fear, and flying, and the invisible.

While they talked, I asked them as a group to make notes (on a large sheet of paper placed among them) of any really interesting points for the whole class to share. I then asked them to think again about the Green Man figure – mentioning the Sir Gawain legend, Robin Hood, the way things may be felt to have a spirit, the spirit of place in woods, trees and other natural forms, and buildings. They were asked to write a rather longer note in their journals, to record their thoughts about the Green Man. Within just five minutes they all produced their own essential notes; these were then shared among everyone and more talk followed. Eventually, they were used for a more extensive piece of individual writing, but the notes themselves – written without strain, directly from the 'buzz' of the lesson – showed already how ideas were being organised, and a picture was being composed, as the following examples (chosen more or less at random) revealed:

(a) Tall. Thin. Dark green. A giant rising. Somewhere between Elixir and Warlord. Odd man. Confused. Lonely. Earth and creature. Controlled like robot. Frightened. I think he is a good character. In the story I think he would have been very nice if not for the warlord. He's halfway between life and death. He's alive because he can do what he wants but he's also dead because the belt owner can rule him. I think he's a chalk man who got wasted away. Robin Hood legend might be mixed up with it. If he roamed the country he might have got the name Green Man. So it might be a mixture between the two legends.

(b) I think he's something like a force between the good and bad, separating the two. He can talk to the earth and trees. Is he alive or dead: both together, partly dead and partly alive because of the belt. Whoever owns the belt owns him, he is the spirit of the hills. He talks to the earth, it opens to the green man, the earth covers him.

(c) WHO IS THE GREEN MAN?

122

Each of these notes shows that the writer is willing to confront the *contradictions* present in what is shown in the actions and character of the Green Man. The notes show, too, that these contradictions were, understandably, not easily resolved. It was not an easy writing topic, even for those pupils who felt that they understood the story well. It was, though, successful in helping them to recognise the contradictions within the text. The elaborated versions of their writing, while pleasingly enough presented to merit a classroom display, did not take their essential thinking about the Green Man much further. This is not surprising, given the author's own ambivalence about the 'character' of the Green Man. Drafting and re-drafting can be important sometimes, but do not *always* produce significant real advances in learning; sometimes it is best to make a swift record of essentials, and then move on. The main attraction of a personal journal, after all, is that it should contain essentially *voluntary* writing. Teacher-led versions of journal-keeping can be useful, but should not intrude too much on the domain of personal choice and directions in writing; having set up personal space for the learner, there is then a requirement to protect it.

Personal writing for student-teachers: resisting the 'survival kit' mentality

> For last year's words belong to last year's language And next year's words await another voice.
>
> (T.S. Eliot, *Four Quartets*)

Since responsibility for initial teacher education has become school- rather than college-dominated, it is increasingly important that teachers themselves should have space for personal, self-directed learning. This involves a great deal more than the obvious rigorous professional induction that teacher education requires.

The personal journal-keeping that a number of PGCE courses have encouraged exemplifies good practice in encouraging personal learning. Such journal-keeping may record a wide range of professional and personal experience, while learning to teach. It was suggested (in Harrison, 1990) that one successful way of introducing journal-writing is through a passage by Doris Lessing, which confronts the problem of 'survival-kit' mentality that can grow among beginner-teachers, especially in the early stages of planning and presenting lessons. It is tempting for students to suppress the inevitable 'stagefright' that they experience at that time, by choosing only the safest routes of imitation and conformity.

In her Introduction to *The Golden Notebook* (new edn, 1972) Lessing asked why people who have spent so many years inside the training system of schools and universities still fail to develop powers of imaginative, original judgement. Her answer was that the system, far from developing this essential faculty, suffocates it by teaching people to distrust their own experience, to adapt to authority and to 'received opinion a marvellously revealing phrase'. It may be, she surmised, that there is no other way of educating people, but she refused to accept this. Meanwhile, teachers should, at least, be honest with their pupils in telling them what they are about to receive:

> You are in the process of being indoctrinated. We have not yet evolved a system of education that is not a system of indoctrination. We are sorry, but that is the best we can do. What you are being taught here is an amalgam of current prejudice and the choices of this particular culture. The slightest look at history will show how impermanent these must be. You are being taught by people who have been able to accommodate themselves to a regime of thought laid down by their predecessors. It is a self-perpetuating system. Those of you who are more robust and individual than others, will be encouraged to leave and find ways of educating yourself – educating your own judgement. Those that stay must remember, always and all the time, that they are being moulded and patterned to fit into the narrow and particular needs of this particular society.
>
> (p. 13)

It is, of course, not easy for them to see how they have been shaped, smoothed and sometimes rough-hewn into various moulds of personal behaviour, examination performance, moral and political outlook, religious attitudes and practice, and so on. Nor can they expect support here from schools and colleges; these will not risk subverting their own established values, even though they stand most to gain from teachers who have developed independent and original judgement.

Perhaps student-teachers should face the possibility that the teaching profession recruits almost invariably from among the more successful toe-holders of the educational line. School patterns have already been strongly imprinted through their own years of schooling. Little wonder that they may be tempted to think, above all, in terms of survival, to adapt to the 'right' approach. Out go questioning, reflective, exploratory modes of enquiry; in comes the 'way to do it', a hard-nosed professionalism directed by what Gadamer once termed the 'false idolatry of the expert'. Or that is what can happen, if student-teachers can find no support or resistance in themselves.

Radical changes in teacher-training were introduced in the early 1990s; these aimed, both to enhance the quality of actual teaching experience for students (to which nobody could reasonably object) and to reduce what government disparaged as unnecessary 'theory' on teacher-training courses. Again, where 'theory' really was inappropriate, who could object? Yet 'theory', at best, provided a focus for independent reflection on all that is involved in the complex art of teaching. How else may a profession develop systematic critical reflection on its practice? When courses in initial teacher education become too tightly packaged, out of a strict concern to 'deliver' professional competences, then they carry the same dangers as the National Curriculum itself, in that the principle of 'negotiation' between the prescriptions of the course and the actual concerns of the learners is placed at risk.

Stephen Rowland reflects on this 'dilemma of negotiation' in his book *The Enquiring Tutor* (1993); he suggests that

> deception and manipulation occur when an appearance of negotiation is offered merely to seduce the participants into a sense of ownership of the course without actually empowering them to make strategic decisions concerning the course of events
>
> (p. 42)

The rhetoric of the 'negotiated curriculum' then becomes merely a 'manipulative device', used to stifle critical or creative contributions from learners and teachers alike. Rowland points out that, while some elements of any professional course will be 'technical and predetermined', all those areas that concern personal and professional *values* are likely to require negotiated agendas, so that 'there is a limit to the extent to which we can know what is going to happen' (p. 42).

Reassuringly, many student-teachers recognise the dangers of an exclusively 'technical and predetermined' approach to professional development. They do not wish to see their career in terms of a conformist progress along lines that are never to be questioned. They know that they still have much to learn, both professionally and personally; an induction into teaching that took no account of *both* these areas would be poor indeed.

Given the opportunity to look *critically*, through self-directed writing, at their own education, student-teachers can reveal fine professional judgement. Consider, for example, these contrasting accounts by the same student, of how and how not to teach:

(a) The teacher who introduced the handwriting class was also my English teacher for my first two years at secondary school. Her approach to English was not dissimilar to Miss Creedle's:

'This morning,' cries Miss Creedle
'We're all going to use our imaginations...

At one, we wipe our brains completely clean;
At two, we close our eyes;
And at three, we imagine!'
This mirrored her approach to handwriting: 'Here on the blackboard is the right way to do it. Follow this set of rules and you too can achieve this'. Thus she drew up a table divided into two halves, subject and predicate, and then sub-divided further into other, ever more meaningless categories. After a few swift examples, we were then set for homework the task of deconstructing ten sentences to fit the table. The faces of the class and the layers of Tippex on the books the next morning showed how little we understood. It was left to Cindy to explain, for she had her elder sister's old, corrected exercise book for reference. (Cindy was an old learning partner of mine. She had taught me long division at the age of eight, when Mr O., too busy putting his feet on the desk and strumming his guitar, had refused to explain 'yet another time' how to do it.) It was ironic when, in later years, this same English teacher cited my 'sound grasp of grammar' as one of the reasons for my academic success...

(b) The third year at secondary school was to change my whole life. We had a new English teacher, an American who had gone to Oxford some time before and had remained in England since. She reintroduced creative writing into our studies, long forgotten since primary school. We wrote stories based on our reading of Keats' *'The Eve of St Agnes'*, a poem of frustrated young love. My response was a Lingard-esque tale of romance across the Catholic/Protestant divide of Northern Ireland. We tried to emulate Austen's *Northanger Abbey* by writing our own parody of the Gothic genre. We discussed articles from newspapers; and wrote discursive pieces on animal rights, soap operas and the 'youth' of today. We went to the theatre and composed critical reviews of the plays on our return to the classroom, after many heated discussions.

We imagined different settings for stories and composed lists of onomatopoeic words to conjure up the atmosphere:
the fair: fizz, whirl, wizz, brandysnap, squeal
school: shuffle, chatter, slam, bang, moan
breakfast: clatter, crackle, munch, crunch, sizzle
We aspired to write an equally vivid description of a room, having encountered Bronte's Red Room in *Jane Eyre*. Everything we did was done in context and for a real, non-arbitrary purpose. We knew what simile, metaphor, oxymorons, onomatopoeia, alliteration were because we saw them in action in plays, poems and novels we read. It was aspirational rather than prescriptive learning, and all my enthusiasm for English rushed back...Previous to her class my imagination had been reserved strictly for use at home, as far as English was concerned. Yet, having captured my imagination, she and her two colleagues helped me to channel this enthusiasm into developing my own personal style of language and approach to literature.

(Christine)

Could there be a more complete contrast of classroom experience, in the English teaching of just one school? In the first case, the teacher might be comforted by some of the more fussy requirements for Writing in the National Curriculum, but daunted by its (modest enough) demands for varieties of writing and of audience. In the second case, the teacher was unconstrained by the National Curriculum, or any other conventional restraints, in providing high-level teaching and inspiring high-level response from her pupils. It is clear, too, from this account that Christine has already been inspired as a potential teacher herself, to provide nothing but the best for her classes. She acknowledges that there is a self-directing, self-responsible imaginative centre in each learner, for which all teaching must provide space. The same thesis was expressed, with graceful strength, by another student-teacher in this passage from a poem written by her in her PGCE year:

> Janice could dance,
> Really dance, if she wanted to,
> Could sing the songs,
> The real moon songs,
> And make those comments sing back,
> Could hold the sky through that twinkle in her eye –
> *But only, only if she wanted to*
>
> (from 'Jan', by Ellenor Craig)

If, through critical reflection, the errors of past generations of teachers can be put right by those who are preparing to teach, then the powerful curiosity that learners can *bring* to learning may be exploited, in contrast to the experience of Emma who recalled, when aged five,

> asking my teacher where the word 'husband' came from, and how objects were assigned sounds as meaning (though I didn't use those words, of course). She obviously did not understand my infant question, or else did not have an answer, and so she told me to get on with my work and stop stalling the lesson with silly questions.

Small incidents, clumsily handled by adults, may loom disproportionately large in a child's mind:

> It seems amazing, the types of sarcastic comments that one remembers from schooldays, and the sometimes devastating effect they could have on your learning development. During the first year at secondary school I was running down to the library. A large teacher stopped and told me off. I must have said I was going to use the library and her bellowed reply to me was, 'You're not the sort of boy who looks as though he reads books!' This comment seemed to frighten and crush me, it created a lack of self-confidence in myself, she had made me feel small and had taken away a piece of my soul. I wandered

around school thinking that you had to look a certain way to be able to read books in the library.

(Simon)

Both the powerful inner energies of children and their vulnerability to outside interference were captured by Emma, who recalled how art had a prime importance for her:

> Art at school: painting with thick brushes and powder paint; making calendars, clocks, dolls and models (and through this learning to interpret ideas on to a three-dimensional medium). Then the story pictures, project pictures, science pictures, history pictures (these were the aspects of the more 'academic' subjects that were pursued with relish in primary schools). If it had not been for that interest I might not have learned as easily as I seemed to. The focus for art at home was dad. All the rainy days, evenings and weekends spent with my twin, sharing scrap paper, Berol pens, brushes, plasticine, cow gum, sweet wrappers and paint with my dad. Any train journey or car journey always leant itself to keeping our minds occupied with art.
>
> Reading: I became a good silent reader. Taken out of that inner enjoyment to the reading corner created all types of fear and anxiety. I always stumbled on words, my mind could not coordinate with my tongue and I dreaded the moment when the teacher would correct me. I managed to muddle through but I have never overcome this problem totally.

Another student, Helen, conveyed the sheer, relentless energy that children can bring to learning and making sense of their world:

> I would read anything: the back of cereal packets at the breakfast table, my father's horse racing form book. To me:
> I II Desert Orchid BG Desert Storm Wild Orchid H. Cecil 8.4 P. Eddery meant
> > Desert Orchid, a bay gelding, was sired by Desert Storm out of Wild Orchid. In his last three races he has come first and second respectively. Trained by Henry Cecil, he will be ridden by Pat Eddery and carry eight stones four pounds as his handicap.
> At an early age I had learned how to decode a technical manual.

Teachers, wrote Helen, were felt to be dangerous;

> one of my earliest memories of school was complete fear and 'respect' of the teacher – *never* answer back, *never* speak out of turn, and the best way to get approval, I seem to remember, was to be the fastest in the reading class.

Her suspicions at the time that the reading-scheme books were 'deadly boring, stereotypical and thoroughly uninteresting' was confirmed only later, when she came across some of them on a second-hand bookstall. Her real reading experiences happened at home:

I would rifle through my brother's schoolbag to see what books he had brought home, and on one occasion I found something called *Animal Farm*, by George Orwell. I read it whenever he brought it home, unbeknown to him. I can vividly recall being totally wrapped up in this most wonderfully strange fairy tale – for I thought I recognised the genre even before I read the subtitle, 'A Fairy Story'. School, however, worked in a different way. By night I read *Animal Farm*, by day I rushed to finish 11C of the Ladybird Reading Scheme so as to keep ahead of all the other bright children in the class. We would read a book to 'get off it', not to enjoy or learn from it...

A teacher once smacked me on the back of the hand for doing the next few exercises in my course book in my own spare time. I was more confused than upset. Any other teacher would have been pleased, I thought. A control-freak, she would direct our playtime by ordering us to follow her in skipping exercises round the playground, chanting songs as we went. But perhaps the greatest sin of all was to fill our reading corner with wonderful books yet never allow us to touch it. It was a giant carrot promised to us if we were 'well behaved'. Yet in the whole year I spent there I never once remember any child even touching a book in that little library.

By contrast, some rare teachers inspired enthusiasm through their own need to ransack learning and language. Christine recalled Miss B., who

had a deep thick woollen blanket of a voice. She brought Christmas plays that didn't involve baby Jesus and an all male cast bar Mary. She taught us songs we could sing without rupturing our larynx or falling asleep. She played Holst's *Planet Suite* and asked us what pictures it drew in our heads...When I told her that her voice was a bonfire toffee-brown, she understood what I meant, and went on to build an identikit of several other voices that I understood too...that's when I knew I loved her.

In conclusion, Christine dwelled on the complex processes of making sense of experience, with (to invoke Ptolemy's phrase, which he used to explain puzzling planetary movements) the 'loops of retrogression' that learning involves. She wrote, too, of how she has become gradually *empowered* by learning:

If I were asked to present a personal linear timechart, that pinpointed my learning peaks, squeaks and troughs, I could produce one. However, when it came to the end of my timechart, the enforced linear progression would no longer be valid. My reading, my understanding of what I have learned has changed or, rather, reverted back. The books I have read more recently have reached into me now, and reached back to me then, are reaching outwards, taking me with them.

Missing pieces have been filled in and scratched edges smoothed. Doors have opened and old baggage has been unpacked; hung up; squared up; stripped of its hold. Language has power again for me, one that I can control, see under, over and through. Language is thought and feeling, its written form is its image and beyond it is a depth of inexhaustible possibility.

I had realised that language could do things, that it was powerful and, most important, that because of this it might be guarded jealously (its secrets to withhold), distributed in measured dollops with a caution not to jar, break or dismember your bit; to make the best of what you are given. This language still frustrates. But now I know why, and half the battle is what it is you're fighting and why. And why it feels good to be fighting, not retreating any more. I feel I have a voice now, not the one prescribed for me, not the one that dulled and tied up my tongue, but one that I am enjoying learning to use. *I am sharpening my tongue.*

These early journal notes by the students show a discerning professional eye, including sharp criticism of poor practice, and warm appreciation for the work of successful teachers. Their insights may not necessarily make their own professional development any easier; after all, their criticism implies exacting standards for teaching. Yet neither, I suggest, will those standards be easily dislodged, since they are so clearly based on the experience of the students themselves. And, for present purposes, they provide eloquent evidence that personal writing and journal-keeping are valuable, arguably essential activities in the development of a literate imagination.

In following the spirit of this book's title, discussion of the 'secondary' language acts of reading and writing has preceded attention to the 'primary' act of talking. Yet important points have already emerged, about interpersonal aspects of reading and writing, and the *conversations* that these involve. The next chapter will argue that, far from any disrespect being intended for the place of talk in learning, it is on talk that all learning, literacy and imaginative communication must depend.

CHAPTER 7

Realising Through Talking

This chapter examines the place of talk, as a basis for achieving *readiness to learn*, and *confidence in reading and writing.* It explores:

- talking to *think*;
- the challenge of *managing* classroom talk;
- mismatches between principles and practice in developing learning through talk;
- the value of talk in *developing the mother tongue*;
- encouraging *rich diversity* in the spoken language;
- *'the silent minority'*, by Janet Collins: the plight of quiet/withdrawn pupils in the classroom.

I only armed wit muh human breath
but human breath
is a dangerous weapon
                    (from John Agard, 'Listen, Mr. Oxford Don', 1985, p. 44)

This chapter on talk aims to provide a link between the main explorations of the book into literacy and imagination in learning, and the important accompanying issue of how to ensure a *readiness* to learn, and an *engagement in the process* of learning. That task, which was explored in Chapter 4, will also be the focus for the next chapter. While speech is a pre-condition of literacy it is, just as crucially, a pre-condition for any learning; the attitudes of learners and their teachers to talking must, then, be of pivotal importance to issues in this book.

The importance of learning through talking has been reiterated in many ways since the pronouncement, in the Newbolt Report (BoE, 1921), that the only way to get pupils to think about a problem is to get them 'to talk about it'. That enlightened Report, which deplored tongue-tied learners and fixed packs of knowledge, made only gradual impact, however. Successive generations of learners and teachers accepted that to be quiet was to be well behaved; quiet pupils might, at least, look as though they were learning, while any talk that was not teacher-dominated might risk disorder.

Yet what real learning can take place, without interaction through talk? Where learning is a matter of conforming to the teacher's directions, then pupil-directed talk presents a danger of disrupting the conformity required. Where, however, acquiring knowledge is not seen as a didactic transmission of pre-formulated knowledge, but as an '*interaction* between the new and what is already known...between the learner and the teacher...[and] amongst small groups of learners' (Wells, in Wells and Nicholls, 1985, p. 19), then learners will be encouraged – indeed, required – to join in talk. It is through dialogue, with teachers and with peers, that learners interrogate their world, and take possession of it; from this point of view, talk enables us to 'transform the world by naming it', so that 'dialogue is thus an existential necessity' (Freire, 1972, p. 61). As was argued in Chapter 5, there is a crucial social dimension to literacy; while private space for a private world is essential for reading, learners also need a further world, where reading can be shared with other readers.

There has been a wealth of good advice since the 1970s, on the virtues of classroom talk; the best of this, from writers such as Douglas Barnes (1976; Barnes and Todd, 1977), Michael Stubbs (1976; 1983) and Andrew Wilkinson (1975; 1982; Wilkinson *et al.*, 1990) sought honestly to show how pupils need to talk, in order to think. They also sought to address the challenges to a teacher's skills in classroom management, that classroom talk presents. Such work as theirs was influential in securing a place for speaking and listening, within the National Curriculum Framework for English, so that all schools must now, at least, acknowledge the rhetoric that talk is of value in learning.

Yet, despite these developments, evidence still emerges (for example, Wray and Medwell, 1991; Marbach, 1992) which suggests that teacher-directed talk, based on pseudo-questions to which the teacher already has the answer, remains the dominant form of talk in schools. Moreover, research by Janet Collins (1994, on which the latter part of this chapter is based) showed that, where class or group discussions occur, they may be dominated by a small number of assertive, yet not necessarily articulate or thoughtful pupils, who actually hinder interaction amongst the class. Other children may remain silent, frequently showing reluctance to speak to either pupils or teacher. This can happen with pupils who seem to be doing well, from their teacher's viewpoint, as in the case of Justina, when learning French:

Throughout the lesson, including during oral work, Justina was hard at work writing in her exercise book. She had even taken the initiative to devise her own dictionary of 'new words' in a separate book. Judging from the comments in her exercise book the teacher was highly delighted with her progress. On page after page Justina was complimented for the neat presentation of her writing. Encouraged by this praise, she had armed herself with a number of coloured pens, rubbers and paper whitener, in a quest for ever higher standards of neatness. Yet, despite her diligence, I felt that Justina had missed the central point of the lesson, since she *did not speak a single word of French*. Her one interaction with the teacher was conducted in English; this was on a point of detail about setting out her work. He seemed oblivious to her lack of participation in talk. When, out of sheer frustration, I asked Justina to read what she had written she said, 'I don't speak French because it confuses me'. Justina's compliance with her teacher's expectations for her written work was matched by an equally stubborn refusal to *share* the language with anyone.

(derived from Collins, 1994)

At least Justina was working hard on her own terms. Even worse than this, some quiet, 'withdrawn' pupils may complete a bare minimum of work, with little interest or investment in the outcome. Like the pupils observed by Barnes (1976, p. 17), 'They conform, and even play the system, but many do not allow the knowledge presented to them to make any deep impact upon their view of reality.' The causes of failure in using talk effectively for learning may not lie with teachers who dominate classroom talk; more crucial, perhaps, is how classroom talk is *managed*, and when and how teachers should intervene, in fields of guided and independent learning. For example, in a chapter on 'Reading Choice: a Question of Gender?', Elaine Millard (1994) drew attention to the different reading tastes of boys and girls which, if left uninvestigated by the teacher, can result in damaged reading development for both girls and boys:

In the middle years, where the reading of fiction is largely a question of voluntary reading and personal choice, the divergent tastes of boys and girls are reinforced rather than thrown into question. Sometimes reading itself can be caricatured as a girl preferred activity. One boy...only lightly veiled his contempt for the books he knew the girls in his class choose to read. When asked about the 'good readers' in his group he mentioned immediately the girls in front of him who are 'a bit clever' (pulls a face). 'They read Judy Blume books and soppy things...I read tougher books that you can really get into. Things that happen. Their books have got romance and all that and I don't like that'.

(p. 101)

Clearly, the influences of gender attitudes and stereotyping, that have influenced this boy's view, need to be aired in his classroom; and, like all controversial issues, they will need skilful handling by the teacher, to ensure that there is genuine investigation of them. Yet, as Elaine Millard shows in her earlier chapter on 'Building Communities of Readers', it is perfectly natural to exchange views on books with friends and family. She interviews, for example, twelve-year-old Christine, who describes her vigorous interest in what her friends and other members of the family are reading, and how their views influence each other: her mother now reads 'books that I read' on her advice, while 'my brother had the autobiography of Malcolm X and I read that as well. I don't agree with everything that he wrote but there's something, he had a way of saying things that he really, you know, you thought about deeply' (p. 60).

By drawing on this kind of natural exchange of views, and the ways in which it can open up genuine new areas of learning, teachers can help to build 'communities of learners', through talk. An abundance of examples of good practice in tactful yet effective intervention into small group discussions was contained in documents from the National Oracy Project. One of these, *Oracy at Forest Gate School* (NOP/NCC, 1993), featured a 'whole-school' approach to classroom talk. In the art room, pupils at key stage three are comparing some postcard reproductions of Picasso:

Steve: What's yours, then?

Nila: Dunno, face maybe (peers more closely). Yeah, a woman's face – she's crying, I think.

Steve: Let's see...Oh yeah!...it's weird innit...her eyes are too big and they're a bit spidery.

Nila: Yeah, but look at mine. It's a woman too...I think...is it...yeah, it is (giggles now). Look at her fingers – what a mess – she's not normal. They're like sausages...

Soon, the teacher intervenes with a question, then produces a book on Picasso, with a competent conventional portrait painted by the artist:

Teacher: He could work like this if he wanted to (shows image). But he's obviously chosen not to in this range of pictures. Why do you think that is?

(p. 28)

At this point, the pupils took over once more, to hypothesise on why Picasso used unconventional styles, and to consider what is meant by 'real' and 'reality'. The teacher noted that, from the fun and naivety of their opening remarks the pupils moved to serious engagement, through 'expressing their personal responses, exchanging ideas, formulating opinions and developing their critical faculties' (p. 28).

To 'read' as these students are reading is, in a broad sense, to interpret, in the sense of 'I read you'. We read maps, faces, the weather, dreams, landscapes, and political climates, as well as books. It is natural to confer with others, to share clues and ideas, in order to 'read' as well as possible, and we are at a disadvantage when we cannot share all kinds of reading experience through talk. John Dixon (1994), in a rebuttal of John Marenbom's foolish proposal (to NATE, in 1993) that 'we simplify the English curriculum by leaving speaking to be learned in the home' (p. 3), proposed a 'performance model of reading', which 'places human interaction at the core of literary interpretations'. Such an approach, he suggested, indicates 'that readings are a matter for social exploration by a group of students, not isolated individuals'.

Dixon proposed, here, an enlightened approach to handling literary (and other) texts which many teachers would be glad to adopt. They and their students, however, must still face the one form of assessment of achievement in English studies that dominates and virtually excludes all others – that is, the capacity to 'stand and deliver' answers in terse-and-cogent writing, against the clock, and ensuring that nobody 'cheats' by conferring. Given that universal constraint, in examinations at virtually every level, how wide has good practice actually spread, in handling classroom talk?

Patterns of talk in teaching the mother tongue

Men and women spoke long before they learned how to write. The signs we inscribe or print should bow down to the sounds we utter. Our highly visual civilisation is reversing reality. But language was conceived in the dark...
(Burgess, 1993, p. 340)

Aya Marbach (1992) investigated mother-tongue teaching in British and Israeli secondary schools. Despite a wide difference in theory and rhetoric about the value of talk in the classroom – its widespread acceptance in Britain was not matched in Israel, even where teaching the mother tongue was concerned – she found that there was little difference in actual practice, in the classes that she saw. Out of a total of eighty-two lesson sessions observed, she recorded only six lessons in Israel, and seven in Britain, where pupils were encouraged to talk to each other. In neither country did she observe designated lessons, where the declared objective was to encourage talking in its own right.

This might seem astonishing to British educationists, given the many contributions by practising teachers on the value of talk, in journals such as *English in Education* and *The Use of English*. Reflecting on this,

Harrison and Marbach (1994) invoked Barnes's question to teachers:

> Are they teaching their younger pupils to learn to accept factual material passively and reproduce it for matching against the teacher's model, to be judged right or wrong?
>
> (Barnes, 1977, p. 27)

– to suggest that many teachers still need to move beyond the kind of 'class discussion' which involves no more than their own talk, with the occasional participation of a minority of pupils.

Following all the research evidence, the provisions of the National Curriculum and the many accounts of good classroom practice in encouraging useful talk in the classroom, all trained and experienced teachers have received the 'message'. There are widely known techniques for successful handling of small discussion or paired groups; co-ordinating plenary sessions; organising role-play, 'hot-seat', or 'talking heads' activities; devising large-scale 'parliamentary', 'law court' or 'public meeting' sessions, and so on. Such expertise in these many areas of learning through talk requires, still, to be given a secure place in mother-tongue teaching, so that all learners and the whole curriculum may reap the obvious benefits of enlightened policies on developing talking skills.

At risk, then, of re-stating what is already well known by teachers: learners need confidence and expertise in talk, so that they can –

- listen to, convey and share ideas and feelings;
- listen to, convey and share information;
- understand, convey and share the 'story' (their own, and others');
- listen to, present, defend and interrogate points of view;
- consider questions, raise questions, work towards answers;
- understand accounts of processes, be able to describe and evaluate processes;
- be sensitive (as listener and as speaker) to appropriate tones and rhythms of voice – for example, sometimes reflective and exploratory, at other times assertive and persuasive;
- be aware (as listener and as speaker) of the need for clear expression;
- know when to be tolerant, when to support, and when to challenge in talk with others;
- be confident in providing a personal presence in talking, without letting self-consciousness intrude on what you want to say – and accept the personal presence of others, while respecting what they have to say (rather than how they say it).

These ten requirements for learning through talk are a tall order for learners. To help them, all that teachers now need to do is to match the rhetoric with good practice; reform of our present examination system would help them, through a large infusion of oral and collaborative presentations, to replace the present absurd over-emphasis on a narrow range of writing skills in GCSE and at A level.

Claiming one's place through talk – and celebrating diversity

In Samuel Beckett's play *Not I* (1973) a mouth, detached from its body, speaks to an audience. Even though we are used – through phone conversations, or listening to the radio, or talking in the dark – to voices without bodies, Beckett's technique is disturbing, surely, because we expect at least a head, if not a whole body, to be part of the speaker's presence; we are likely, also, to take careful note wherever we can of the speaker's facial expression and body language, while we listen.

An obvious point to infer from this, is that what we say, and how we say it, is inextricably bound up with who we are; and, because of the immediate presence of the listener, this is even more true about our talking than about our writing. When, for example, we feel comfortably equal with a listener, speech is likely to be relaxed. Any formality of relationship, which imposes a degree of 'them' and 'us' between those who are talking, will introduce degrees of constraint on free discourse. Tony Harrison explores a version of such constraint in his satirical poem 'Them & (uz)':

I chewed up Littererchewer...
and used my *name* and own voice: (uz) (uz) (uz)
ended sentences with by, with, from,
and spoke the language that I spoke at home.
RIP RP, RIP T.W.
I'm *Tony* Harrison no longer you!
You can tell the receivers where to go
(and not aspirate it) once you know
Wordsworth's *matter/water* are full rhymes,
(uz) can be loving as well as funny.
My first mention in the *Times*
automatically made Tony Anthony!

(1984, pp. 121–2)

Tony Harrison mounts his amusing attack on RP (received pronunciation) by occupying the 'lousy leasehold poetry' of the literary establish-

ment. With his new-found authority as poet and respected 'literary' figure, he makes us ask ourselves: what do we mean by 'educated' speech?
Is it when a speaker shows clarity, intelligence and power; or is it simply
when talk conforms to the norms of standard English? These questions
will be investigated in Sue Dymoke's discussion of Jackie Kay's vernac-
ular poetry, and her encouragement to write in variant dialects (in
Chapter 9, on 'Creativity').

Language belongs to a community; yet each person in that community
has an individual claim on it. Speech proclaims personal identity, as well
as the norms of the group. For that reason the ugly jibe, that 'she (or he)
seemed fine until she opened her mouth' is a personal insult, not just
criticism of language usage. Those who throw such insults may reveal
more about themselves than about their victim. They betray, perhaps, an
over-anxiety about 'correctness' in speech, instead of a concern for what
is being said and for the power to communicate that.

The insult may also be felt to be directed at a whole community.
Writing on language issues in multi-ethnic schools, David Gillborn
(1990) quoted an account in Mac an Ghaill (1988), by a young
Caribbean woman student in a British sixth-form college, about being on
the receiving end of language insults:

> It's the fact that they made you reject yer own way of talking. That really got
> me. It was rejecting another part of you, being black you know, being part of
> you. Like the teacher at junior school got mad when I said, wha instead of
> pardon and all that and I found out that if you did not want to be laughed at,
> the best way was to keep in the background and was to try and speak the best
> English I could.

This student reveals how an attack on her speech pushed her to avoid
speaking in front of a teacher – and therefore to avoid the interplay of
learning. Others, when attacked, might react more aggressively – for
example, rejecting 'correctness' by exaggerating points of accent and
dialect in the classroom. She continues:

> So, I learnt to stop saying things like filim and all that business, coz when I
> was in junior school and the teacher asked, what did you do at the weekend? I
> stood up and said, well, I went to see a filim and the whole class started
> laughing. I felt so bad inside, you can't understand. I mean the teacher as
> laughing as well. I mean they're laughing at me, they're laughing at my par-
> ents, they're laughing at everything concerned with Patois, with everything
> black.
>
> (in Mac an Ghaill, 1988, p. 29)

The choice of a language for learning, together with methods used to
teach that language, are politically loaded decisions. This is inevitable,

since language is the medium for knowledge and culture, and hence for power. Given that it is so, a universal principle emerges for all discourse in learning: that rigid distinctions between standard ('acceptable') and non-standard ('inferior') versions of a language are, themselves, not acceptable. First, rigidity should be resisted on behalf of fair and equal opportunities for all; and second, on grounds of good strategies for language and learning development. Having argued elsewhere (Harrison, 1992c; Harrison and Marbach, 1994) that to treat non-standard versions of a language as inferior is to inflict a kind of linguistic apartheid on individuals and on whole groups of people, I am attracted to Berel Lang's view (1991), which concludes a chapter on 'The Rights of Black English', that it is 'not Black English that is the problem, but English. Or, more precisely, language itself' (p. 32). Perhaps so. Yet could the blame be placed more exactly on intolerance of groups and individuals, rather than on language as such? The insults suffered by the young Caribbean woman in a British sixth-form college (in the account quoted above) were, after all, unnecessary; she had on her own account, been making herself perfectly clear. As her fellow country-woman and poet Grace Nichols claimed (1990, pp. 234– 84), to retain the 'valid, vibrant language' of her childhood is to accomplish 'an act of spiritual survival', since 'difference, diversity and unpredictability make me tick'.

The sense of difference and diversity savoured by Grace Nichols is echoed in this account by a student teacher, of feeling enriched by her bilingual experience:

> I know that I could once speak Gaelic, though I soon forgot every single word once home. I met my father at Euston station and impressed him with the words for a 'red cow' and a 'blue pig'. I remember going back into my old school in the East End, and realising that the sounds I'd produced were different from those of my peers, even when I spoke English. I thus lost my cockney accent at seven years old, never to regain it. Instead I retained some hint of an Irish accent and many of the idioms, much to my classmates' amusement and bewilderment. 'Ah musha' (equivalent to the french 'alors') caused a stir, as did my inability to say 'any' like the rest. But when they said 'any' it sounded like 'eny' to me! I knew why my teacher rolled her eyes when they uttered 'siy' for 'say', though they remained bemused...
>
> (Helen)

Helen's teacher was, of course, right to be concerned that her class should be skilful in handling 'standard' English, given its universal currency as a language of commerce and public affairs; for this reason, her concern is shared by teachers all over the world. She was also right, not to condemn whatever languages, dialects and accents that her pupils brought to the classroom – since these variant versions *belonged* to her pupils, and could not simply be left at the school gate, any more than they could leave their bodies there, while their minds go inside to learn.

Where classroom talk is concerned, the following principles should act as a safeguard on behalf of all learners, whatever their language background happens to be:

● encourage *flexibility* among all speakers, in mediating between non-standard (usually colloquial) and standard (usually written) forms of the mother tongue;
● *empower* all speakers to range over the whole universe of discourse – intellectual and affective;
● encourage a full sense of *ownership* of all the versions of language that may be required by speakers;
● instil *confidence* in the use of these versions of language;
● bencourage *respect* for the variant versions of language that may be used by other individuals and other communities, for their own particular needs.

(based on Harrison and Marbach, 1994)

These principles should apply to both individuals and to whole language or dialect communities. They have, though, come under renewed pressure in Britain, since the introduction of the National Curriculum. While the original specified attainment targets for talking and listening in English won the broad acceptance of teachers and parents, the further restrictions of 'correctness' in language and 'appropriateness' in literacy materials introduced in the 1993 New Order caused wide dissent. They constituted an attack on those same forms of linguistic and cultural diversity, on which good teaching and learning must build, in order to be effective.

Going 'back to basics' requires teachers to work from where learners really are, in order to take them where they need to go. Learners need to learn, in order to inherit the world. In a study of attitudes to learning among non-standard English speakers I suggested that, in the overriding need to learn, the actual clients of schools – learners and their parents – look above all for an emphasis on what is taught and what learned. From the client's point of view, education should provide preparation for and openings into the world to be inherited. 'In the case of a child who has newly arrived with her parents from a rural Pakistani village...her education should aim to equip her to take a place in an advanced industrial community' (Harrison, 1992c, p. 37). The learning needs of this child are no different from those of all non-standard (multilingual, multidialectal or monolingual English speakers with variant dialects), nor from all standard speakers of the language.

This simple truth is sometimes neglected, among contentious issues about the status of languages and dialects. From one point of view, the sheer unfairness of cultural or linguistic hegemony in a multilingual society such as modern Britain is faced: 'Usually the more powerful groups in any society are able to force their language on the less powerful...In Britain, the British child does not have to learn Panjabi or Welsh, but both these groups are expected to learn English' (Romaine, 1989, p. 23).

Yet from another viewpoint there are 'powerful arguments – advanced not least among many minority groups themselves – for ensuring that learners should, above all, be fluent in the dominant national language, so that they may claim their full share in the commercial, industrial, professional and political life of the nation' (Harrison, 1992c, p. 38). While learners rightly expect to receive unqualified respect for their various cultural and linguistic backgrounds, they must also have full access to the power base of their adopted community. This includes, inevitably, opportunities to gain full command of the dominant language. Yet a further point needs to be made, about the vast potential that various languages and variant dialects have, to enrich the mother tongue. Similarly, individuals and whole communities of learners can enrich education, wherever education is open to their voice.

Teachers need a better lead in building on this rich diversity, than was given in the proposed New Order of 1993. It was encouraging to note that flexible and sensitive attitudes to linguistic variety were common among the teachers of English interviewed by Aya Marbach (1992), as revealed in this view of a head of English in a comprehensive school –

> I try to set up a system which will allow teachers to bring in as many language experiences into the classroom as they can, and to produce as much variety as they can – spoken and written English – in the children. I do not see it as being defined in any narrow sort of way...that the children use standard English dialect.
>
> (p. 311)

Such a view will help to ensure that differences of class, culture, gender or ethnic background will not degenerate into inequalities, where talk and learning are concerned. Yet, even when teachers may have done all that they can in this direction there remains the significant minority of children, represented earlier in this chapter by the case of Justina, who have their private reasons for electing to be silent in the classroom. While, of course, there is a great range of 'normal' behaviour in talk, from extremes of loquacity to taciturnity, such pupils may be putting their learning progress at risk, through refusing to join in talk. What can be done for them? In her study of the school and family circumstances of quiet pupils (1994), from which she draws in the following account, Janet Collins dwells on the need for teachers to listen, to give individual attention, and to be aware of personal and family factors that may explain silent behaviour:

The Silent Minority by Janet Collins

the frustrations of the inarticulate go deep

(Wilkinson, 1965, p. 40)

Many of the case studies in my research into the 'silent minority' in middle-school classrooms suggested that much of the silent classroom behaviour witnessed by teachers may have its origins in a pupil's family experience – through anxiety or conflict with parents and other significant people in their lives. These experiences may affect their willingness or even their ability to relate to learning in school.

Obviously, teachers can have no direct influence on the quality of relations between parents and children. Yet some awareness of these, together with a whole-hearted attention to what pupils may be wanting to say when at school, can have a dramatically beneficial influence. The pupils with whom I worked cited a fear of ridicule or rejection as main reasons why it was difficult for them to join in class discussions.

Heather's vivid account of the frustrations that she felt, when 'shut in and quiet' in her primary school, may illustrate this:

> But at the same time you're screaming inside and you're shouting at people inside and nobody can hear you and you can't really them, because...you're that far away inside yourself. You, like, you shut yourself off, don't you, you bury yourself really deep until you can't really see yourself, or you can't really see out.

Heather recalls the distress that she experienced when she refused to talk; in her self-imposed solitary confinement, she felt that she ceased to exist at all. An individual's language development is linked with growth towards self-realisation; when one of these is interrupted, so is the other.

Since, as this chapter argued earlier, language is the medium for knowledge, culture and power, it is not surprising that those who have been given cause to fear knowledge, culture and power may wish to avoid the livewire of language, along which these are transmitted. Teachers, especially those who work in inner-city schools, are caught in a dilemma here. Their desire to respect the home language and background of all pupils, and to encourage them to 'name the world, to change it' (Freire, 1972, p. 61) may be in conflict with the pressure on them to deliver a prescribed curriculum through the medium of standard English. When pupils are encouraged to talk on their own terms, they may challenge this pressure to conform.

The fear that pupils who are allowed to talk might 'answer back' (Wilkinson, 1985) and challenge school authority goes beyond sensitive issues of classroom discipline. When they are encouraged to ask questions, pupils will invariably raise subjects beyond the expertise of the teacher, so that the teacher can no longer maintain the pretence of being custodian-of-all-knowledge.

The way in which teachers may be threatened by pupils' insatiable curiosity is illustrated in a poignant episode in *Petals of Blood* (1977), by Ngugi wa Thiong'o. Godfrey Munira, who teaches in the village school, takes his pupils out of the classroom one day for a botany lesson, in order to provide his pupils with 'hands on' learning. However, the fragile social order between himself and the children is maintained by nothing more substantial than his factual knowledge and his academic language. This begins to crumble when the children use vivid poetic metaphors to describe the flowers; when they notice that some flowers are worm eaten, they ask their teacher disquieting questions about why beauty gets destroyed, and why God allows it to happen. His answers do not satisfy the children, who respond with formidable questions about humankind and nature:

> man...law...God...nature: he had never thought deeply about these things, and he swore that he would never again take the children to the fields. Enclosed in the four walls he was the master, aloof, dispensing knowledge to a concentration of faces looking up to him. There he could avoid being drawn in...But out in the fields, outside the walls, he felt insecure.
>
> (p. 22)

Munira needs, himself, to learn how to handle passionate reflection, dialogue and argument amongst his learners, for learning cannot be confined to classrooms, to didactic instruction, or to deferential note-taking. He needs to risk himself, too, in the pursuit of understanding.

The importance of learners taking possession of their own learning was brought home to me in an incident from my own teaching, which demonstrated how open-ended small group activities can empower all pupils to play an active role in their own learning. For the purposes of the study, I was working on a special learning-through-talking programme with twelve 'silent minority' pupils, aged twelve. We were moving towards the end of a lesson which had focused on the needs of disabled pupils in ordinary schools – a theme that I had introduced through my account of the problems faced by my own mentally handicapped nephew had experienced in his school. We also talked about Christy Brown's *My Left Foot* (1989), which had been recently filmed on television.

When the pupils were arranged in small discussion groups, their conversation revealed that they had been too animated by the issues raised, to confine themselves to the questions I had asked them to consider. Roxana, for example, posed her own urgent question:

> Like, say if you were pregnant and you'd just found that if it were going to be disabled, well, like would you divorce it?...what...have it abortioned, like.

She was so intent on finding an answer to her question, that she hardly noticed when one of the other pupils corrected her terms. As each of the group members answered 'no' to her question, Roxana remained quiet. It was only when Owen said this might be worth considering, that she was prepared to suggest herself that an abortion might be a humane way to reduce suffering; this led to further vigorous examination of the question that she had put.

In this supportive and reflective atmosphere, members introduced their own stories to the discussion. Susie found the courage to talk about the death of her two-year-old, brain-damaged sister; she talked so quietly, however, that background noise from other groups made it difficult for her own group to hear her; indeed, only Natasha seemed to hear what Susie said. Yet this disclosure was significant; it was the first time that she had talked about the death of her sister in school. It is difficult to imagine that such a confidential disclosure, or indeed the initial question that led up to it, could have happened in the context of a teacher-directed, whole-class discussion.

The way in which Susie chose to reveal the story of her sister helped to confirm a conviction that grew in me during these teaching sessions: that having a regular 'talk partner' provides quiet pupils who have emotional or behavioural difficulties with a much-needed degree of security, and that teachers should remember this special requirement when organising classroom talk.

As for my observations of teachers handling classroom talk, these confirmed insights recorded by many who have researched into small group classroom interaction, such as Barnes and Todd (1977), Edwards and Westgate (1987), Walsh (1988) and Galton and Williams (1992), that successful teachers in this field have a number of common characteristics:

1. They show understanding of *principles* that underlie the value of talk for learning;
2. They *make their views clear* to their pupils, both in the ways they act, and in explaining their expectations of classroom talk;
3. They provide pupils with lessons that contain appropriate *security and challenge*;
4. They are aware of *difficulties experienced by quiet pupils*, and are prepared to make provision for this;
5. They show a genuine interest in the progress of *individual* pupils.

Finding reasons for talking

Just as Susie found things to disclose, in order to move more confidently into learning through talk, some important reasons for my own choice of research topic have emerged. As my study progressed and I worked towards an explanation of quiet behaviour I realised that in some fundamental areas I, too, had been silenced throughout childhood.

I was born with a congenital heart disease. My parents' accounts of my childhood, of which I remember very little until I was six or seven, are a catalogue of illnesses which were, because of my condition, life threatening. In addition to these periods of illness, as I grew older the condition itself became increasingly debilitating. For example, shortly before undergoing corrective surgery when I was eleven, walking the short distance between home and school would leave me in a state of near collapse.

Undergoing the surgery itself was the climax of years of intensive medical care. I remember with some affection a team of nurses who showed tremendous compassion during that time. However, despite their best efforts the kind of treatment appropriate to my condition is intrusive, frightening and unpleasant.

Believing it to be in my best interest my parents were always brutally honest about my illness and about the long-term prognosis. For example, I grew up with the knowledge that there was a fifty-fifty chance of the operation being successful, and that failure would mean permanent paralysis or death. Even as a small child I knew that my parents' relative briskness was due, in part, to the fact that they were experiencing major difficulties in addressing their own anxieties over my future. Consequently, whilst we talked at length about my condition and related medical procedures, I knew instinctively that it was inappropriate to discuss my feelings and fears. Essentially, *we coped with anxiety by denying its existence*. This denial continued in school where, because many of my teachers were not told about my debilitating illness, my physical and emotional 'special needs' were not recognised.

It is only recently that I have been able to give voice to those fears, and to regard them as an integral aspect of my life. A major turning point in this process was the harrowing experience of seeing my father destroyed by cancer. Watching his obvious distress at facing both his own mortality and the indignities of illness finally legitimated my childhood anxieties. After years of denial I was free to talk about my anger and hurt.

During the course of my study I observed (both during lessons and in one-to-one interviews) a number of instances in which pupils were able, perhaps for the first time, to give voice to their concerns. The following examples featured two pupils who might be regarded as representing different extremes on a continuum. (a) *Diana* (described in the study as 'ready to learn') talked freely in one-to-one interviews and soon developed the confidence to express her feelings in the relative security of small group activities. By comparison, (b) *Angie* (described in the study as 'excluding') experienced difficulty in talking to me even during one-to-one interviews.

Diana

During a series of one-to-one interviews Diana begins to re-examine the nature of her relationship with her younger sister. She starts by wondering how far their close relationship is a product of their parents' divorce, and how far it is due to the fact that Dawn is small for her age and therefore appears vulnerable.

> Yeah, I think we're closer than other brothers and sisters 'cos sometimes they've got their mums and dads but me and Dawn we've got each other really haven't we?...but I think that if my mum still lived with us we'd still be close as well – because she's smaller than her age and – don't know why – but I'm close to her.

Diana is clearly protective towards Dawn. Her father goes so far as to describe her a 'little mother'. In assuming the role of surrogate mother, Diana is fulfilling a female stereotype in which she perceives herself in relation to others.

One effect of the close relationship is that Diana is preoccupied by sister's needs. Her relationship with her sister certainly takes up a lot of

Diana's time. It may not be an over-exaggeration when Diana says 'if I go out she is always with me'. Moreover,

> As soon as she's out of my sight I get worried and I go looking for her, right. Yesterday I were at my friend's house right, listening to a tape and she weren't in the bedroom and I went downstairs and I'm shouting her and everything and she were in the front (room) playing...She'd got me right worried and I said 'come upstairs with me Dawn because you got me worried when you are on your own'

This is a relationship of mutual dependency, Dawn looks to Diana to help her solve practical problems, such as bullying at school. Diana needs to be sure of Dawn's physical proximity. Perhaps unconsciously Diana feels that she could lose Dawn, in the same way that she has lost her mother. Certainly, Diana is afforded a certain status as the capable older sister.

In a subsequent interview Diana reveals that she is aware that her relationship with her sister is one of dependency. She also anticipates a time when her sister will want to be more independent. Indeed, Diana suggests that she is beginning to facilitate this process. When I ask Diana how she will feel as her sister gets older, she answers this in terms of a growing independence:

> I know, that's what I'm thinking about like, she's got to stick up for herself in some ways and I'm, I'm just doing all the sticking up for her. I've got to like tell her now she's got to do things for herself, be a bit more independent.

Diana seems increasingly aware of the need for independence in relationships especially as this relates to her relationship with her sister.

Not surprisingly, although close, Diana's relationship with her sister is not without its tensions:

> But I think it's better to have a little sister, even though she does get spoilt more. Well she don't really get spoilt more, it's just that sometimes I feel left out but I'm not.

Diana has obviously spent some time reflecting on her relationship with her sister. She is sensitive enough to believe that relationships are both complex and fluid. Perhaps she needs to be encouraged to look beyond the relationships with others and establish her own personality, needs and ambitions.

In addition to talking with Diana in one-to-one interviews she was one of a group of pupils withdrawn from their class to participate in small group discussions. During a small group discussion of *The Trouble with Donovan Croft* by Bernard Ashley (1977) Diana was so confident that she frequently drew analogies between the issues raised and her own lived experience. For example, when discussing Donovan's experience of fostering, Diana immediately related this to her friend's experiences in a similar situation.

> I knew a girl called Kelly once and she was fostered. And I don't think it were fair 'cos she had to go to different houses. And when she was in this house that I knew her in the parents weren't treating her right, well foster parents they weren't treating her right...and her sister, well her foster sister, she knew were getting more attention than Kelly and when Kelly just got a bit of attention Joanne, her foster sister, got all jealous and they had to get rid of Kelly she had to go to a different house...and Kelly said that she felt all miserable and horrible and that she wanted to find her parents again.

It is significant that in telling her story Diana is prepared to go beyond the actual facts of the case. She talks about how being rejected by yet another foster family made Kelly miserable and long for a family of her own. Diana also expresses her own point of view. She does this directly, with phrases such as 'I don't think it were fair', and also in her implied criticism of Joanne's jealousy when Kelly 'got just a bit of attention'.

I felt that this expression of personal experience was useful to the whole group, in that the other pupils could learn from Diana's experience in a way which would enhance their reading of the text. Moreover, Diana was providing an excellent role model for her peers.

Interestingly, it was later in the same session that Diana felt confident enough to challenge me about what she saw as an incident of blatant racism in the book. She said that it was inappropriate for Donovan's foster family to believe that the fact that Donovan was black might be a problem for a white family. Turning to her West Indian friend for support, Diana stated that black and white people were the same and should be treated as such.

Interestingly the two West Indian pupils present had little to say on the subject of racism during the subsequent discussion. However, they were prepared to talk more freely during one-to-one interviews. As on numerous other occasions during the study, I appreciated the benefits of supporting my teaching with the opportunity to have 'private conversations' with pupils. This luxury is not ordinarily available to class teachers but my experience would suggest this should be a more familiar technique for handling the special needs of quiet/withdrawn children.

However, some pupils were so withdrawn that they found it difficult to talk freely even in the relative privacy of one-to-one interviews.

Angie

Angie's strained relationship with her teachers was evident in the first of a series of one-to-one interviews. In this one-sided conversation (despite my best efforts to listen to what she had to say) Angie was extremely reserved. Her responses were characteristically short and often difficult to hear. Our difficulty in initiating a flowing conversation is illustrated when Angie was asked about her recent trip to Jamaica. An open-ended question such as 'What is Jamaica like?' led to a long pause and eventually to the response 'I don't know.' However, Angie gradually warmed to the subject and described some of the bird-life she had seen.

> We saw some big birds...like storks...and we saw...we saw two humming birds. They like, they hover over like sticks with wings coming out...they stay in one place, then they start moving again.

This short description is represented in the transcript by five lines of speech interjected with lengthy silences and encouraging noises from me.

Yet, during the series of interviews, Angie moved towards sharing some of her inner feelings. In the first interview it was notable that Angie described a shy person as someone who 'didn't talk a lot' and went on to say that whilst being shy was 'normal' it could be a disadvantage in social situations.

...it's normal but you get scared out of your wits...like when we go to this woman's house, I didn't know her very well...she was asking if I wanted this and I went...I just shook my shoulders.

Angie is clearly frustrated at being silenced by fear in social situations, and one can imagine the way in which parents and other adults might criticise what they perceive to be rude behaviour on her part. The possible importance of her version of 'shy' was self-evident during the interview. However, the relevance of other comments from her emerged more gradually, as I became able to make connections through my thinking of her and interviewing her mother.

One such example occurred at the start of the first interview when Angie talked about learning to swim and temporarily losing her confidence. Perhaps because of her quiet and expressionless style of speech it was only on transcribing the interview that it became clear that Angie linked this loss of confidence with her mother having to go to work.

...then she had to...sometimes she had to go to work then I was a...then when I had to go to the swimming baths again I was afraid to go in the water...

If it is difficult to hear and respond appropriately to Angie in a one-to-one situation how much more difficult it must be for teachers to 'hear her' in a busy classroom. Compared to Diana, Angie's progress towards a confident exchange of talk was remarkably slow; this, of course, provides all the more reason why her school should respond to this special need of hers, to be released from the imprisonment of her own shyness, in order to learn. (Text derived from Janet Collins, 1994.)

Janet's study reveals how realising through talking is a precondition for readiness to learn, and for the confident development of a literate imagination. The next chapter will examine further aspects of special learning needs in schools, which require the attention of all teachers who believe in fair opportunities for all their students.

Part III

APPLYING THE PRINCIPLES

CHAPTER 8

Listening to Special Needs

This chapter considers a range of difficulties and special needs encountered, in achieving *readiness* in language and learning. It examines:

- the *duality of language;* its capacity to empower, but also to restrict;
- studies by Beth Mercer of the *success of 'normal' pupils with temporary problems,* in encountering adverse circumstances in language development, through teacher and family support;
- teachers' views on providing support for *learners with long-term disabilities;*
- *learners' views* on handling their difficulties;
- *issues arising* from interviews with teachers and learners.

Some problems with language

Language at one and the same time helps and hinders us.

(Sapir, 1921)

It is a truism that we need language to liberate us into full humanity; but a truth less often acknowledged is that many psychic, social and cultural conflicts can underlie its use. As well as freeing us, language can also oppress, by imposing rules and restrictions – social and cultural, as well as linguistic. Understandably, the power that language may have to weaken, rather than enhance a learner's capacity for independent thought, and for the acts of symbol-making that we call creativity, is given much less attention in education systems than is given to the powers of language for good. Yet the fact, that language can sometimes prove to be bad for our health, is of the greatest importance to teachers and learners – especially to those concerned with difficulties in learning language, and learning through language.

Behind the welcome commonplace, reiterated in *English for Ages 5–11* (DES, 1988) that –

> English should enable children progressively to widen their language competence from the uses of home and family to those of the school, the work place and society at large
>
> (3.26)

– is an acceptance of the *interrelated* qualities of talking and listening, reading and writing. Furthermore, language development grows through real people and their real lives. Writing on special needs in language work, Barrie Wade (1992) argued against the testing of discrete 'skills' in the four language areas. He pointed out the particular damage that may be done to children with difficulties in language and learning, when the complex yet unitary process of language development is compartmentalised, as in National Curriculum testing. Children with reading difficulties, for example, need 'more than anyone to experience the pleasure and satisfaction that poems and stories can give' (p. 51).

When systems for teaching or assessing language actually place barriers against such access, by refusing to recognise the particular nature of a special need (which might be simply met, perhaps, through tape cassettes or, with partially sighted children, through large-print books), then there may be retardation, not development. Testing the language of children with special educational needs can produce, as a study by Wade and Moore showed (1993), such degrees of strain and fear of failure, that low self-esteem and confidence are further eroded by the testing itself. Children who were consulted in this study wrote that tests made them 'all hot and bothered', 'like pulling my hire out', 'upset if I get a low mark and everyone else as resblie (reasonable) marks' and 'very nervis because I sometimes don't no wot to put' (pp. 186–7).

Such dangers to those who are vulnerable in language development are not only located in teaching and assessment, but in all fields of language use. Brian Friel's play *Translations* (1981) examined the powers that language may have, to enhance or to harm human lives. Any one of the major characters in the play could justifiably see Sapir's comment – that language may hinder, as well as help – as a reflection of their own plight. Sarah, as one of the most obvious examples of this, is introduced by Friel in the opening stage directions: 'Sarah's speech defect is so bad that all her life she has been considered locally to be dumb and she has accepted this: when she wishes to communicate, she grunts and makes unintelligible sounds.'

Like so many learners with language difficulties, Sarah longs to talk well, and works hard with her teacher-mentor Manus to achieve this. Her teacher responds with enthusiasm:

> Come on, Sarah. This is our secret...nobody's listening. Nobody hears you...Get your tongue and your lips working. 'My name...' Come on. One more try. 'My name is...' Good girl...Raise your head. Shout it out. Nobody's listening.
>
> (Friel, 1981, p. 12)

She is unwilling to use language in front of strangers or even her peers, since it is easy enough to make herself understood with the signs and sounds that she has always used. The will is there, however, and when she discloses her name to a stranger she is 'elated at her success' and wants her mentor to know of her achievement – 'I said it, Manus!'. Ironically her acquisition of language, combined with her loyalty and affection for Manus, who is in some ways her Pygmalion or Svengali, combine to deprive her of her mentor. We are left to wonder whether she will, therefore, be deprived of her language once again, since it is only with her mentor that she feels confident enough to experiment with language patterns and sounds. With other people, Sarah will use only her name or sentences already rehearsed with Manus.

Later in the play, when Manus is preparing to leave, Sarah's speech becomes clear and self-motivated, although at times hesitant. In a reflection of the opening of the play, Manus asks Sarah her name, encouraging her to speak but without any of the warmth or enthusiasm of the earlier occasion. Now that she is speaking more fluently he tells her: 'Very good, Sarah-Johnny-Sally. There's nothing to stop you now – nothing in the whole wide world'; but his words have a hollow ring and, significantly, her parting words to Manus – 'I'm sorry...I'm so sorry, Manus' – are the last words she actually speaks in the play, reverting instead to the sign language by which she has made herself understood in the past.

Sarah, although speaking few words during the course of the play, manages by her movements, actions and limited speech to engage the full attention of the audience. They feel her frustration and share her anxieties. She lacks two essential capacities of speech – to say *what* she wants to say, *when* she wants to say it; and to command an audience (since it is the playwright, not she, who commands the audience of the play itself). Only with Manus does she have the confidence to try out new discourse, and the will to keep trying.

Translations dwells on many issues to be considered in this chapter, about experiences of learners and teachers in handling difficulties in language and learning. These include: the importance of relationships in learning; the need for special support – but also the need for a *general* climate of support; the importance of giving praise for effort; and the importance of understanding an individual's needs, within the complex interstices of discourse of a whole community (for further examination of this, see discussion of other characters in *Translations*, in Harrison and Mercer, 1992).

Success in overcoming language difficulties: two cases by Beth Mercer

While this chapter has made some opening criticisms of the ill effects of inappropriate testing of children with language difficulties, it should also be insisted that *appropriate challenge* is of the essence, as with all learning, where language and learning problems are concerned. In interview the teacher, Beth, who worked with the two cases to be reported below made her views clear:

> Because they are labelled 'slow learners'...people do accept less from them and, given any chance to opt out, some of them do. One can't blame them; if you're not expected to work, why should you? So they give in work which is totally illegible, they can't even read it themselves. It's only when the teacher brings it to me and says, 'Can he do better than this?' that something can be done.

The same group of allegedly low performers, however,

> have just made a video and some more have put together a guide for Chesterfield that involved various kinds of written work. It also involved taking pictures and they had the wit – and I was most impressed, because I couldn't do this at all – they took some photos of the crooked spire and, in order to get it all in, they took four photos that fitted together exactly...That takes a degree of sophistication that is thoroughly impressive, and people didn't believe who'd done it when I showed it to them.

As a teacher and also as a disabled person herself, Beth believes that people who are challenged 'in any way, shape or form, are always anxious to prove themselves', whatever previous discouragements they may have endured. It is on that drive to 'prove themselves' that she based her own teaching of these learners.

Case one: Mohammed

Mohammed came to stay in Britain with relatives, to learn the language.

Like Sarah in Friel's play, he was unwilling to speak out in public, the class-room of his boys' comprehensive school, but happy to talk freely with his support teacher. In front of other teachers and boys he professed not to understand English; he was uncommunicative, apart from monosyllabic answers and simple statements. Fortunately he found an aware support teacher, who gave him great personal encouragement, as Sarah's teacher does in *Translations*. With this teacher he soon showed a good command of the language, both spoken and written. He began to talk freely among his support group, and made oral presentations to them with little hesitation or error.

Not all his teachers were aware that he could speak and understand English as well as he did. Some would often ignore the fact that he had done no homework, since they thought he had not understood that it should be done. The support teacher, however, took advantage of the good communication system among teachers in the school, to convey essential information about his competence in the language. She pointed out that he had not been behaving manipulatively – at least, not initially. The combina-tion of a strange environment with an alien culture, and the fact that he missed his family and resented having to leave them, led to his unwilling-ness to communicate with most of the school.

It was only the support teacher, however, who had been finding time to relate to him. Once he he had recovered from his initial surprise at being told what to do by a woman, he had begun to open out, and would approach her with news, problems or simply chatter. All this was living evi-dence of Barnes' view that

a child's participation in lessons does not arise solely from his individual charac-teristics – 'intelligence', 'articulateness' or 'confidence' – but includes the effects of his attempts to understand the teacher and the teacher's attempts to understand him.

(Barnes, 1976, p. 33)

Mohammed's frustrations in the school led to aggressive behaviour. If he was nudged in a queue, he did not voice a protest, but merely punched the offender in the mouth – which, predictably, won him no friends among either pupils or staff. Yet his struggle to declare a place for himself in the school must have seemed steeply uphill. Not only was he facing his first term in a large comprehensive school, in common with the rest of his year group, but he found that he was also faced with a curriculum delivered in a foreign language, much of which was of a specialised and technical nature. The problem here was to give him success without making the work so easy that he felt success to be meaningless.

For Mohammed, success beyond the protection of his support teacher came through the catalyst of Jamie, an American boy with a variety of learning difficulties and with problems of physical coordination, who joined Mohammed for extra English lessons. Their friendship led them both to col-laborate and to compete. Mohammed's communication skills grew rapidly through Jamie who, preoccupied by his own learning problems, had no cause to mock Mohammed's mistakes.

Although they became inseparable friends, by the time that Jamie left the

156

school to return to America, Mohammed was able to move on to other relationships in a way that Friel's Sarah never achieved. While she remained in her private world, Mohammed and Jamie were former isolates who came to provide interaction and support for each other. Their mutual support helped each, in their own social development and self-confidence, towards integration within the whole class group. For once, life ended more happily than art sometimes allows.

Mohammed had no disabilities in language or learning, nor other disabilities, as such; he found himself, as almost all learners may do at some stage in their learning, having to confront difficult circumstances. Expert support, combined with his own native ability and drive to relate to his world, soon helped him to overcome these.

Case two: Simon

Every word, no matter how neutral...exercises some effect on personal relationships and upon learning. We show ourselves as individuals through talk. Not until we have done this can we establish identity within a given group.

(Walsh, 1988, pp. 13–14)

The case of Simon concerns parental support, rather than teacher support, in overcoming language and learning problems. Simon was born in Belfast, during the 'troubles'. When he was eighteen months old his family moved from a part of the city that had been uninvolved in violence to a house opposite a garage/filling station; this proved to be an irresistible target for terrorists and was regularly bombed or became the victim of bomb hoaxes. After some months there, it was noticed that Simon's speech was not developing normally. He had begun to speak quite early, saying 'da' for daddy at six months; now his speech had become hesitant and unclear. He became introverted, preferring to play on his own, building Lego or doing quite complicated jigsaws, a skill he developed so well that, at the age of three, he was helping his grandfather with jigsaws of a thousand pieces or more.

It became increasingly clear to his family at this time that the pattern of Simon's speech, as well as his word formation, had undergone a change. He no longer formed words completely, but would leave the initial letter or first syllable off any word. For example , 'Can I have a cup of tea?' became 'An I 'ave a 'up of 'ea?' At the same time, other words seemed almost unrecognisable, such as 'aillet' for table and 'Ilo' for umbrella. Since his speech had developed normally until this point and was, in fact, advanced for his age, this seemed to be as puzzling as it was worrying.

As his problem became more obvious his father began to monitor his behaviour and speech patterns. This showed how Simon was beginning to turn more and more into himself, shutting out those around him while he played his solitary games. He became moody and started bed-wetting. If things were not going his way, he would fly into uncontrollable rages; he was becoming a disturbed child. At two and a half he was walking well and had good dexterity and imagination. His speech, however, seemed to be regressing, not improving.

When the family moved to England, Simon was referred to a children's hospital, where he was assessed as gifted; the child psychologist also suggested that, following his disturbing experiences in Northern Ireland, Simon recognised more about what was going on around him than his family realised. Since he had no trouble with hearing or actual sound production or comprehension, he was referred to a speech therapist. Because it was assumed that he was too young to understand, no-one explained to him why all this was happening. Simon became frightened and confused, realising what was happening, but not the reason why.

The speech therapy waiting-list in the area was very long; Simon's appointments were spaced far apart, so that after consultation with the therapist, his mother embarked on a home-based remedial programme for him. This would involve his returning to the beginning of his language development, so that he could 'learn again' the language which he appeared either to have forgotten or to have repressed. The work involved much activity – trips to the museum, bus journeys, activity games and nature trails – all of which required planning and discussion with Simon, both before and afterwards. Simple games were developed to tell stories from pictures, putting pictures in the right order, singing games to develop sound patterns, nursery rhymes, talking games – all designed to stimulate talk.

At the same time it was made clear to his sister that, much as her kindness to Simon was appreciated when she explained his needs, it would be helpful to him if she could wait until he made himself understood before she gave him what he wanted. This was already the pattern for playmates at school, since they were simply not prepared to give him their attention unless he made himself understood. The playgroup staff were, of course, aware of his problems; they only intervened when necessary.

Close family members had to steel themselves to insisting on Simon's making himself clear, without pre-empting him even when they understood what he intended. Friends, too, had to be encouraged to follow the same pattern. Initially, Simon was discouraged; the bed-wetting problem remained and, if anything, he became more insular. His solitary games increased unless he was invited into games and activities by an adult. At this point it was tempting for all concerned to give in, and to do what he wanted; the family felt guilty about the 'cruel to be kind' policy, but they continued to help each other to maintain morale and determination.

Perseverance began to pay. After three months of the home-based and playschool programme, Simon began to progress. Not only did he complete words, but his vocabulary expanded to include more complex words; 'elly-ishun' developed from 'elly' to become 'television'.

Once the individual words became more recognisable, Simon's sentences and grammar could be more easily followed. Speaker and listeners began to form a close, benign circle; as Simon was able to trust more in an attentive and sympathetic audience, he became more adventurous in his talk. The family learned not to put too much pressure on him, lest it revive old discouragements and make him fearful of developing new language

158

patterns. They talked to him while everyday tasks were being performed, just as one might talk to a young child who was attempting to acquire language for the first time. Simon was re-learning the language that he had already acquired before his problems began. He needed more encouragement than other children, in play as well as in talk; lacking in confidence, he was still unwilling to accept new words and constructions, and even anxious when using familiar words. yet by the time he was five, Simon's vocabulary was wide; his speech was clear, and while he remained diffident in social meetings, his language and play were much more within the boundaries of 'normal' child behaviour. In school he proved to be a sensitive, creative learner, who eventually made his way to art college.

While Mohammed and Simon exemplify very different kinds of need, it is clear that both depended on the care and expert intervention of supporting adults; while each needed to be challenged, in order to make their claim on language, this had to be arranged within a skilfully devised framework. We turn, now, to consider the views of support teachers, on their work with pupils who have language and learning difficulties, and who also have to face more long-term disabilities than in the cases considered above.

Listening to teachers

That the causation of a child's learning problems is frequently multiple must again be stressed...Any deficit or defect usually affects the child's adjustment and leads to further deficits. Fortunately the reverse also holds true: amelioration of one deficit often leads to the establishment of a better emotional and physical balance, to access to new energy, and to improvement in other deficits.

(Frostig and Maslow, 1973, p. 10)

One of the many causes for special language needs in learning is disability; this word, in turn, covers a huge range of challenge – physical, intellectual and emotional. In the teacher interviews for her study of 'Disabled Learners' and Teachers' Attitudes to Learning' (1993), Beth Mercer reported on the high level of awareness that special needs teachers showed, in meeting this great diversity of need:

What became immediately clear was the great sensitivity towards the children in their care exhibited by the various teachers I interviewed. All displayed an awareness of both the physical and emotional problems of the children. What became obvious simultaneously, however, was their lack of dogmatism concerning how those children should be taught effectively.

(Mercer, 1993)

They were, moreover, strong in their optimism – from the experience of their pupils, and from their own experiences of disability – that challenges of disability can be overcome. However, while they all supported policies followed since the Report by the Warnock Committee (DES, 1978) for integration, wherever possible, of children with special needs into mainstream education, the *ways* in which integration are achieved were open to some criticism. A support teacher, on a temporary contract, cited one of many examples given of unnecessary underachievement among learners with special needs; in this case, the learner had no intellectual or language problems as such, although her eyesight problem inevitably affected her actual performance in reading in the classroom:

C, who is very bright, is dealt a rough hand because of her eyesight. We all know that if her eyes were O.K. she'd be in an academic group with all the best teachers. Instead, because she needs extra help to produce her best work, she gets less – daft, isn't it!

This criticism, that those with most needs often end up with least resources, recurred in the interviews with teachers; it is one that is often made by special needs teachers and by studies in this area. Mortimore and Blackstone (1982), for example, stressed that because of learning problems, such children may find themselves placed, inappropriately, in a lower ability stream; from there, a process of 'labelling, teacher expectations and the self-fulfilling prophecy' will ensure that they perform at the level expected of them, which may well be below what they can really achieve. How many schools, one wonders, are willing to follow, say, the policies of those in medicine, and target the greatest resources for the most pressing educational needs in a school? The injustice has been obvious for decades; the essential point against it was made unanswerably by Clegg and Megson (1973):

John knows and accepts that James is cleverer than he is; he does not accept that James is therefore entitled to better treatment in the school. Equality of opportunity is a myth. Equality of concern is not.

(p. 91)

One of the teachers, who was head of a special needs department in a comprehensive school, was unwilling to renounce the ideal of equal opportunities (which does not, after all, assume that everyone is equal). She did, however, feel that some re-focusing by teachers was required; she emphasised, above all, the need for appropriateness of challenge to learners:

Instead of saying we will have equality of opportunity and aiming everything at the mean, we need to rethink our ideas and aim work at children at their own level, not above or below it. Yes, it means hard work but only then will we have equality of opportunity.

The need discerned here for more flexibility of approach by teachers was precisely what was missing in the school of one of those interviewed:

It's an old grammar school. Many of the teachers taught as grammar school teachers and they really haven't changed their policy since, and there are some teachers who have absolutely nothing to do with slow learners at all...There is a certain level at which some teachers will aim their teaching and it doesn't deviate up or down.

While it would be absurd to expect one person to be a specialist in all kinds of special need there should at least, as one interviewee claimed, 'be much more discussion between mainstream teachers and special needs teachers', and altogether much more real work done on behalf of genuine integration of children with special needs in language and learning into mainstream classrooms. The extra help, special encouragement and often different approaches to work that are required should be worked out at 'whole-school' level, not just within a designated department. The case for a whole-school approach to curriculum issues in special needs learning was made persuasively by Peter Clough (1988, p. 336), who called for:

- framing issues of learning difficulties in the *whole context* in which they are recognised;
- providing a theoretical framework which draws on a *variety* of sociological, psychological and other theories, not just relying on any one of these;
- recognising the *experience* of all participants – teachers, pupils and parents – in handling research and teaching issues in learning difficulties;
- *systematic reflection* on experiences of teaching and learning, in order to improve principles and practice.

To place the debate about learning difficulties in the centre of discussion about the whole curriculum and whole-school policies is to recognise *in practice* that those who have learning problems are at the heart of the concerns of the school. Learners with special needs are both 'normal' *and* special, declared one teacher:

Yes, in a way they are singled out and exceptional, but by this means they are able to achieve an 'ordinariness' which they cannot achieve in a Special school.

The day-to-day task of making effective working relationships and finding appropriate working levels with these pupils was acknowledged to be demanding and often highly frustrating. Part of this comes, as with parenting, with the job:

> Some of them don't make the least effort unless you actually sit beside them dictating every word. The ones that make you really cross are the ones that have some ability but just won't use it. They're the ones that drive you up the wall. I could shake them.

Some of the teachers blamed themselves, too:

> I know that when I am not there, my slow learners produce work which they would never produce for me, and when I challenged one of them he admitted that he could get away with it when I was there, so he did.

There were, however, just as many accounts of success and reward in teaching:

> I suppose there are times when I feel like tearing my hair. Sometimes when you've tried to get the child to do something six times and they're still not getting there, you feel as if you have been banging your head against a brick wall. Then, just when you're at your wit's end, they get it right, and that's what makes it all worthwhile.

Others spoke of the special pleasure shared by both teacher and learner, when a new task is successfully performed. For the teacher, it may be the sense that 'you have actually got through to the child where others have failed; it's an amazing experience really'. For the learner,

> I can remember seeing Chris's face when he got the hang of division sums. It was just as if someone had lifted a great weight off his shoulders. He was grinning from ear to ear, like a Cheshire cat.

The illumination of new learning produces its own kind of elation:

> It's an amazing feeling. Your teaching can transform a lifeless face into a bright, smiling one. It's almost like turning on a light. It's hard to explain really but you have this feeling, or at least I do, that it's a great gift to be able to give such pleasure to another person. There's no feeling quite like it and it's worth all the frustration.

These teacher interviews highlighted seven points, in particular, that deserve the attention of all teachers and curriculum planners, so that fair conditions may be achieved for those with special language and learning needs:

- there must be *accurate assessment* of special language and learning needs;
- *appropriate resources* must be targetted where they are most required;

- intelligent concern for special language and learning needs is shown through choosing *appropriate tasks and appropriate levels of task, so that pupils may engage with enthusiasm and imagination in learning;*
- while appropriateness is crucial, pupils with special needs deserve as *rich and imaginative curriculum* as all others;
- while special attention is required by those with special needs, the discourse and relationships of learning and teaching must also respect the *essential social ordinariness and personal normality of the learner;*
- support teachers need *constant support themselves, including consultation with all 'mainstream' teachers,* in order to develop expertise in overcoming frustration and failure in handling special needs;
- there should, throughout the school, be a *celebration of all achievement;* achievement and competence are not only to be measured by 'normal' standards, but also by what is normal to the individual.

Such views were, not surprisingly, endorsed by the many witnesses, from a range of educational and professional organisations, who gave evidence to the Parliamentary Committee of Enquiry into Meeting Special Educational Needs (House of Commons, 1993). In particular, witnesses who were called to the Committee emphasised requirements for resources; for expert assessments; and – in order to avoid unnecessary statementing – for recognition and provision within schools of a broad area of need among pupils who have specific needs, from time to time.

Listening to the pupils

I see through your eyes pity for me
I don't want your pity or your lies
You see my chain instead of me
You see many things wrong with me, instead of me.
(disabled seventeen year old, quoted in Exley, 1981, p. 23)

Without exception, the pupils interviewed in Beth Mercer's study 'spoke of their support teachers in terms of real affection', as they reflected on their efforts to claim a space for themselves in the social and academic life of the school. Often these support teachers provided some protection from a sense of being lost in the large classes and sprawling buildings of a comprehensive school. They felt able to discuss problems about work, other pupils, home relationships, and (within professional limits) their relations with other staff. The three summaries of case studies provided below illustrate three distinct kinds of language and learning needs; each of the studies was based on classroom observations, as well as on interviews with the pupils.

Case study: Pupil A

Pupil A is fifteen years old, although he looks no more than eight or nine. He is closely monitored by the local hospital, since he is so light and undersized. He suffers serious motor problems, and had to have special coaching to hold a pen properly when he reached the secondary school. Because of his motor problems, he gives the impression (wrongly) that he was never taught to write properly, since he seems unable to form letters correctly, despite every effort on his part. Writing takes him a great deal of time, with very little reward to show for himself or for the teacher. Among other discouragements he suffers is being habitually compared at home with a younger brother who has none of these problems. Yet he has advantages, too – including a father whom he greatly admires and who gives him a great deal of encouragement (although dad lives away from home). This close relationship may help to explain why his reports regularly showed the highest grade for effort in almost all his school subjects.

His lack of co-ordination makes sport of any kind difficult, yet his enthusiasm overcomes a great deal here. When team games are played he is picked early for a team; he is popular, despite his lack of prowess. He makes friends easily and is rarely involved in arguments – although this is partly explained by a notable unassertiveness in the classroom.

In interview, however, he revealed his feelings about school and learning with candour. In particular, he resented any teacher who mistook his problems for lack of effort: 'some teachers tell you off even if you are trying your hardest and that makes me really mad'. Criticism of his writing performance is especially painful:

> I hate everything that needs lots of writing. I really hate it. I can't keep up and it gets me in a real state. That's when my writing gets really bad and I make lots of spelling mistakes – even really easy words...Then the teachers have a right do on me but it only makes me worse.

When asked whether he was embarrassed about being withdrawn from the main class for special learning support, he declared his appreciation:

> No, it's dead good. Lots of other people would like to come. They're dead jealous...I can ask if I don't understand and no-one shouts, 'How thick', like they do in the full class. And you can read my writing, so I don't have to keep writing things out over and over again. Some teachers don't really try very hard to read my work. I think they give up before they've started, if you ask me.

Clearly, it is any failure to *try* that brings down his scorn; and that goes for teachers, too. His heroic efforts to hold his own in adverse conditions shine out of this case study. When conditions work in his favour, and allow him to speak his mind, he does so with clarity. Confidence in discourse will grow with confidence in achievement; while his writing problems will not disappear over night, there are ways of compensating for this, when it comes to choosing a career – including word-processing skills, dictaphones and expertise in writing brevity – all of which require appropriate school provision.

Case study: Pupil B

Pupil B, aged fourteen, was born partially sighted; after several major operations, she still has only 25 per cent vision in each eye. She is rated as a bright girl by her comprehensive school, where the only concession to her disability is a visiting support teacher, provided by the County. She has been encouraged by her family to lead as 'normal' a life as possible, and she expects no favours in social, academic or even sporting life. Although she cannot play full team sports, she joins in simple games such as French cricket. While she has no language problems as such, she had inevitable problems in learning to read. However, by the use of her own powerful glasses and a magnifying glass she learned, with difficulty, to read at an early age, without the use of braille – a skill of which she is justifiably proud. When she plays the piano she has learned to commit notes quickly to memory, as a way of avoiding having to peer at the music sheet.

When in school, instead of having to work from the blackboard, her teachers prepare special worksheets for her; with these, she finds no problem in keeping up with her classmates. She is well organised in her work, shows great determination, and is showing the kind of academic promise that could lead to a university place.

When she was asked whether she had any worries about being interviewed, her social confidence was revealed at once, as she neatly turned the table on the interviewer:

I don't mind. I went out to interview some women in the street the other day and they weren't too keen, so I know how you feel...One woman asked if we were from the DHSS. I don't know what she's been up to, but she wouldn't say a word into the microphone and she wasn't very nice.

Reflecting on her academic work, she revealed that the word-processor on her computer 'is very useful to do my homework because my handwriting is not very neat'. English has become one of her favourite subjects, 'because the teacher is very understanding. He was the first teacher who let me use a cassette recorder to do my work, so that I could record some of my essays instead of writing them.' She rated this teacher highly because he is 'really understanding. He seems to know just how I feel and why I get frustrated.' She also spoke of her special enjoyment of drama, where the teacher is 'ever so funny and very patient'.

While she appreciated the element of extra support she receives from both fellow-pupils and staff ('I think it must be because my glasses show how blind I am. I think it makes them feel sorry for me'), she emphasised the importance of feeling normal:

I don't know about anyone else but I know that I'm better in a comprehensive school. I don't want to be treated as someone 'special'. There's hardly anything wrong with me. It's only my eyes, after all. The rest of me is OK – fine, in fact. I would hate to be in a school that thought about the difficulties all the time.

When she was involved in classwork, the observer noted that 'she is confident both in discussion and when she acts, and does not feel inhibited by her disability when she moves around the room'. During a history lesson, she was observed devising her own radio programme. This had involved her in some time-consuming information-searching and reading. The flexibility of her teacher had, however, allowed her to work on a radio programme, rather than writing up the project, which had saved her time and made the work more enjoyable. Because of the special demands of her project, she had decided to work alone, rather than take up the time of the friend with whom she had originally planned to collaborate. The observer noted:

The tape starts with 'Nimrod' from Elgar's *Enigma Variations* and goes into a general introduction to the Victorian age before specialising on travel at the time. In order to make the recording more interesting, she has added sound effects with the help of the Drama department. These include crowd noises, market cries and carriages going along roadways and through puddles. She is hoping that, when it is finished, she can take it to the local Cheshire home for some of the residents to listen to, as she visits every weekend to talk to some of the old people.

Clearly, this pupil provided an example of integration at its best – including a clear understanding among all concerned of the special need; imaginative teaching provision to meet this; close consultation between home and school; and effective use of outside agencies. Result: a confident, happily 'normal' pupil, with an impressive range of social, linguistic and academic competence.

Case study: Pupil C

The case of Pupil C, however, will be familiar to all non-selective schools: a slow learner, aged twelve, with a reading age of seven, who finds both the academic and social demands of school life very hard. He is a gentle boy, craving affection; yet while he tries to please his teachers, he is usually passive, as if in a daydream. He rarely says anything in front of the whole class. Having only recently been diagnosed as having a hearing problem, he now has a two-way transmitter, which matches one worn by his teacher, to amplify her speech. While this has been successful when he actually uses it, because of teasing by other children he sometimes hides it and pretends he has left it at home.

He is one of four pupils in his class who are statemented as having special needs; in contrast to his reluctance to speak, the other three are noisy and aggressive. During classroom observation it was noted that he was

in awe of the teacher, who tends to shout if the noise level rises...With some children this tends to make them more noisy; with him, it has the reverse effect and he becomes quiet and withdrawn.

He began the interview by sympathising with the interviewer, who would have to write up the interview: 'I hate writing. It's really hard.' Much of the interview was then taken up by his complaints about teachers who shout. He liked his support teacher because

> he never gets cross with me even when I'm being dim. I like him 'cos he doesn't talk to me as if I'm stupid. like the rest of them do. Him in science is always shouting – all the time.

Although he liked most teachers, he said he would like some teachers better if they did not shout so much – 'Why don't they shout at the people who make the noise?' He also resented unfair criticism, and thought that one teacher

> is a bully too. She tells me I'm lazy but I'm not really. I just find it ever so hard. I think it's 'cos my hands are so big. They're good for gardening but not much good for sewing. My fingers get in the way and then I prick them with the pins. I hate it. I really do.

Indeed, if gardening were in the curriculum, he would shine. He talked with gentle enthusiasm about his successful part-time gardening business:

> C: I garden ever such a lot. I've got my own round, like Jim...I have ten old people who can't do their own gardens, so I do them. I've got some tools of my own that I got for Christmas, and the man next door sold me his lawn mower for five pounds, so that means I don't have to keep borrowing me dad's.

> Interviewer: Do you get paid for all your hard work?

> C: Yes, I get fifty p from everyone for cutting their lawns...I don't do it for the money, 'cos I enjoy doing it. Anyway, the old people haven't got alot of money, have they?

As for his school work, he said that he received 'some nasty remarks' from other pupils, when he first received extra help for his reading and writing, but that his friend 'thumps anyone who does it now'. On the whole, he thinks he survives quite well, although ' I'm just worried that people can be pigs. They laugh at me sometimes.' He feels that this is not well understood by anyone, except for his support teacher:

> On the whole, I wish they'd just leave me alone to get on with it. I know they only want to help but it really gets me fed up at times. At least when I'm grown up I'll be able to get a bit of peace in the garden. I think that's why I like gardening so much. No one nags me when I'm out there, they just leave me alone to get on with it.

While it may be tempting to place the blame for this boy's plight on the sheer size of classes in comprehensive schools, this would not be entirely fair. Even so, his hearing disability was diagnosed late; some of his teachers are less patient than others, in responding to his reticence, problems with reading and writing, and general lack of achievement; and he is left too often to look out of the window and day-dream. He might be one who would benefit especially from continuous small group education – within, rather than separate from, the mainstream school. This would, of course, have resource implications.

While his plea to be left alone may be understandable, anyone who is in a support role also knows that it is unacceptable. Confronting the issue of what is involved in providing effective support, Ben Morris (1991) declared that the essential thing is

caring – LOVE as we ought to call it – not in any sentimental sense but as George Lyward used it – 'strong love' as he used to say – the love that gives us the courage to say 'No' to child or colleagues when no is the appropriate thing to say.

(pp. 13–14)

So long as that caring is expressed through skilful provision by teachers and parents, this claim by Morris cannot be disputed. It is, however, also true that pupils, too, need conditions where they can find the courage to declare their feelings and needs (including their own right to say No); otherwise, they will withdraw from, rather than assert their rightful place in the world. The case of Pupil C provides further confirmation of findings by Von Tetzchner *et al.* (1989), that such pupils need, above all, to have *conversations*, where they will be provided with the rich linguistic environment and conditions of intimacy through one-to-one exchange.

These interviews with pupils disclosed a wide range of disabilities and needs; some of these were so severe (including gross neglect and abuse) that the details would be inappropriate for the present broad language-and-learning concerns of this chapter.

Returning to the points that emerged from the teacher interviews (above), the seven points that they highlighted are all endorsed, implicitly or explicitly, in these interviews with pupils. Seven further related points also emerge, that:

● those concerned with special needs learners should respect and reward *effort*, even where achievement may not always be evident;
● these learners appreciate *patience* from those who teach and support them, and depend on it;
● *flexibility* in teaching provision is needed; for example, 'whole-class' writing tasks are not always appropriate, where there are learning difficulties;
● *good links* between school and parents are important;
● the partnership should also include the pupil, *as a respected partner*;
● the curriculum should reflect, where possible, *the interests and capabilities of the learner* (for example, Andrew and his gardening);
● as *trust* grows between these pupils and their teachers, the pupils are

more likely to cope with challenge and disagreement, in the process of developing a rich and imaginative curriculum;
- respect for the individual learner should extend to providing the right conditions for *self-assertion*; where smaller learning groups are required for this, they should be provided.

This chapter has raised large and complex issues, which deserve their own full book. The argument and examples provided here have dwelled on achieving readiness in language and learning, and have sought to place critical issues in a *whole-school* and *whole-curriculum* context – as was seen, also, in the parent's account by Kath Green, of her son's difficulties in learning, in Chapter 4 of this book. For a full account of providing an imaginative secondary English curriculum for children with special literacy needs, the work of Bernadette Walsh (1988; 1989) is especially recommended.

Having examined, over four chapters, particular aspects of language in learning, the next chapter will focus on creativity in learning.

CHAPTER 9
Creativity in English Studies

This chapter examines creativity in learning, especially in English studies. It considers:

● *compliant* versus *spontaneous* behaviour in learning;
● creative *being* and creative *action*;
● creative *play* in learning;
● accounts by students of *constraints* on creative action;
● features of creativity;
● *'hands-on'* creative learning;
● study by Sue Dymoke on *'Writers into Schools'*: creating poetry with a writer-in-residence.

Realising through play

...behind the spindly words
a child's tentative
                first footsteps
a small voice stuttering
                at the sky
'bird – bird'...
they leap in shafts of sunlight
through the mind's
shutters

(Dorothy Livesay, from 'The Children's Letters',
in *Collected Poems: The Two Seasons*, 1972)

In dwelling on creative being, and on creative activity, this chapter seeks to celebrate the working of creativity in language and learning. In the light of earlier chapters which have confronted the dangers to be faced by learners whose teachers demand passive compliance with a fixed curriculum, a suitable text to launch this discussion of creativity is taken from Winnicott's classic *Playing and Reality* (1971); in a chapter called 'Creativity and its Origins', Winnicott claimed:

> It is creative apperception more than anything else that makes the individual feel that life is worth living. Contrasted with this is a relationship to external reality which is one of compliance...Compliance carries with it a sense of futility for the individual...In a tantalising way many individuals have experienced just enough of creative living to recognise that for most of the time they are living uncreatively, as if caught up in the creativity of someone else, or of a machine.
>
> (p. 65)

Fear and anxiety were, for Winnicott, enemies of creative being (if not of all creative activity); compliance was, he declared, a 'sick basis for life'. On this view, a friendly chat between friends in the school cloakroom that savours the moments of a good weekend, is evidence of creative living; while listlessly attending, but not attending *to* a school assembly; or carrying out, without involvement, some routine classrooom exercise is *not* creative. Such enforced compliance, which allows no element of choice, is maintained by a compliant, false self, with no access to creative being or action.

Winnicott, it may be recalled, wrote as a specialist children's therapist. His views were, in some essentials, close to Freud's, whose great contribution to understanding children was to recognise profundities in their psychic lives. For Freud, the child was 'not a blank sheet of paper, but a very developed, curious, imaginative, sensitive being in need of stimulation...a passionate being, with sensuous drives and fantasies that give his life a dramatic quality' (Fromm, 1973, p. 62). Yet, as Fromm further pointed out, Freud reverted from these insights, and adopted the traditional Augustinian view of the 'sinful child', who must be moulded into civilised behaviour.

Winnicott, however, retained a view of children as complex, autonomous individuals, who are capable of responsible behaviour. Moreover, in offering a conjunction of the terms 'playing' and 'reality', Winnicott challenged Freud's dichotomy between 'pleasure' and 'reality' principles in life, where there must be a barrier between the inner drives of individuals and their daily work. While Freud's dichotomy reflected well enough the 'profit motive' outlook of a market economy, where boredom or exploitation of labour must be alleviated by 'reward', Winnicott sought to close the gap between (personal) 'being' and (impersonal) 'doing'. Through encouraging personal response in learning – a gesture from the inner self to the outer world – we develop a genuinely personal sense of responsibility for what we do, in the world. Winnicott's view, that *playing has its own reality,* was shared by eminent educationists such as Gadamer (1975), Bruner (1976) and Bolton (1982), all of whom showed how play is essential to imaginative-creative activity. In identifying the 'fundamental connectedness of thinking, feeling and language in imagination', Neil Bolton claimed: 'It is language born of imagination which serves the development of thinking'(p. 13). Imagination is the 'fulfilment of pre-reflective intelligence' (p. 16) and, being so fundamental to thought, it is 'the most capable of development and cultivation' (p. 14).

The implication of this for learners, that they need a 'protective perimeter' – which provides both freedom to 'play' and also expert support and guidance – is crucial for the teacher, in working out strategies for classroom activities. While accepting that Freud was right when he claimed that significant achievements, including great works of art, may be created at the *expense* of the creator, teachers must be concerned only with work which reflects and also encourages the personal growth of the learner. 'Genius', suggested John Macmurray (1962), 'is simply human spontaneity, the expression of personal freedom...The artist is not abnormal, but simply the normal human individual' (p. 157). This version of the artist, as an ordinary person who may achieve extraordinary things when given the opportunity, should guide the teacher, in providing creative conditions in the classroom.

The energetic creator

In it there is a space-ship
and a project
for doing away with piano lessons...
...There is a river
that flows upwards...
...There is much promise
in the circumstance
that so many people have heads.

(Miroslav Holub, from 'A Boy's Head', 1990, p. 102)

Although Winnicott's work made a deep impact on a number of writers and teachers, its effect was, arguably, not wide enough. Kieran Egan (1986), for example, complained that 'imagination' and 'the sense of the child as an energetic creator of mental images of what may never have been experienced' has had 'no influence at all' on mainstream educational principles and practice (p. 7). This view was disputed by D.J. Hargreaves (1989, p. 9), who found evidence of 'an explosion of research on creativity' since 1950. Yet Hargreaves also acknowledged that much of this research was psychometric, with an emphasis on creativity as a 'general, abstract characteristic' (p. 11) which can be measured by testing – and with the inevitable implication that creativity is a fixed entity, rather than, as Winnicott held, a whole attitude to living.

There were welcome developments during the 1980s in the field of reflective/critical thinking as advocated, for example, by Nisbet and Shucksmith (1984), who wrote about 'The Seventh Sense'. The notion of a seventh sense was based on Flavell's (1970) notion of 'metacognition'. This is an awareness of one's own thought processes; it may be developed and used to monitor thinking, and to learn how to learn. The reflective/critical thinking movement was also advanced by Matthew Lipman and his colleagues (1980), who campaigned for schoolchildren to learn philosophy through critical reflection, and by texts such as Robert Fisher's *Teaching People to Think* (1990).

Yet, in placing a special emphasis on 'problem-solving' aspects in imaginative play, and on controlling channels of thinking, the area of wonder – where the purpose of play is, simply, play – may have been neglected. The spirit of the times has not been in favour of the imagination; Sara Meadows' text on *The Child as Thinker* (1993, pp. 361–2), for example, devoted just two pages out of nearly five hundred, on 'imagination', where she apologised for the bias that she herself followed, towards 'deliberate cognitive effort', in neglect of 'imagination', and also criticised Egan's account of imagination for relying on 'some value-laden judgements' (p. 362). What other kinds of judgements are possible, one wonders; and how can existing traditions of educational psychology, as presented in Meadows' impressively full account, possibly contribute to the understanding of imaginative processes in learning?

It is difficult, even, to find vigorous *objections* to the notion of imagination in learning, either in published texts on learning and cognition, or – as a student, Shelagh, discovered during her PGCE course – in actual classrooms. In her training department this student found that, far from the much criticised exposure to 'theory' that she had been warned about, intellectual or creative enquiry was not on the menu:

> Knowing, partly, that I held a creed long outworn, too vague yet too demanding (for who now believes in the primacy of imagination, creativity, expression?), I had long since prepared myself for direct confrontation, argument and dissent. But those were not my opponents. The northern faces blinked at me mildly. At college I was faced by a neutrality which, even in its most busy

duplication and reorganising of its hand-outs, is mild, accepting, acquiescent. Always preparing for the next year and the next, the college grows too preoccupied with its own affairs, distanced from the children and their school worlds, forgetful of the voices and faces that fill the classrooms. Detached, or with a cynical acceptance, the tutors shrug at the school system they have absented themselves from. And their students are allowed to shelter in the same corners, never seriously expected to question, extend their own understanding or engage their own humanity as a 'resource' in the complicated business of dealing with young people...The students soak up a year's worth of Professional Qualifications...the newly trained teachers shuffle out to schools, prejudices unchallenged, ideas unexplored, questions unasked and unanswered.

Things were no better when she arrived in a school for her teaching practice:

All the while, racing with clarity and suppressed vitality through your head, circling, twisting and dancing in silence, is a wealth of ideas, thoughts, questions and offerings, such a desire to be thorough, directed and strong in my work, a keen knowing and condemnation of my inadequacies and inefficiencies – but also a need for the keener articulation, and intelligent suggestion from an experienced voice.

Instead:

'When I was at college I wrote down pages and pages of my aims and objectives. I didn't like to be vague.' Or, 'It's all very well saying that you had some good (corruption of my term 'interesting') talks with the children. But they should be working.'

You learn not to reply, partly because of the preoccupation of them all – dashing to get things done; and, somewhat grumpily but urgently, to 'do' something stops anyone who speaks to you from being in the same place or still listening by the time you draw the necessary breath to reply – and partly because you feel that reply is not what is wanted.

You are being told.

(with acknowledgement)

Did Shelagh expect too much of both college and school? Or was she unusually unlucky in her choice of training course? An important inference from her account, I suggest, is that a whole system of education/training can conspire to stifle creative involvement in teaching and learning. Even the study of poetry may suffer from a suspicion of imaginative/metaphoric/creative modes of language; a former student who became engaged in doctoral research on poetry wrote that her supervisor was, at least, honest in his reasons for discouraging creative modes of language:

I think he'd like me to produce a text which is guaranteed metaphor-free.

Despite the fact that word-play is germane to my topic, he worries that the external examiner will pick on any form of non-literality. And, as he always tells me, 'the external examiner is God!'

The supervisor was, perhaps, doing his best to defend his student in the face of 'academic standards'; yet this rigid opposition of creativity to academic discipline is no less absurd than, say, to claim that metaphors must be accepted uncritically because they cannot be evaluated. Metaphor, like creativity itself, cannot be measured by any known instrument, and is best understood through *enactment*. Ironically, as Sternberg (1990) and Baer (1993) showed, we can only think about creativity *through* metaphor; how else may poetry be understood? It is unfortunate for the rigid academic mind that the good (or poor) quality of a metaphor must be fully experienced, rather than simply measured according to a tried formula.

Launching creativity

Tom Stoppard's character Henry, in *The Real Thing* (1984), has a role in the play as guardian of the language. Sometimes he shows a finicky concern for points of grammar. More importantly and less pedantically, though, he condemns jargon that misrepresents real events; he also condemns the misuse of words, that is committed in a confused metaphor – 'I don't think writers are sacred, but words are.' Art, explains Henry, is for launching ideas, and the actual instruments used for launching are metaphors. In order to clarify what he means by the art of language, he compares a good and bad metaphor with a cricket bat and a cudgel: 'What we are trying to do is to write cricket bats, so that when we throw up an idea and give it a little knock, it might...*travel*'. In the spirit of Zen, but with a metaphor from rural England, Stoppard shows how a well-delivered idea which is delivered with economy looks, sounds and feels right; there is no need to measure its impact.

The accounts by students, above, of what they saw as fundamentally timid handling of imagination and creativity in learning, prompts the question: *what is creative teaching and learning, and what blocks to creativity do teachers and learners need to overcome?* John Baer (1993, p. 14), writing on divergent – thinking versions of creativity, cited the influential work of Guilford (1967), who identified four categories of factors which enhanced divergent thinking: *fluency* of ideas; *flexibility* in producing a wide variety of ideas; *originality* in producing unusual ideas; and *elaboration* in developing ideas. These look useful, in seeking an answer to the question; but in order to give some human shape to such abstract characteristics, an answer might be given in some form like this:

Creative learners/teachers	Those who block creativity
• are curious, interrogate, speculate, examine	• accept directions, enjoy routine
• enjoy 'play' in learning, risk imaginative ventures	• prefer literal/factual versions of knowledge
• are non-conforming, independent, will take risks	• like strong guidelines, are custom-bound
• make connections, see relations, are flexible	• prefer to work step-by-step, are rigid
• enjoy uncertainty, take risks to compose their own order	• prefer order, tidiness and a given framework
• have a rich blend of feeling and reasoning	• mistrust feeling and intellectual venture
• are sensitive, bodily aware	• are dull in sensory life
• like to day-dream, wonder, incubate ideas	• are anxious to plod to conclusions
• enjoy complexity, can qualify, modify	• prefer simple binary, either/or solutions
• are confident, tenacious in self, sense of place, and claiming their place	• are anxious about work, lack assertion, discouraged by criticism

In *Jumpers* (1972) another of Tom Stoppard's academic characters, George, moves beyond academic hesitations, to argue that people have a spiritual aspect which transcends reductive – such as Darwinian or Marxist – versions of humanity. George suggests that this spirituality is creative living itself, which may be found in quite ordinary moments of recognition:

> And now and again, not necessarily in the contemplation of polygons or new-born babes, nor in extremities of pain and joy, but more probably in some quite trivial moment, it seems to me that life itself is the mundane figure which argues perfection at its limiting curve. And, if I doubt, the ability to doubt, to question, to *think,* seems to be the curve itself – cogito ergo deus est.
>
> (pp. 62–3)

It may be trusted, for example, that as the above list is vigorously examined, extended or amended by readers, then this itself is evidence of their creative engagement with the world.

The kind of fulfilment to be achieved through creative action – when 'being' and 'doing' are in harmony – was identified by Ted Hughes (1967), in a widely quoted note on 'Learning to Think', which compares creative thinking with angling:

> Your whole being rests lightly on your float, but not drowsily: very alert, so that the least twitch of the float arrives like an electric shock. And you are not only aware of the float. You are aware, in a horizonless and slightly mesmerised way, like listening to the double bass in orchestral music, of the fish below there in the dark.

So far, Hughes puts an emphasis on 'being' – on the relaxed pleasure of the experience; but as thoughts and connections quicken, he also identifies the pleasurable discomfort of 'doing':

> At every moment your imagination is alarming itself with the size of the thing slowly leaving the weeds...And the whole purpose of this concentrated excitement...is to bring up some lovely solid thing like living metal from a world where nothing exists but those inevitable facts which raise life out of nothing and return it to nothing.
>
> (pp. 60–1)

For Hughes, this pool of being is exactly where the mind 'connects' to form symbols. This is not just the preserve of the established creative poet; indeed, as Marjorie Hourd (1974) and Margaret Meek (1985) argued, all children who are ready to learn are ready precisely because they have this capacity. The capacity of learners to symbolise provides the capacity to relate to their world, and to enact their talents. Symbol formation is, therefore, crucially a harmonising agent (rather than compromising, as in Freud's view that we only symbolise what we have repressed); without it, learners cannot make the world their own.

'Hands-on' creativity in learning

Chapter 3, on 'Metaphor', reflected on the problems of 'our entirely visual civilisation' (Montale, 1976, p. 21), where learning is restricted by an undue dependance on sight, at the expense of other senses, and other modes of experience. In *Windows on the Mind* (1982, p. 222) Harth suggested that a whole tradition of science had relied on the kinds of observation that take place when looking at marine life 'through an underwater port of heavy plate glass, with the observer on one side, fish and shells on the other, unconcerned and undisturbed'. The scene outside the window is taken to be objective reality, since it seems to exist independently of the observation, and 'because it looks the same to any observer peering from their port'. In post-quantum mechanics, however, the observer can no longer take this picture for granted, but reaches out and, activating all senses, 'manipulates and participates in the goings-on'. This participation between observer and world brings about changes that are unavoidable and usually unpredictable. It is this peculiar interaction between the consciousness of the observer on the one hand, and physical reality on the other, that dominates the stage (p. 222). These new laws of physics require all the senses to explore a rich variety of experience, so that the investigator is made to feel that 'the dynamics of (personal) consciousness may not be separable from the dynamics of the world' (p. 224).

What is true at the frontiers of knowledge also applies to all classrooms. Genuine creative writing, for example, may have its beginnings in the simplest of exercises, as with a year seven group, newly arrived in their secondary school, whom I asked to describe anything they learned, from handling a few objects that were passed round the class – some chestnuts, large leaves, apples, eggs, paper weights and so on. When a boy described his egg as 'oval', and was asked what 'oval' meant – 'like an egg', he said, inevitably – the class began to warm to the idea of looking around words, as well as objects, with a view to closer accounts of what these felt, sounded and 'tasted' like. Luke volunteered that his own name is an Icelandic word for 'hand'. The water in the Icelandic springs, he reminded his study group, was as warm as human blood, or 'lukewarm'. Suzanne capped this with the information that her name was from the Hebrew 'Shushan', like a lily. Another group was keen to explore textures of fabrics, under headings of touch, smell, sound (when rubbed) and even taste, as well as sight. Jim, the boy who had described his egg as 'oval', began to parody the lesson by describing an apple as 'shaped like a square with rounded sides', but noted in his journal:

> surrounding the stalk is this muddy green patch which has ecaped the sun, and at the other end the dead blossom creeps out like a hairy spider. One of the sides is a peach colour, red mingled with yellow – the other side a vivid red...

This was attentive observation, but still confined to vision. He ventured further with the next object, a seashell:

> It looks like a brown-and-white crab, with black claws. The brown looks as though it has been put on in streaks with a stiff paintbrush. On the bottom there is a lot of mauve streaks which look like the hairs of a sea

anemone...The shell smells of the sea and also of fish – it has a not altogether clean kind of smell. When I rub my hand over the shell it feels very bumpy. It is very hard all over, the bottom is very smooth and shiny. When I tasted the shell it is hard on the tongue, nearly tasteless, then a creamy kind of taste with a sharp feel of salt.

– still too many adjectives for the spirit of the lesson, but Jim has moved far beyond 'oval' and 'square' definitions, into a richer, less predictable world altogether. It is a world that *he* enters and composes, as he investigates it. This modest, yet authentic encounter with experience shows how Jim has profited by taking a full part, and engaging with 'hands-on' learning. Although he did not choose to write in verse form, his writing has an essential poetic quality, in Holub's sense, that 'a poem is being as against emptiness' (in 'Although', 1990, p. 129); Jim's 'being' is now beginning to be part of his learning-through-writing. This, as Sue Dymoke shows in her account of pupils writing poems with a writer-in-residence, is at the root of all creative thinking and writing, throughout the school:

Writers into school: the Jackie Kay experience by Sue Dymoke

Language...in poetry, fable, myth and story...achieves forms that constitute (if anything does) the foundation of English as a distinctive subject.

(Knight, 1994)

This account explains ways in which a writer-in-residence was used in a large comprehensive school. It also explores the impact that she had on students' perceptions of the writing process. In *English, Whose English?* (1987) David Allen discussed how to focus on profitable ways of organising writing. He argued for the need to 'pay far more attention to the process itself and, from knowledge of how experienced writers behave, develop classroom practices which allow children to behave like real writers' (p. 24). This is a fine premise and one which reinforces the principle that no classroom writing should be completed in a vacuum. Writing in the classroom must reflect the world outside and draw on successful practices; otherwise it remains at the level of a mere classroom exercise.

Preparing for the visit

Encouraging students to write for specific audiences, whether these are younger children or newspaper editors, is an important aim in any English classroom. However, I also think it is not only the teacher who needs that knowledge of how 'experienced writers behave', but also the students. It is not enough to recall second-hand experiences or writers' anecdotes to support an introduction to drafting processes in the classroom. Wherever practicable, young people should be given the opportunity to see and hear established writers at work and to work alongside them. The tradition of bringing writers into schools is by now quite well established. The W. H. Smith 'Writers in Schools' project, and support from regional arts organisations, have made it possible for many schools to invite writers in during 'book weeks' or when the English department wishes to have a drive on one particular genre of writing. Teenage fiction writers seem to be most in demand although I often receive a 'phone call from a colleague who is looking for a 'lively poet'. This request for a 'lively poet' often leads me to question what the purpose of the visit will be and how it reflects the precise aims of the department/class/teacher. In the Preface to this book Bernard Harrison proposed teachers as 'managers of learning'; learning experiences do need to be managed and planned for. Using a poet to entertain a hundred year-nine students in a theatre on a wet Monday afternoon might provide an hour's relief for the teacher but it may not make the most of the potential experience, nor will it encourage the writer to return to the school.

At worst the use of writers in schools is merely a matter of exposure, often coupled with the assumption that the writer can magically perform the role of teacher at the same time: 'Here's Mr so and so who writes crime stories. Has anyone read any? No well... He's going to read you some anyway and then you can ask him some questions. I'll be back in about an hour.' While such an experience may have some limited value (the students have seen and heard a real live writer and some of them may have been encouraged to read his work) a rich opportunity may have been wasted in offering only a tantalising glimpse into another world.

The best use of writers in schools is when all parties concerned (the writer, the students, the teacher and the school community as a whole) are given the chance to develop a rapport, to establish a relationship and methods of working which will remain long after the writer has departed.

A writer-in-residence

During the autumn term, 1993, I was pleased to fulfil a long-held ambition: to introduce the school's first writer-in-residence, the poet Jackie Kay. Jackie's November residency followed months of planning and persuading and, although it was an exhausting experience, I should welcome any chance to repeat it.

Prior to this residency, writers of all kinds, and from many different cultural ethnic backgrounds – including a playwright, a radio journalist, a science fiction writer, numerous poets and several novelists – had been into school and worked with different age groups. The anthologist Anne Harvey spent a practical day in school offering guidance to year-seven students on different ways of performing poetry and sharing her encyclopaedic knowledge of poems with year-ten students, who were compiling their own poetry anthologies for a GCSE assignment. Anne was impressed by the enthusiasm and initiative which both sets of students showed. I felt that the next stage was for the students to be able to work in a more concentrated way, with a writer-in-residence. Anne agreed and kindly offered advice about writers who might be suitable and willing.

Other places to approach for advice might be a regional arts association or the National Association of Writers in Education (Nanholme Centre, Shaw Wood Road, Todmorden, OL14 6DY), both of which keep lists of writers available for readings and workshops.

The kind of experience I sought for my school had a direct bearing on the kind of writer chosen and, to some extent, the way in which funding was acquired. Building on their experience with previous visiting writers, some students had begun to share their 'private' writing notebooks with English staff, while many others had found audiences for their work in the annual English Evenings which the department holds. At these evenings students are given the chance to perform their work for parents and friends. The school needed a writer who could encourage further those who were already confident enough to talk about their writing, whilst giving others the confidence to begin doing so. I wanted to give our students the opportunity to explore and reveal more about themselves and events which were important to them, and to realise the ways in which writing, especially poetry, can be used to do this. I also wanted staff and students throughout the school to make contact with a real working poet, with a view to dislodging the stereotype of the poet which may persist in people's minds.

To achieve such aims required a writer who would be honest yet also sensitive and approachable, and who enjoyed working with young people. In the rush to secure a 'writer' sometimes the latter is sadly ignored. If the children feel uncomfortable with that person in the classroom then the experience can be alienating. In spite of such exacting criteria Anne Harvey swiftly produced two names. Jackie Kay immediately seemed like the best option. As the author of *The Adoption Papers* (1991) and *Two's Company* (1992) a lively collection of poems for children, she was already known to me. I had also heard her give an entertaining reading in the Beeston Poets series, and knew that she would fit in well. Jackie Kay is a black Scottish writer. She uses dialect frequently in her children's poems, particularly to explore the different ways people communicate. Therefore, the ways she looked and also sounded emphasised the idea that poetry has many different voices. The fact that Jackie wrote poems for children as well as her adult collections was important. It meant she could work with students of all ages, reinforcing that this was a whole-school experience, in which everyone could share.

Securing funding for the residency was another task which had to be organised well in advance. Regional arts associations are a useful starting point (although not a successful one in this case) and a school's TVEI(E) budget should be another potential source. My school has a vigorous Parent Staff Association, which regularly raises funds for otherwise unaffordable equipment and will listen to requests for funding from departments. Although I could perhaps have gained help elsewhere I thought that it was essential they were involved in an initiative like this, as it would confirm the sense of a whole-school commitment to the project. The PSA were interested in the proposal but wanted more information before a decision could be reached. Their concern was to ascertain what the tangible results would be; what would the final outcome be? Such questions were difficult to answer. How far in the future would it be, before Jackie's advice or her own poems had an effect? Would the effect be long term or short lived? How many students would actually be influenced by the experience? All this was unpredictable. We hoped the residency would have an enormous impact, yet there was no guaranteed outcome. It is easier to argue over such points when one is requesting a new tape recorder or a set of dictionaries; however, after my assuring the committee that there would be, at least, some kind of publication produced they gave their approval.

Work-in-progress: dialect poems

During Jackie's visit, teachers in the department wanted to use her in a number of different ways. Firstly she would work with five specific classes over a series of lessons. Secondly she would work with much smaller groups of students who had either shown a keen interest in sharing their writing with others in the past or who had taken the initiative to reply to the internal advertisement for workshop members. Thirdly I felt it was important that other students, staff and parents were given the chance to share in the experience. Jackie kindly agreed to do an evening reading.

The sessions with specific classes took a number of different directions. Many younger pupils wrote about early memories, sibling rivalries, or things which frightened them, such as parents arguing, being trapped in a lift or a car accident at night in a foreign country. A year-eight class compiled a class anthology of their own poems on tape and sent Jackie a copy of it. One year-nine class focused on dialects and family languages, using Jackie's poems 'Sassenachs' and 'English Cousin comes to Scotland' (both from *Two's Company*). In the second poem a visiting English girl tries to understand her Scottish cousin's account of an argument between the cousin and her mother. This is retold using many dialect words. The language barrier and the struggle for control in the relationship between the two girls are both cleverly handled in the closing lines:

Whilst I'm saying this, my English cousin
has her mouth open. Glaikit.
Stupit. So she is, so she is.
I says, 'I'm going to have to learn you
what's what.' And at that the wee git
cheers up; the wee toffee nose git says,
'not learn you, teach you,' like she's scored.

These poems led into a discussion on the issue of language and power and the assumptions people make about you as soon as you open your mouth. In order to provide a stimulus for writing in the dialects which students had identified (it is, after all, hard to write solely about language) Jackie asked each member of the group to think of an object and a secret, and to describe each one briefly on separate scraps of paper. The secrets and objects were then reallocated randomly around the class. In many cases they provided starting points for some unusual poems in a number of different dialects; Nottinghamshire and Geordie dialects were the most popular.

Having to create written forms for words that were usually spoken, and to complete initial drafts in a very short space of time, were the two real challenges of this activity. The intensity of the process was heightened by the fact that the poet and both members of staff present were also writing. Clearly it is not always possible for the teacher to be 'on task' in this way all the time too. However, I had assured Jackie that throughout her residency all staff would endeavour to write too, and I think that this added to the experience of the week. By the end of the second lesson Jackie had already worked through several drafts of 'Amber and Chocolate' (a poem which she later dedicated to two students in the class) and many students were well into the process of writing wildly imaginative pieces about such diverse subjects as: fathers in prison; the concealed cigarette which burned the house down; doing 'nuffin' and the thirteen-year-old boy who still takes his battered teddy bear to the pictures. 'Teddy Bear' by Lee Tassi shows a sophisticated use of dialect, humour and an awareness of audience as he asks us to imagine...

Bet sey yer wher a big lad,
Thirteen or soo,
An'yer gooin doon the pitchas,
Wi' yer teddy in y'arms,
Someone's bahrned ter stop yer,
say 'whatcha daein, man?' and goo tell,
All y'mates.

Working with A-level students

For me one of the most satisfying aspects of working with Jackie was the way in which she encouraged children to be adventurous with their writing, to turn things upside down and look at them from a different point of view, to take risks. There was no guarantee that these risks would not reveal painful memories, yet her sensitive approach encouraged students to take a chance. This fact was nowhere more evident than in the long workshop session she ran for our year-twelve A-level students. All the students had been immersed in ways into poetry and prose since the beginning of their course and had been experimenting with writing in different forms. They had also looked at and discussed *The Adoption Papers* (1991) as well as several poems from Jackie's new book *Other Lovers* (1993). In some ways they were prepared, but I don't think that any of them expected to respond to the workshop with the enthusiasm that they did. During the short reading/question and answer session the students clearly warmed to the poet. Many of them commented later that she was nervous (which surprised them and immediately made her 'more human'). They also found that she was amusing, and made them interested in the issues she wrote about through the immediacy and accessibility of her writing. They liked the way she used different voices in the title poems of *The Adoption Papers* and *Other Loves*, and were happier now they had heard these poems come to life with her voices.

Throughout her residency the poet kept coming back to talking about memory and the resource which memory provides for writing. When working with year twelve she asked them each to find a partner and to tell that partner an important or significant memory in as much detail as possible. When both students had given each other a memory they were to 'give it back' by retelling the memory in the second person. Once both memories had been given back, students could then interweave them or use one of them in their writing. I worked on this activity with Jackie and was amazed at its success. Many students found that, without any planning, their memories were about similar events, while others found that their partner's memory was so much more interesting than theirs, that they preferred to write solely about it. By the end of the afternoon initial drafts were complete and students worked on these for several weeks afterwards. I was impressed with their commitment to the writing, and the way that they wanted to make the most of this special opportunity. Two girls found that when very young they had both had the same frightening experience of waking up alone in hospital, recovering from an eye operation. In her poem 'I will always remember' one of the girls, Louise Hipkins, used the experience and reworked it so that the initial anxiety became softened by the realisation, all those years later, that others had the same fears:

Alone and frightened,
in the dark.
Waiting for
mum and dad to come.

Crisp, clean sheets,
Tightly folded
encasing me.

Trapped under layers of white,
woven round and round.

Reaching out
to hold onto something,
anything.

It's lonely here
in the early hours.

May as well wait 'til Day
breaks.
But what's the difference?
No light can penetrate this darkness.

There's a sound.
A muffled whimpering
that comes from deep inside.

It's painfully close by.

184

Two
small islands in an ocean
of blackness.

The idea bobs between us
tentatively.

Reaching out, our fingers touch.
Like sole survivors of a sunken ship,
we cling.

I am not alone.

(reproduced with acknowledgement to Louise Hipkins)

Louise thought of this poem as a break-through. She had found a grasp of structure which went beyond the solid blocks of text used in her previous poems. She had used single lines and the gaps between verses most effectively, to convey the sense of isolation and of someone gradually piecing together a strange and invisible environment. Many other students experimented with structure in ways they had not done before. The fragmented nature of some of Jackie's poems appealed to them. Students also took on the challenge of writing long poems in sections, using several different voices. Several of them used the opportunity to write about intensely personal, disturbing experiences and found that this structure helped them to explore the various viewpoints of those involved. One student wrote about coming to terms with his parents' divorce, and the desperation he had felt. He told me that this was the first time he had ever been able to really think about what had happened to him, and was shocked by how much the rush of words on to paper had upset him. Another student, Claire Jacklin, wrote a long poem called 'Whatever happened to Daddy'. In this extract, entitled 'The Suspicion', the young girl begins to think through what is actually happening to her parents:

Mum and Dad don't really talk.
Not properly.
They don't canoodle or walk
hand in hand.
There is a bitterness.
More from Mum than Dad.

Dad tries to please her,
buys her flowers, washes the pots.
'Thank you,' she replies
in that disappointed, bitter tone.
I know this.

Dad has haircuts too
young for his age,
he smells good, very good.

Always smartly dressed
in modern clothes,
keeps up with the trends.

Then the phone rings or he
rings someone on the phone.
The upstairs phone.
He laughs and talks quietly,
hiding his conversation.
He is not talking to a woman.

Mum is busy, works hard.
Bustles along, strong and bold.
Her non-permeable body
allows no words to stab her feelings.
They are shredded as it is.
She continues life.
Pushes away the problem
or puts up with it.
Which ever?

He is talking again
to a different stranger.
Will he go out tonight?
See his 'friends'.
All of them seem to be male,
so it's alright, he's not
having an affair.
That is how life is.

(reproduced with acknowledgement to Claire Jacklin)

Claire has learned from Jackie, how repetition of seemingly innocent words and observations (and careful juxtaposition of these) can give them a real power and complexity of meaning. In Jackie Kay's poem 'Sign' (from *Other Lovers*), which is concerned with society's refusal to accept sign language as a valid form of communication, she repeats the phrase 'no language at all' in ways which highlight the irony of such a conclusion. I like, too, the way Claire uses questions and short statements to provoke the reader and to indicate how aware the narrator really is about what is going on.

Many of the A-level students went on to use their poems, in all their draft stages, as the basis for a piece of A-level coursework. It is sad to think that, following new SCAA regulations (1994), our next cohort of students will not be permitted to include such original writing in their coursework folders (see earlier discussion of this in Chapter 2).

As well as working with whole groups of students, we built in a number of opportunities for much smaller groups of students, from years seven to thirteen, to show Jackie drafts of poems on which they were working at home, and to seek advice and/or inspiration from her about what they should do with individual poems or their writing in general. She offered help with fine tuning, reworking and ways into publication. The reaction to these sessions was excellent. Many students were surprised and encouraged by the different kind of learning that they provided. A number of talented poets, with folders full of previously unseen material, sought advice. Graham Self, a year-nine student, brought along a sheaf of well-drafted poems, many of which used complex rhyming structures. Jackie was impressed by 'The Execution of Mary, Queen of Scots' which includes a description of the queen paying off her servants for the last time:

> She placed her money in packets,
> with all the servants, names.
> She read a book called 'THE GREAT SAINT',
> and saw all her sins and shames.

Students took full advantage of the opportunities offered by Jackie's workshops. Many have gained in confidence as a result and have begun submitting their work to magazines for consideration. When interviewed for the school newsletter Frances McCarthy from year-nine commented, 'She gave me the guidelines I would need to get anything published. I am really grateful for that chance.' Kate Hargreaves, from year thirteen, who has subsequently been offered a place on the UEA English and creative writing degree course, said that 'after the workshop the five of us talked about our writing for over an hour – something we've never really done before'. The girls' comments really sum up what this whole experience was all about. In March we shall publish an anthology of poems written during or as a result of Jackie's stay. Its title, *Nobody Listens to Vera Lynn Any More!* is taken from a poem by Jamie Collings of year nine. Yet the effect of Jackie's residency runs much deeper than a single publication. Our students lived, breathed and ate school dinners with her. Many of them came along with their parents and teachers to hear her read her own work, and were anxious to know more about her as the news spread from class to class. They saw how her drafts gradually developed into fully fledged poems such as the marvellous 'Teeth'. They shared jokes with her and experimented with the forms she uses. Months later when she appears on *The Late Show* or has a poem in *The Observer* people are still coming up to me, whom I had not realised she had influenced in any way, and saying 'Did you see Jackie on TV last night? When's she coming back?'

CHAPTER 10

Personal Meaning in Language and Learning. with a study by John Hodgson on 'the power of narrative'

This final chapter includes a study by John Hodgson, on the powers of personal history and of narrative in developing a literate imagination. It includes discussion of:

- the need for *teachers, as well as learners*, to engage with personal meaning in learning;
- respect for *varieties of individuals, and varieties of cultures* in learning;
- *the power of narrative* in learning, and in educational enquiry;
- notes from a *personal history* (John Hodgson);
- Coleen's story about school, *'Time to Let Go'*, with teacher's commentary (John Hodgson).

Full circle

The Introduction to this book considered the political context in which the National Curriculum Framework for English was developed, and the conflicts that arose concerning the 1993 proposed New Order. The concluding section to that chapter examined the wider responsibilities of teachers of English – as managers, and as educationists – in contributing to the full professionalisation of teachers. Following this Introduction, successive chapters have dwelled on various ways in which the fascinating, yet exacting task of developing a literate imagination may be achieved in schools.

Teachers of English have, over decades, developed patterns of learning that place a central emphasis on finding personal response and meaning through work in English. Yet the 'privilege' of space for personal response has had to be fought for, not least during the years of this present decade. The fact that there is no space in today's schools for any 'donnish' withdrawal from what might seem to be tiresome or intrusive issues of policy, is revealed in the following conversation with John Hodgson, which prefaces his study of 'the power of narrrative'. John explains how, as a secondary school head of English, he was required to make a public defence of values in English such as this present book has sought to promote:

JH: 'I'll tell you what English is: it's reading, writing, grammar, spelling and Shakespeare.' Thus John Major in a Prime Ministerial statement in 1993, at the time when the government's intentions to impose mandatory testing of English 'skills' on all fourteen-year-old pupils were challenged by teachers. The boycott on tests was initiated by teachers themselves, working with their professional association, NATE. The teacher unions, who were generally represented by the media as the source of disturbance, only became involved when the wave of professional discontent had already gained strength.

In my own school, for instance, a colleague and myself (deputy head and head of department) made a presentation to the governors in March 1993. We identified twelve reasons for objecting to the tests. These ranged from the incompetence of the government agency responsible for organising them (in imitation of the Ministry of Circumlocution, it regularly sent out memos contradicting earlier memos), to the vacuity of the tests themselves. As one of the twenty-eight schools that had piloted the tests, we felt well placed to make these criticisms. The governors, a representative group of the local community, listened sympathetically and agreed to support our professional reasons for not cooperating with an anti-educational procedure. This process was repeated in hundreds of schools across the country; it showed a degree of parental partnership and support for the views of teachers of English that seemed incomprehensible at government level.

BH: So, John, it was a common sense, and a moral sense, that guided teachers and parents in this 'grassroots' protest. Once more, the conflict over the testing of English highlighted a deeper conflict about aims in teaching the mother tongue (which was examined in Chapter 2 of this book). Put crudely, this is between, on one side, those who see English teaching as primarily a matter of drilling pupils in 'correct' language use; once this is in place, the pupils may proceed to receive their standard dose of literary heritage. Shakespeare operates as symbolic representative here; his questionable politics (he raised many awkward questions about 'authority'), occasional obscenities, dubious sexuality and protean variety of spellings (he spelled his own name in several different ways) are all forgiven by those who bend the ears of government, it seems, as long as the text is in the 'canon'. On the other side of this (crude) divide are those who see English teaching as a means of helping pupils become, through developing confidence and expertise in using their language, more fully themselves. Such teachers may also be enthusiastic about including Shakespeare in their teaching programmes – but not for government reasons.

JH: Our earlier conversation (in Chapter 2) sought to show that there need be no conflict between a view of English studies as involving 'personal growth' through language, and a view that recognises the power of good quality literary texts, in developing such personal growth. Such views have much in common; they are a whole world, however, from the finger-stabbing 'I'll tell you what English is' thrust of the Prime Minister. There, the message is that pupils must first be taught and tested on correctness in reading and writing, and then be tested on 'great' texts.

We may see here a reason why parents did not support the government line on English teaching and testing, as politicians expected of them. In their complex duties of child-rearing, they have had to distinguish between genuinely educative and merely coercive modes of up-bringing. Parental firmness in some essentials is vital to the framework of successful family life; yet consultation, reason, respect and flexibility are also essential features of a civilised family. Through the contacts of an effective parent-teacher partnership, therefore, it may be easily discovered that many parents have no difficulties in finding respect for modes of teaching English which attempt to develop their children's natural expressiveness, without authoritarian prescriptions.

The Prime Minister's ex-cathedra pronouncement 'I'll tell you what English is...' represented a severely limited and oppressive view of English studies which was, however, formulated in the 1993 Order for English. Such an intervention at the highest level of government was in marked contrast to what happened in an anecdote related by John Richmond to a NATE Conference (1991): towards the end of the Second World War, Prime Minister Churchill approached R.A. Butler, then Minister of Education, and suggested that something should be done in schools to make children more patriotic. Butler demurred, insisting the the curriculum was the province of the schools and their governors, and that the role of government should be merely as facilitator. 'Oh, quite, quite,' said Churchill, merely adding, 'But can't we at least tell them that Woolf won Quebec?'

Richmond contributed to the ill-fated Language in the National Curriculum (LINC) Project (which was discussed in Chapter 5). No such respect as Churchill's for the autonomy of schools was shown by the government in 1990, which not only refused to publish the LINC Report, but also refused to release Crown copyright; thus the work of hundreds of teachers and academics over three years, at a total cost of some £21 million, was not allowed to reach the light of day. The fault of the Report, it seemed, was that it presented language as a socially conditioned phenomenon to a government whose leader, Mrs Thatcher, had claimed that 'there is no such thing as society'.

BH: The impulse behind the 1993 revision of the English Order was, then, an attempt to impose a particular view of language and culture. This was, of course, also the impulse behind the Cox Report which led to the original 1990 Order. Yet, as you argued earlier, if the Cox Report was a prison, it was at least large and open, with the possibility of finding some interesting and unsupervised pathways. It endorsed some good practice in the teaching of speaking, listening, reading, writing, drama and media studies. In contrast, the revised (1993) Order sought to impose a rigid 'transmission' view of learning; this caused such wide professional resentment that the original 'open' prison of the original Order has, itself, become more widely challenged. No longer is there a comfortable consensus, that a National Curriculum will deliver all that is required of school education.

Coercion in matters of language and culture is politically dangerous and educationally ineffective. The learner-centred approach to education that this book has advocated is not just an alternative among several possible options; it is, simply, the one effective form of learning. Meaning, in order to be effective in the lives of students, must be personally achieved, through whatever cultural channels are available. This is not necessarily an argument against a National Curriculum; but it is to insist that the full range of English studies must reach *beyond* any imposed framework, that personal engagement with the world and with texts is of the essence, and that consultation and true respect on both sides should characterise teaching-learning relations.

JH: Yes; the argument is partly on behalf of individuals, and partly on behalf of the variousness of 'cultures', as lived by communities large and small. A more congenial notion of culture than is allowed in the National Curriculum Framework was suggested by Paul Willis, in *Common Culture* (1990). Willis was primarily concerned with examining people's use of 'common' culture; he aimed to re-evaluate ways in which people use cultural products, whether these be television, the press, fashion, music, or other cultural forms, whether 'high' or 'low'. He argued that people use cultural products for their own purposes, in active and creative ways. They may create fashion, by adapting clothes from charity shops; they may re-record music, to create their own albums of favourite tracks; they may discuss radio/televison soap operas in ways that show that they are well aware of the facticity of these 'soaps'. Without making claims about the quality of what is available (and it is at this point, I suggest, where education might intervene), Willis shows that people's use of cultural products is unpredictable and varied – as varied as their individual identities; since culture, in Willis' view, is a means of shaping identity.

Personal education, then, can be seen as a process of appropriating cultural objects and experiences to one's developing identity, rather than having an identity thrust upon one by an authority-approved version of culture. From this viewpoint, attempts by government to impose reading materials seem unjustifiable – until one recalls Willis' caveat, that people are essentially creative in their cultural receptiveness. Thus it is the *variousness* with which fourteen-year-old boys and girls may respond to the young lovers in *Romeo and Juliet*, that makes exploration of that text worthwhile with a class.

The power of narrative

Thus we build up the being that we are...

Wordsworth, *The Prelude*

BH: The importance of personal writing and of personal histories in learning was explored in Chapters 4 and 6 of this book. In showing how, through narrative, we may learn and also help others to learn, John Hodgson extends the need of learners to 'tell', to the domain of fiction. As was discussed earlier in Chapter 4, the whole field of personal reflection, autobiography and non-fictional or fictional narrative has been exploited by Woods (1993) and many others, as a profitable area for educational enquiry. What Gillie Bolton (1994) identified as the uses of fiction in educational research could be extended to all areas of narrative 'telling':

1. narratives of all kinds provide a framework for composing qualitative evidence in terms that may be widely understood;
2. they provide a means of 'exploring a professional problem that is inaccessible or problematic by any other means';
3. they are 'an excellent vehicle for conveying the ambiguities, complexities and ironic relationships that exist between multiple viewpoints';
4. narratives do not deal with rigid 'facts'. They leave 'gaps for the reader to fill'. In requiring a response and contribution from the listener/reader, they raise 'questions through the unresolved plurality' of meanings.

(adapted from Gillie Bolton, 1994, p. 56)

With this version of educational enquiry, it is easier to see research in Zora Neale Hurston's terms (1986, p. 174), as 'formalised curiosity. It is poking and prying with a purpose'. In this spirit, John undertakes some personal 'research' into events from his earlier life, and in his teaching. He opens his account with a note on his own earlier life, before moving on to discuss a story written by one of his pupils:

JH: Looking back to my own early reading, I was fortunate as a small child to be given many books, from the stories and poems of A.A. Milne, through large collections of Grimm's and Anderson's fairy tales, to the stories by 'B.B.' (Denys Watkins-Pickford), *The Little Grey Men* and *Down the Bright Stream*. These latter two particularly engaged my imagination; this seems, on reflection, to have something to do with their presentation of very small people moving out from their familiar territory to cope with adventures and dangers down the bright stream. Unconsciously, no doubt, I related their feelings to mine. Then, at the age of five, I was taken to the cinema for the first time. The film was the comedy *The Titfield Thunderbolt*. I was utterly entranced by the large, coloured moving picture, and this visit sparked a love of film (and, more recently, of video) which has never left me. By the age of twelve I had acquired a cine camera and was beginning to make films. Quite deliberately I experimented with various genres, over the following few years, on 9.5mm black-and-white cine film, pastiches of commercial thrillers, comedies, travelogues and documentaries.

None of this was known to anyone outside my family and friends. School seemed to me mainly tedium. The only moments of genuine pleasure I remember from primary school were finding, in a cupboard, an elderly (abridged) copy of *A Christmas Carol*, which I read at one sitting; and, in the top class, writing plays which were acted by other children in the class. English at grammar school had occasional oases of imaginative nourishment in a desert of clause analysis and reading such texts as Conan Doyle's *White Company* around the class (where *was* all the wild, progressive teaching of the 1960s happening, so disparaged in our post-Education Reform Act age?).

In the second year, an energetic teacher got us to act the Pyramus and Thisbe scenes from *A Midsummer Night's Dream*, and to write a letter from one of the men who discovered Gulliver, to the Emperor of Lilliput. We also had to paint our favourite scene from *The Rime of the Ancient Mariner*. This was a good year. Nothing happened in the third year, apart from weeks and months spent copying down figures of speech, with examples, from dictation. Then came O-level preparation. The teacher I had at this stage later became an HMI; after he had left, and I was in the sixth form, he wrote to me, saying he hoped that I was keeping up my writing. I did not, at first, realise what he meant. The stories and essays I had produced in school seemed to be done because they had to be done, not to be 'writing' in the sense that I hope students such as Coleen (whose work is described below) may view their writing – that is, as an important opportunity to engage with all kinds of experience and issues that concern them in their world.

It was not until the sixth form that I discovered what adult literature could mean to me, when I encountered some newly arrived teachers who combined academic prowess with a strong sense that the only meaning worth having was, in Keats' words, that which was 'felt upon the pulses'. It was here, in fact, where I developed a sustaining passion for Romantic poetry, particularly that of Blake and Wordsworth, and where seeds were sown for the kinds of satisfaction in teaching and learning that were expressed later by one of my own students, Sian, in her work on Wordsworth (see Chapter 2). The *Songs of Innocence and Experience*, some of the prophetic books (particularly *The Marriage of Heaven and Hell* and *Visions of the Daughters of Albion*), and *The Prelude* – all of these, to invoke Wordsworth, 'spake to me/Rememberable things'.

They were 'rememberable' because they seemed to be companions in my journey to meaning. In these writers (and, as time went on, in many others) I found friendly voices which expressed feelings and thoughts which chimed with my own. In other words, my pleasure in literature was not merely 'aesthetic' or 'cultural': my reading was a force in my life.

One aspect of Wordsworth which interested me from the beginning was his concern with moral growth. In my late teens and early twenties, when I was thinking of becoming a teacher, I underwent a crisis of confidence about the basis of morality. This was related to my emerging awareness of my sexuality, and is probably a not unusual preoccupation of adolescents. At Cambridge, reading for the 'English Moralists' paper – which, perhaps quaintly, included Plato as an English Moralist, I sought an answer to the question of whether a moral sense can be regarded as innate, or is imprinted by social conditioning upon the tabula rasa of the mind. In Plato's *Dialogues* I found a notion of pre-existence that sent me back to Blake:

Innate Ideas are in Every man, Born with him; they are truly Himself. The Man who says that we have no Innate Ideas must be a Fool & Knave, having No Con-Science or Innate Science.

(1925, pp. 24–5)

Blake's linking here, of 'Innate Ideas' and 'Con-Science', was a step towards what I was looking for – reassurance that the moral sense is more than a function of the kind of fear felt, for example, by Wordsworth when he took the shepherd's boat. Yet I was still unconvinced and, as I read Wordsworth and Coleridge, I found that they, too, had doubts. Coleridge's letters and notebooks show him wrestling to confute Hartley's doctrine, as expressed in *Observations on Man*, that 'passions' and 'affections' were no more than simple ideas united by association, from which the moral sense is 'generated necessarily and mechanically'. He found the answer in Kant's distinction between the phenomenal will, as determined according to natural causes, and the noumenal will, as morally free. Reading his letters written at that time, I shared Coleridge's relief and sense of liberation, at having found an answer to 'necessitarianism' and an escape from the 'labyrinth-Den of Sophistry' (1956, p. 536).

Preoccupied as I was with these questions, I found Wordsworth's passage about the nursling baby, in Book II of The Prelude, to be a remarkable evocation of the kind of primal experience which allows a natural moral sense to grow. Wordsworth describes the baby who

sinks to sleep
Rocked on his Mother's breast; who with his soul
Drinks in the feelings of his Mother's eye!

This relationship, says Wordsworth, creates within the 'infant veins' a sense of connection with 'the world', which allows a natural playfulness and tenderness:

Is there a flower to which he points with hand
Too weak to gather it, already love

Drawn from love's purest earthly fount for him
Hath beautified that flower; Already shades
Of pity cast from inward tenderness
Do fall around him upon aught that bears
Unsightly marks of violence and harm.

Now, with twenty-five years of teaching experience, and working as head of department in a large rural comprehensive school, I find that my interest in Wordsworth has been rekindled. Recent psychoanalytical thought has celebrated the originality and power of Wordsworth's insights, written a century before Freud's accounts of early experience. Ronald Britton, of the Tavistock Clinic, writes directly about *The Prelude* in a forthcoming book; other writers, such as Trevarthen (1993), report empirical investigations of infancy which support Wordsworth's insights of two centuries ago:

> however feeble and dependent a newborn infant is...there is, right from the beginning, an exuberance or outgoing creativity and inventiveness and an autonomy and coherence of consciousness.
>
> (p. 68)

In Wordsworth's terms, this is the 'first poetic spirit of our human life'. Tremarthen writes that play has an 'educational function' for human beings:

> Mothers, if they are happy, play with their babies from birth, fathers are often very good playmates for a baby from two or three months and siblings soon join in. Play, of this kind, does nothing at all for looking after the baby as a biological organism. It is communication with a known companion and with a curious, active and creative partner in cooperative consciousness.
>
> (p. 75)

Or – to echo Neil Bolton (cited in Chapter 9) – the purpose of play is, simply, play. The same may be claimed for 'education', too, in some essentials. It is not, I think, too idealistic to ask that the English studies classroom should have some of the qualities of play, as described by Tremarthen. The glimpses of my personal history, provided above, represent a 'play' of reflection, which also help to move my argument forward. The need to tell 'my' story – of events in both the 'actual' world, and the 'imagined' world of fictions – is fundamental to all human beings; for all learners, it is their way of composing new experience into personal meaning (see, for example, Harrison's account of 'Telling' in Learning Through Writing, 1983a).

Coleen's story: 'Time to let go'

These personal notes, on 'why' I became the teacher that I am, return me now to the 'how' of the classroom – and how learners may find personal meaning *there*, through narrative forms. To illustrate this, I shall draw on some writing by Coleen, a year-ten student, who seems to me to express at the same time the exuberance and seriousness of creative play. The writing shows a student in a comprehensive school English classroom, using original narrative to play with the possibilities of life, as she moves forward to adulthood. In doing so she confronts, in her own imagination, such fundamental aspects of life as the achievement of autonomy and the responsibilities that attach to personal relationships.

Few teachers would disagree that children should have plenty of opportunities to tell stories. Both simple, spoken anecdotes and lengthy, complex written fictions have an assured place in the range of activities encouraged by most teachers (and which are now expected in the National Curriculum). This is partly a matter of tradition: mother-tongue teaching in Britain has tended to give a higher value to narrative than has, for example, been the practice in the United States, where expository writing maintains a higher status. This is despite evidence, not least from American teachers and researchers, that students without experience of narrative writing may experience difficulty in writing fluently; perhaps an exclusive emphasis on expository forms may fail to engage sufficiently their imagination in learning and writing.

There has been, since Tolstoy's time, plenty of theoretical justification for children's story-telling. Barbara Hardy's well-known description (1968) of narrative as a 'primary act of mind' has been influential, as was D.W. Winnicott's notion (1971) of a 'third area' of imaginative play as being important in children's development. 'Cultural experience begins with creative living first manifested in play,' wrote Winnicott (p. 100), and James Britton applied this claim to children's reading and writing of stories. He saw such activity as characteristic of Winnicott's 'third area' of experience, 'an area of free activity lying between the world of shared and verifiable experience and the world of inner necessity', the purpose of which will be to relate, for the individual self, 'inner necessity with the demands of the external world' (1971, p. 46). In recent years, however, a further tendency in the teaching of narrative has taken strong root in the practice of English teaching. Influenced by the practice of media education, teachers have asked their students to examine formal aspects of narrative: to see it in terms of *genre*. From this viewpoint, of course, narrative form may be seen as potentially limiting students' thoughts and imagination. Andrew Stibbs declared (1993, p. 38) that 'teachers may need a subtler justification for stories than as templates for shaping our experience into significance. What if it were argued that stories may pervert, edit, idealise or stereotype our experience in ways which could disable us?'

I wish, in the final section of this book on the developing of a literate imagination, to seek this 'subtler justification', through examining the work of a year-ten student, Coleen. Coleen has been known throughout her school career as a prolific and talented writer of stories; her work has been admired by a succession of teachers. I shall argue that her skill in fact involves, at the same time, awareness of narrative forms and strategies, and a need to play out, in her imagination, various possibilities of experience.

The story is called 'Time to Let Go'. It was written early in the first term of her tenth year she was fourteen. Her class had just read Jack Rosenthal's play *P'tang Yang Kipperbang*, which was written originally for a television series entitled *First Love*. It deals with a fourteen-year-old boy's struggles with understanding his sexuality and relating with girls in a co-educational grammar school shortly after the Second World War. The play is always successful in class: it is wittily and sensitively written, and the period setting gives readers both a sense of history and of continuity: this is the climate of feeling into which their parents were born, and they recognise the characters' emotions.

We read and dramatised the play, watched the television film, and discussed the characters' relationships, both in groups and as a class. *P'tang Yang Kipperbang* is not a play which I wish to interpret in any particular manner to a class, so that my students had, I hope, time and space within which, in Witkin's words, 'to find their way in (the text), explore all its possibilities, or, more correctly, all the possibilities it has for (them)' (1974, p. 47). I attempted to encourage this freedom of response in the title of the written assignment which I then set. I merely asked the students to write a story, partly or wholly set in a school, which was true to life. I hoped that this would enable them to find their own centre of interest and motivation, within manageable limits. Coleen wrote on the cover sheet of her story (this was a GCSE-coursework assignment):

> As *P'tang Yang Kipperbang* was set in a school, our topic was to write a school story which was true to life. I started by doing a rough draft and then a final draft in which I made corrections and added things. I did most of the work at home.

Coleen's story starts:

> Dear Scott,
>
> I don't know why I'm writing this, it seems like a strange thing to do but somehow I just know it's going to help. Writing down my feelings always did help me. Remember how you used to make fun of my almost religious ritual of writing in my diary every day?

From the beginning, then, Coleen's story implies one of the functions of narrative for her: 'Writing down my feelings always did help me.' It is a way of making contact with what Britton (1971, p. 46) called 'the world of inner necessity'. But at the same time as she is aware of this need, Coleen is equally aware of ways of telling. She draws upon her cultural experience of narrative to write a story within a story. She tells Scott, in her imaginary letter:

> I'm going to tell you a story. It's a story that you should know well, a story that we, you and I, lived through. Didn't they always tell you in those endless English lessons that I loved and you hated that the only place to start a story is at the beginning? But the thing is, I don't know where the beginning is...So I'm going to start with the day we met, all those years ago ...

Within her narrative, Coleen reveals the importance of English lessons to her, and a subtle sense of the meaning of beginnings. Her narrative-within-a-narrative begins:

> My first day at school was a cold September day which I can only just remember. I stood outside the classroom, clinging desperately to my mother's leg as my new

teacher tried to coax me inside. Through my hot tears, which flowed so freely when I was young, I could sense myself being watched, and I peered past my teacher to see a boy, the same age as myself, looking at me curiously, a puzzled expression on his freckled face.

'Clinging desperately to my mother's leg...Through my hot tears, which flowed so freely' Coleen taps into the literary culture to find her expression. This seems an accurate way of putting it, because, of course, culture is the unified experience of individuals, and individual experience can find its expression through received forms. This is illustrated a little later in Coleen's story. The boy tells her not to be a cry-baby:

Well, I might have been shy and scared of the unknown, but even at age five I had my pride...I wiped the tears from my cheeks and marched, head held high, inside the classroom.

The expression here is little more than cliché, but it gives Coleen the form in which to express the conflict between staying with her mother and finding her pride. This kind of conflict, between the needs of security and of individuality, is indeed the theme of the whole story; it thus expresses, imaginatively, an important aspect of Coleen's development.

For the friendship between the fictional children grows over several years, until, when they are both thirteen, Scott shows Hannah (the girl narrator) a new side of himself. She has asked him what he wants to be:

'A doctor,' he said softly, so softly I almost didn't hear him.

I was puzzled for a moment before I realized what he was talking about.

'No, my dad wants me to be a doctor,' Scott said, wearily. 'Just like him and David,' he added bitterly.

Coleen's – or Hannah's – reaction to this revelation is, again, expressed in a conventional narrative form, as Coleen, the author, experiments with phrasing:

And then, when I looked at Scott, I felt as if for the first time in all those years of friendship I really understood him. Understood that under his don't-care exterior and constant laughter he was mixed up inside. And understood that all he ever wanted to be was the son his father wanted him to be. Just like David.

I think Scott gave me a glimpse of his soul that day and looking back I wonder if I could have helped him that day. Helped him to become the person he wanted to be, not a carbon copy of David but himself. And helped him to understand that whoever that person was, I would always be his friend.

Characters in imaginative narrative have, surely, the same status as characters in dreams as seen by Fritz Perls (1971): they all express aspects of the writer's psyche. 'Every aspect of...(the dream),' writes Perls, 'is a part of the dreamer, but a part that to some extent is disowned and projected onto other objects' (p. 27). The two characters, Hannah and Scott, express for Coleen two possibilities for herself: the possibility of becoming herself, and the possibility of not becoming herself. These alternate potentials within the self are suggested in a later paragraph of Coleen's narrative:

It was as if, in a way, we'd changed roles, Scott becoming my quiet, shy self and me taking over his part as the more outgoing, cheerful one.

And in the penultimate paragraph quoted, 'Hannah' is clearly the part of Coleen which will guard Coleen's own individuality, as it grows: 'whoever that person was, I would always be his friend'.

The next part of the story deals directly with the difficulties of emerging from a family environment which is felt to be both nurturing and limiting. Hannah and Scott are doing homework together in Scott's house:

> I stopped abruptly as I felt the presence of Scott's father looming over me. Although I'd known Dr. Baxter since I was just a little girl, I couldn't help feeling just a bit intimidated whenever he was in the room.

Coleen's story is full of 'presences': the presence of the boy looking at her on the first day of school; the presence of Scott's father; later, the presence of GCSE examinations. All these represent aspects of mental life with which she has to cope: other possibilities of the self, represented by Scott; intimidating authority, represented by Scott's father; the need for success in the world, represented by the GCSE examinations. At this stage of the story, she focuses on Scott's reaction to his father's presence:

> I saw that his face had taken on that look I was beginning to know better and better. Tight and pinched as if all his anger was imprisoned inside his body and fighting to get out.

The psychological insight here seems to me remarkable: Coleen senses the anger which is created by a sense of dependency on a controlling parental figure. This is an aspect of her mental world of which she is implicitly and, indeed, consciously – as her writing shows – aware. And she is also aware of the possible outcomes of this struggle: a resolution through the establishment of an individual self; or submission and despair. Her character Scott expresses for her the latter possibility, one of which she is, in her narrative persona – and, I would guess, in herself – deeply afraid:

> I ask myself over and over every day now – why didn't I ask Scott what was wrong? Not only on that day but on so many others too. I think I was just too afraid of what I might find out if Scott confided in me. Because I knew, oh I knew, that something inside of Scott's mind wasn't quite right, that an evil little doubt had planted itself there and was slowly eating away at Scott until he gave up hope in himself completely.

The identification of Scott and Hannah as possible aspects of a single self is emphasised in the next part of the story. One of Hannah's friends tries to get her make more friends, and Hannah tells her 'that all Scott and I need is each other'.

The story then moves ahead three years, to when the couple are about to take their GCSE examinations. This experience was, of course, two years ahead of Coleen when she wrote the story; it is another aspect of life which she is playing out in her imagination. The Hannah self prepares carefully for the exams, and sleeps soundly before the first one. But her sleep is interrupted by a 2 a.m. phone call from Scott:

> 'The GCSE's, Hannah!' he exclaimed. 'I can't take them!'

Hannah is silent, and then hears 'Dr. Baxter in the background, demanding to know why his son was using the phone at two o'clock in the morning'. Hannah's silence here introduces into the story another aspect of 'the world of inner necessity': betrayal and guilt. Coleen experiments in her imagination with the conflicts that, in the real world of lived experience, make such feelings inevitable:

> Those were my exam days, days which passed much quicker than I'd expected. I've found that, in the last few months leading up to them, my memories of Scott have grown fuzzier and fuzzier, while my memories of school have grown sharper and more clear. Maybe that shows how school can take over your life, changing you into someone whose whole existence is concentrated on working for those ever-important exams. At least that's how you are expected to be in those final months leading up to the GCSE's.

In her imagination, Coleen is considering what might happen if she took seriously the rhetoric of her teachers, concentrating her whole existence on the self-interested pursuit of examination success. What might be the cost in relationship with others, and, indeed, with part of herself?

For the Hannah figure is now concentrating entirely on worldly, external success, while the Scott figure is carrying inner pain. It is at this point, writes 'Hannah', that their roles seem to have reversed, 'Scott becoming my quiet, shy self and me taking over his part as the more outgoing, cheerful one'.

Fritz Perls writes of the effect of disowning a certain part of ourselves, and suggests that if we 'want to own that part of ourselves again, we have to use special techniques by which we can reassimilate those experiences' (1971, p. 27). The special technique, for Coleen, is surely her story-writing. When Scott hangs himself, Hannah has to confront the emotions she feels as a result of having disowned part of herself. Coleen contemplates, imaginatively, Hannah's grieving, anger and guilt:

> I was angry at you for so long. Because you left me, Scott, alone in a friendless world with no-one to talk to, and I hated you for that ...
> One thing that hasn't left me and that I've almost given up hope ever will is my guilt. I think I'll always feel guilty because I didn't help you to believe in yourself.
> I've been told, over and over again, that nothing I could have done would have stopped you committing suicide but I don't believe it and I don't think I ever will.

Within Coleen's mind, we may suggest, the guilt is also stirred by contemplating the possibility of not believing in herself: of giving too much credence to worldly success, as represented by examinations.

But Hannah sees the possibility of resolution:

> I'm ready to admit now that it's time to let go. It's time to put our friendship away to be brought out only when I need cheering up. Because that's who you were for me. Someone who made me smile, someone who gave me so much happiness in my life.

Coleen's story can be seen as formulaic, predictable, very much the product of a fourteen-year-old mind. But it represents so much more than a rehearsal of narrative clichés. It cannot possibly be adequately judged by the behavioural criteria of the National Curriculum – even as expressed in original, 'Cox' version of the document. Coleen is working, with a deep seriousness, in the 'third area' of imagination: the area in which she can experiment with the possibilities of life. Her story deals with issues of the deepest importance to the growing self: the possibility of other identities; the pressure of parents and school authorities; guilt and betrayal; and, most important of all, the question of whether or not a fuller, autonomous self will in fact come to pass. As a highly capable school pupil, she senses the danger of losing herself through her own success – as her character Hannah nearly does. English lessons, which Coleen has always loved – as 'Hannah' indicates – offer her the possibility of another kind of growth besides the purely academic. Her story – writing is a crucial element in her life – is a process of ensuring that her own developed self will, in fact, come to fruition.

To conclude

> Joshu: Have you eaten your porridge?
> monk: Yes, I have.
> Joshu: Then you had better wash your bowl.
>
> (from the Zen text, *Mumonkan*)

John Hodgson's account of Coleen's story provides a vivid demonstration of Kieran Egan's claim, in *Teaching as Story Telling* (1986), that 'the story form is a cultural universal...it reflects a basic and powerful form in which we make sense of the world' (p. 2). Indeed, Egan argued for the power of the story form across the whole curriculum, 'in order to teach any content more engagingly and meaningfully' (p. 2). From his focus on the imaginative powers of children he concluded, 'perhaps ironically', that 'a more academically rich curriculum is appropriate during the early years' (p. 18), when children are, arguably, at their most inventive in using their imagination. Yet, in his eagerness to promote the uses of stories across the curriculum, Egan was tempted to consign imaginative stories such as Coleen's to the 'affective' domain of meaning, in seeking a 'comprehensive' version that brought 'cognitive' and 'affective' together (p. 37). John's commentary on Coleen reveals, however, the complexity and power of her story; there is no doubt that she was thinking at least as hard, and as comprehensively, about difficult problems as she would need to think, say, about why the path of light is reflected through a prism – even though she may have been involved in different balances and patterns of thinking, while she wrote.

In celebrating the place of the literate imagination in learning, this book has dwelled on the special importance to learners, of hearing and reading imaginative texts, as well as encouraging the telling and writing of narratives. Arguing that creativity and imagination are fundamental to learning, Margaret Meek suggested (1985) that, while the case for a gen-

Coleen
Gordon
10S2

Time To Let Go   18th Oct '93

Dear Scott,
I don't know why I'm writing this, it seems
like a strange thing to do but somehow I just
know its going to help. Writing down my feelings
always did help me. Remember how you used to
make fun of my almost religious ritual of
writing in my diary every day?

Sometimes I wish that I'd let you read my
diary, especially the parts where I wrote
about what a special friend you were to
me, but I suppose now you never will. So I'm
writing to you, as the next best things to
talking to you and I'm going to tell you a
story. It's a story that you should know
well, a story that we, you and I, lived through.
Didn't they always tell us in those endless
English lessons, which I loved and you hated
that the only place to start a story is at
the beginning? But the thing is, I don't know
where the beginning is. Not the real
beginning anyway. So I'm going to start with
the day we met, all those years ago......

My first day of school was a cold Septemb
day which I can only just remember. I stoo
outside the classroom, clinging desperately
to my mother's leg as my new teacher
tried to coax me inside. Through my hot tears,
which flowed so freely when I was young, I
could sense myself being watched and I

eral functional literacy is self-evident, 'it is equally evident that those who have become aware of a variety of narrative discourses, who "possess" known texts as metaphors for deeply felt emotions' will continue to seek further imaginative enrichment through their reading:

> the effective texts say 'suppose' – that great invitation to imagine which is felt as a desire to articulate things differently, a desire that lies behind the most memorable hypotheses and the most memorable poems.
>
> (p. 57)

To support its case for developing the literate imagination, this book has also argued the case for open learning, in every sense, throughout education. In its challenge to an existing emphasis on uniformity, conformity and a rigid curriculum, it has proposed a view of learning which now seems to be winning wider recognition. The 'Statement of Purpose' (1993) from the *Education Now* Movement, for example, advocated acceptance of Einstein's proposal that *imagination is more important than knowledge* in our modern and constantly changing world; it maintained that people learn best:

- when they are self-motivated;
- when they take responsibility for their own lives and learning;
- when they feel comfortable in their surroundings;
- when teachers and learners value, trust, respect and listen to each other;
- when education is seen as a life-long process.

(April 1993)

Finally, this book rests its case with a reflection from Ngugi wa Thiong'o, in *Decolonising the Mind* (1986). Ngugi's account of the effects of colonial alienation on his own people in Kenya, and of the quest to transcend those effects, has relevance for all human communities in the world. Explaining why he chose to write his books in the Gikuyu, not English language, Ngugi declared that he wished to restore harmony 'between all the aspects and divisions of language', so that Kenyan children may be helped to find their own sense of place in their world. He wished to see 'Kenya people's mother tongues...carry a literature reflecting not only the rhythms of a child's spoken expression', but also the struggle that children must experience between nature and their social nature. Once harmony is achieved between children, their language and their environment, they can 'learn other languages and even enjoy the positive humanistic, democratic and revolutionary elements in other people's literatures and cultures', without suffering 'complexes' about their own language, self or environment (pp. 28–9).

From such a clear sense – gained through the spoken language, and through the written literature – of personal being, meaning and belonging, may grow a genuine *world* view of what it is to be human.

References

Abbs, P. (1979) *Reclamations*. London: Heinemann.

Ackroyd, P. (1990) *Dickens*. London: Sinclair-Stevenson.

Agard, J. (1992) 'Listen Mr. Oxford Don', in *Mangoes and Bullets: Selected and New Poems, 1972–1984*. London: Pluto Press.

Aitken, D. (1993) 'The Effect of the Introduction of the National Curriculum for English and the Standard Assessment Test on Reading Literature in the Classroom', unpublished M.Ed. thesis. Sheffield: Division of Education, Sheffield University.

Allen, D. (1981) 'The Myth and the Pot', *The Use of English,* 33/1, 15–24.

Allen, D. (1987) *English, Whose English?* NATE Pamphlet. Sheffield: NATE.

Arendt, H. (1978) *The Life of the Mind* (two volumes). Volume One: *Thinking*. London: Secker and Warburg.

Ashley, B. (1986) *Terry On the Fence*. Oxford: Oxford University Press.

Ashton-Warner, S. (1980a) *Spinster*. London: Virago.

Ashton-Warner, S. (1980b) *Teacher*. London: Virago.

Ashton-Warner, S. (1980c) *I Passed This Way*. London: Virago.

Atwood, M. (1981) 'Spelling', in *True Stories*. Toronto: Oxford University Press.

Axtell, J. (1988) 'The Power of Print in the Eastern Woodlands', *The William and Mary Quarterly,* 44/2, 300–9.

Baer, J. (1993) *Creativity and Divergent Thinking*. New Jersey: Lawrence Erlbaum.

Bakewell, J. (1986) 'The Quiet Child', in B. Wade (ed.), *Talking to Some Purpose*, Educational Review Occasional Publication, no. 12. University of Birmingham: School of Education.

Barnes, D. (1976) *From Communication to Curriculum*. Harmondsworth: Penguin.

Barnes, D. and Todd, F. (1977) *Communication and Learning in Small Groups*. London: Routledge and Kegan Paul.

Barrow, R. (1993) *Language, Intelligence and Thought*. Cheltenham: Edward Elgar.

Bateson, G. (1979) *Mind and Nature. A Necessary Unity*. London: Wildwood House.

Beard, R. (1987) *Developing Reading, 3–13*. London: Hodder and Stoughton.

Bearne, E. and Farrow, C. (1991) *Writing Policy in Action: the Middle Years*. Milton Keynes: Open University Press.

Beckett, S. (1973) *Not I*. London: Faber.

Best, D. (1992) *The Rationality of Feeling*. London: Falmer.

Birch, D. (1989) *Language, Literature and Critical Practice*. London: Routledge.

Birmingham CCED (1992) *Key Stage 1: National Curriculum Assessment*. Birmingham: Birmingham CCED.

Black, M. (1981) 'Metaphor', in M. Johnson (ed.), *Philosophical Perspectives in Metaphor*. Minneapolis: University of Minnesota Press.

Blake, W. (1925) *The Poetical Works of William Blake*, edited by G. Keynes. Volume 3. London.

Bleich, D. (1978) *Subjective Criticism*. Baltimore: Johns Hopkins University Press.

Bloom, H. (1962) *The Visionary Company*. London: Faber.

Board of Education (BoE) (1905) *Suggestions for the Consideration of Teachers and others Concerned in the Work of Public Elementary Schools*. London: HMSO.

Board of Education (BoE) (1921) *Report on the Teaching of English in Secondary Schools* (Newbolt Report). London: HMSO.

Board of Education (BoE) (1927) *The Education of the Adolescent* (Hadow Report). London: HMSO.

Bolton, G. (1994) 'Stories at Work. Fictional-critical Writing as a Means of Professional Development', *British Educational Research Journal*, 20/1, 55–68.

Bolton, N. (1982) 'The Lived World', *Journal of Phenomenological Psychology*, Spring issue.

Britton, J. (1971) 'The Role of Fantasy', *English in Education*, 5/3. Reprinted in M. Meek (ed.) (1977) *The Cool Web*. London: Bodley Head.

Brown, C. (1989) *My Left Foot*. London: Cox and Wyman.

Bruner, J.S. (1962) *On Knowing. Essays for the Left Hand*. Cambridge, Massachussetts: Harvard University Press.

Bruner, J.S. (1976) 'Nature and Uses of Immaturity', in J.S. Bruner, A. Jolly and K. Sylva (eds) *Play*. Harmondsworth: Penguin.

Bruner, J.S. (1984) 'Language, Mind and Reading', in F. Smith, H. Goelman and A. Oberg (eds), *Awakening to Literacy*. London: Heinemann.

Buckroyd, P. and Ogborn, J. (1992) *Coursework in A Level and AS English Literature*. London: Hodder and Stoughton.

Burgess, A. (1993) *A Mouthful of Air. Language and Languages, Especially English*. London: Vintage.

Burney, F. (1907) *The Early Diaries of Frances Burney*, 1776–1778, edited by A.R. Ellis. London: Bell.

Calkins, L. (1983) *Lessons from a Child*. Portsmouth, New Haven: Heinemann.

Calkins, L. (1986) *The Art of Teaching Writing*. Portsmouth, New Haven:

Heinemann.

Calouste Gulbenkian Foundation (1983) *The Arts in Schools*. London: Calouste Gulbenkian Foundation.

Camus, A. (1961) 'On receiving the Nobel Prize', in *Resistance, Rebellion and Death*, translation by J. O'Brien. London: Hamish Hamilton.

Carter, A. (1991) *Wise Children*. London: Chatto and Windus.

Carter, R. (ed.) (1990) *Knowledge about Language and the Curriculum. The LINC Reader*. London: Hodder and Stoughton.

Cashdan, A. (ed.) (1979) *Language, Reading and Learning*. Oxford: Blackwell.

Centre for Learning in Primary Education (CLPE) (1993/4) *Language Matters. The Early Years, no. 1*. London: Southwark Council.

Chalfant, J. (1989) 'Learning Disabilities. Policy Issues and Promising Approaches', *American Psychologist*, 44, 392–8.

Ching, M.L. (1993) 'Games and Play: Pervasive Metaphors in American Life', *Metaphor and Symbolic Activity*, 8/1, 43–65.

Clark, C. (ed.) (1960) *Home at Grasmere. Extracts from the Journal of Dorothy Wordsworth and from the Poems of William Wordsworth*. Harmondsworth: Penguin.

Clay, M. (1982) *Observing Young Readers. Selected Papers*. Auckland: Heinemann.

Clay, M. (1988) *The Early Detection of Reading Difficulties*. Auckland: Heinemann.

Clay, M. (1991) *Becoming Literate. The Construction of Inner Control*. Auckland: Heinemann.

Clegg, A. and Megson, B. (1973) *Children in Distress*. London: Pan Books.

Clough, P. (1988) 'Bridging "Mainstream" and "Special" Education: a Curriculum Problem', *Journal of Curriculum Studies*, 20/4, 327–38.

Coleridge, S.T. (1956) *Collected Letters of S.T. Coleridge*, edited by E.L. Griggs. Volume 2. Oxford: Oxford University Press.

Coles, G. (1987) *The Learning Mystique*. New York: Pantheon.

Collins, J. (1994) 'The Silent Minority. Developing Talk in the Primary Classroom', unpublished Ph.D. thesis. Sheffield: University of Sheffield.

Collingwood, R.G. (1938) *The Principles of Art*. Oxford: Oxford University Press.

Cowie, H. (ed.) (1982) *The Development of Children's Imaginative Writing*. London: Croom Helm.

Cox, B. (1992) 'English Studies and National Identity', in M. Hayhoe and S. Parker.

Culler, J. (1975) *Structuralist Poetics*. London: Routledge and Kegan Paul.

Dearing, R. (1993) *The National Curriculum and its Assessment. Final Report*. London: SCAA.

DES (1975) *A Language for Life* (Bullock Report). London: HMSO.

DES (1978) *Special Educational Needs* (Warnock Report). London: HMSO.

DES (1988a) *Report of the Committee of Enquiry into the Teaching of English* (Kingman Report). London: HMSO.

DES (1988b) *English for Ages 5 to 11* (Cox Report). London: HMSO.

DES (1989) *English for Ages 5 to 16*. London: HMSO.

Dewey, J. (1897) *My Pedagogic Creed*, quoted in J.S. Bruner (1962).

DFE (1993) English for Ages 5–16. London: HMSO.

Dickens, C. (1852) *Bleak House*. Norton Critical Edition (1977). New York: Norton.

Dickinson, E. (1955) *The Poems of Emily Dickinson*, edited by T.H. Johnson (three volumes). Cambridge, Massachussetts: Harvard University Press.

Dixon, J. (1994) 'A Simpler Model for English?', *English in Education*, 28/1, 3–8.

Drabble, M. (1966) *Wordsworth*. London: Evans Brothers.

Dyson, A. (1989) *Multiple Worlds of Child Writers. Friends Learning to Write*. New York: Teachers' College Press.

Eagleton, T. (1983) *Literary Theory*. Oxford: Blackwell.

Earl Marshall School (1992) *Valley of Words*. Sheffield: SUMES/Earl Marshall School.

Earl Marshall School (1993) *Lives of Love and Hope. A Sheffield Herstory*. Sheffield: Earl Marshall School.

Education Now (1993) 'Statement of Purpose'. Nottingham: 113, Arundel Drive, Bramcote Hills, NG9 3FQ.

Edwards, A.D. and Westgate, D.P.G. (1987) *Investigating Classroom Talk*. Lewes: Falmer.

Egan, K. (1986) *Teaching as Story Telling*. Ontario: Althouse Press.

Egan, K. and Nadaner, D. (eds) (1988) *Imagination and Education*. Milton Keynes: Open University Press.

Elbow, P. (1986) *Embracing Contraries. Explorations in Learning and Teaching*. New York: Oxford University Press.

Elkind, D. (1987) *Miseducation*. New York: Knopf.

Elley, W.B. (1992) 'New Zealand', in J. Hladczuk and W. Eller (1992), 225–36.

Ellison, R. (1965) *The Invisible Man*. Harmondsworth: Penguin.

Exley, H. (1981) *What It's Like to be Me*. Watford: Exley Publications.

Fanthorpe, U.A. (1987) *A Watching Brief*. Calstock, Cornwall: Peterloo Poets.

Firth, J.R. (1930) *Speech*. London: Benn.

Firth, J.R. (1937) *The Tongues of Men*. London: Watts.

Fisher, R. (1990) *Teaching Children to Think*. Oxford: Blackwell.

Fitter, R.S. (1992) 'Lesotho', in J. Hladczuk and W. Eller (1992), 206–23.

Fitzpatrick, J. (1982) 'Lonergan and Hume: Epistemology', *New Blackfriars*, Oxford, May.

Flavell, J.H. (1970) 'Developmental Studies of Mediated Memory', in H.W. Reese and L.P. Lipsitt (eds) *Advances in Child Development and Behaviour*, five volumes. New York: Academic Press. Volume five, 182–211.

Fowles, J. (1977) 'Notes on an Unfinished Novel', in M. Bradbury (ed.), *The Novel Today*. London: Fontana.

Fox, C. (1989) 'Divine Dialogues: the Role of Argument in the Narrative Discourse of a Five-year-old Story-teller', in R. Andrews (ed.), *Narrative and*

Argument. Milton Keynes: Open University Press, 206–23.

Freire, P. (1970) *Pedagogy of the Oppressed*. London: Steel and Ward.

Freire, P. (1973) *Education for Critical Consciousness*. London: Steel and Ward.

Friel, B. (1981) *Translations*. London: Faber.

Fries, C. (1962) *Linguistics and Reading*. New York: Rhinehart and Winston.

Fromm, E. (1973) *The Crisis of Psychoanalysis*. Harmondsworth: Penguin.

Frostig, M. and Maslow, P. (1973) *Learning Problems in the Classroom*. New York: Grune and Stratton.

Fry, D. (1985) *Children Talk about their Books. Seeing Themselves as Readers*. Milton Keynes: Open University Press.

Fugard, A. (1974) *Three Port Elizabethan Plays*. Oxford: Oxford University Press.

Furth, H. (1987) *Knowledge as Desire: an Essay on Freud and Piaget*. New York: Columbia University Press.

Gadamer, H.G. (1975) *Truth and Method*. London: Sheen and Ward.

Galton, M. and Williams, J. (1992) *Group Work in the Primary Classroom*. London: Routledge.

Gardner, H. (1974) 'Metaphor and Modalities', in *Child Development*, 45, 84–91.

Gardner, H. (1982) *In Defence of the Imagination*. Oxford: Oxford University Press.

Gardner, H. and Winner, E. (1986) 'Attitudes and Attributes: Children's Understanding of Metaphor and Sarcasm', in M. Perlmutter (ed.), *Perspectives on Intellectual Development*. Minnesota Symposia on Child Psychology, 19. Hillsdale, New Jersey: Lawrence Erlbaum.

Garforth, F.W. (1979) *John Stuart Mill's Theory of Education*. London: Martin, Robertson and Co.

Gass, W.H. (1970) *Fiction and the Figures of Life*. New York: Knopf.

Gilbert, S. and Guber, S. (eds) (1985) *The Norton Anthology of Literature by Women*. New York: Norton, 832–4.

Gillborn, D. (1990) *Race, Ethnicity and Education*. London: Unwin Hyman.

Gillborn, D., Nixon, J. and Rudduck, J. (1993) *Dimensions of Discipline*. London: HMSO/ DFE.

Gomes de Matos, F.G. (1992) 'Brazil', in J. Hladczuk and W. Eller (1992), 25–44.

Goodman, K. (1986) *What's Whole in Whole Language?* Portsmouth, Newhaven: Heinemann.

Goodwin, A. (1992) *English Teaching and Media Education*. Milton Keynes: Open University Press.

Gordon, H. and Harrison, B.T. (1991) 'George Sampson and the "National Mind": a Lesson for the National Curriculum?', *The Use of English*, 42/3, 15–27.

Graham, J. (1990) *Pictures on the Page*. Sheffield: NATE.

Gray, W.S. (1956) *The Teaching of Reading and Writing*. New York: UNESCO.

210

Gregory, M. (1993) 'Metaphorical Comprehension. From Literal Truth to Metaphoricity and Back Again', *Metaphor and Symbolic Activity*, 8/1, 1–22.

Grene, M. (ed.) (1969) *Knowing and Being*. London: Routledge and Kegan Paul.

Grene, M. (1974) *The Understanding of Nature*. Boston: D. Rejdel.

Guilford, J.P. (1967) *The Nature of Human Intelligence*. New York: McGraw-Hill.

Haffenden, J. (1981) *Viewpoints. Poets in Conversation*. London: Faber.

Hall, N. (1987) *The Emergence of Literacy*. Portsmouth, New Hampshire: Heinemann.

Hannon, P. and Weinberger, J. (1990) *Ways of Working with Parents to Promote Early Literacy Development*. Sheffield: USDE publication, Division of Education, University of Sheffield.

Harding, D.W. (1963) *Experience into Words*. London: Chatto.

Hardy, B. (1968) 'Towards a Poetics of Fiction', in *Novel: A Forum on Fiction*. New York: Brown University.

Hargreaves, D.J. (ed.) (1989) *Children and the Arts*. Milton Keynes: Open University Press.

Harper, F.E.W. (1872) 'Learning to Read', from *Sketches of Southern Life*, in S. Gilbert and S. Guber (1985).

Harrison, B.T. (1979) 'Literature in the Secondary School', in A. Cashdan (1979), 88–104.

Harrison, B.T. (1980) *Poetry and the Language of Feeling*. TRACT no. 27. Lewes, Sussex: Gryphon Press.

Harrison, B.T. (1983a) *Learning Through Writing*. Windsor: NFER/Nelson.

Harrison, B.T. (ed.) (1983b) *English Studies, 11–18. An Arts-based Approach*. London: Hodder and Stoughton.

Harrison, B.T. (1983c) 'Literature for Children: a Radical Genre', in B. Ford (ed.), *The New Pelican Guide to English Literature*, volume 8, 365–79. Harmondsworth: Penguin.

Harrison, B.T. (1984) 'A Sense of Worth: Seven Days with *Hamlet*', *The Use of English*, 35/3, 21–34.

Harrison, B.T. (1986a) *Sarah's Letters; A Case of Shyness*. London: Institute of Education, Bedford Way Paper no. 26.

Harrison, B.T. (1986b) 'The Pleasure of Writing', in A. Wilkinson (ed.), *The Writing of Writing*. Milton Keynes: Open University Press, 60–74.

Harrison, B.T. (1990) 'Realising through Writing', *Aspects of Education*, 42, 36–57.

Harrison, B.T. (1992a) 'From Conformity to Criticism: in Search of a Moral Basis for Management in Education', in T. Simkins *et al*. (1992), 262–76.

Harrison, B.T. (1992b) 'Values in English Studies as Values for Management in Education', *The Use of English*, 43/2, 109–18.

Harrison, B.T. (1992c) 'Encouraging Positive Attitudes to Language and Learning among Multilingual/Bilingual Speakers in Schools: Principles and Practice', in M. Hayhoe and S. Parker, (1992).

Harrison, B.T. and Gordon, H. (1983) 'Metaphor is Thought: does Northtown need Poetry?', *Educational Review,* 35/3, 265–78.

Harrison, B.T. and Marbach, A. (1994) 'Mother Tongue Teaching in Israel and Britain', in M. Hayhoe and S. Parker (eds) (1994), *Who Own English?* Milton Keynes: Open University Press.

Harrison, B.T. and Mercer, E. (1992) 'Friel's *"Translations"*: Applying Insights from a Literary Text to Therapeutic Language Teaching', *Educational Therapy and Therapeutic Teaching,* 1/1, 9–21.

Harrison, B.T. and Mountford, D. (1992) 'Negotiating Patterns of Guided Learning in A-level English Studies', *Educational Review,* 44 /2, 195–204.

Harrison, T. (1984) 'Them & (uz)', in *Selected Poems.* Harmondsworth: Penguin.

Harth, E. (1982) *Windows on the Mind.* London: Harvester Press.

Harvey, A. (1991) *The Language of Love.* Harmondsworth: Penguin.

Harvey, A. (1994) *Criminal Records. Poems About Crime.* Harmondsworth: Penguin.

Hayhoe, M. and Parker, S. (eds) (1992) *Reassessing Language and Literacy.* Milton Keynes: Open University Press.

Heaney, S. (1986) 'Among Schoolchildren', *Signal,* 49, 3–17. Stroud: Thimble Press.

Hladczuk, J. and Eller, W. (eds) (1992) *International Handbook of Reading Education.* Westport: Greenwood Press.

Hodgson, J.M.P. (1983) 'Film and television in the English Lesson', in B.T. Harrison (1983b).

Hoffman, R.R. and Honeck, R.P. (eds) (1980) *Cognition and Figurative Language.* New York: Lawrence Erlbaum.

Holbrook, D. (1980) *English for Meaning.* Windsor: National Foundation for Educational Research.

Holmes, R. (1989) *Coleridge. Early Visions.* London: Hodder and Stoughton.

Holub, M. (1990) *Poems Before and After.* Newcastle: Bloodaxe Poets.

Hourd, M. (1974) *Relationship in Learning.* London: Heinemann.

House of Commons Paper (1993) *Meeting Special Educational Needs: Statements of Needs and Provision,* volumes I and II. London: HMSO.

Hughes, T. (1967) *Poetry in the Making.* London: Faber.

Hurston, Z.N. (1986) *Dust Tracks on the Road.* London: Virago.

Janks, H. (1992) 'Critical Awareness of People's English', in M. Hayhoe and S. Parker (1992), 50–9.

Jenkins, H.O. (1991) *Getting It Right. A Handbook for Successful School Leadership.* Oxford: Blackwell.

Jenkinson, A.J. (1940) *What do Boys and Girls Read?* London: Methuen.

Johnson, S. (1757) Review of Soame Jenyns' 'A Free Enquiry into the Nature and Origin of Evil'. *The Literary Magazine; or Universal.*

Kafka, F. (1948–9) *Diaries* (two volumes), translation by J. Kresh and M. Greenberg. London: Secker and Warburg.

Kafka, F. (1949) 'Up in the Gallery', in *In The Penal Settlement: Tales and*

212

Short Prose Works. London: Secker and Warburg.

Kafka, F. (1954) *Wedding Preparations in the Country*, translation by E. Kaiser and E. Wilkins. London: Secker and Warburg.

Kay, J. (1991) *The Adoption Papers*. Newcastle-on-Tyne: Bloodaxe.

Kay, J. (1992) *Two's Company*. London: Blackie.

Kay, J. (1993) *Other Lovers*. Newcastle-on-Tyne: Bloodaxe.

Knight, R. (1992) Editorial, 'The "Case" for Reviewing National Curriculum English', *The Use of English*, 44/1, 1–8.

Knight, R. (1994) 'Free the Native Spirit', *Times Educational Supplement*, 18.2.94, Extra Section, v.

Kohl, H. (1988) *Reading, How to*, second edition. Milton Keynes: Open University Press.

Kundera, M. (1984) *The Unbearable Lightness of Being*. London: Faber.

Landsberg, M.E. (1986) 'Iconic Aspects of Language: The Imitation of Nonlinguistic Reality', *Quaderni di Semantica*, VII/2, 321–31.

Lang, B. (1991) *Writing and the Moral Self*. London: Routledge.

Langer, S. (1953) *Feeling and Form*. London: Routledge and Kegan Paul.

Leavis, F.R. (1943) *Education and the University*. Cambridge: Cambridge University Press.

Leavis, F.R. (1948) *The Great Tradition*. London: Chatto.

Leavis, F.R. (1957) *'Anna Karenina' and other Essays*. London: Chatto and Windus.

Leavis, F.R. (1969) *English Literature in our Time and the University*. London: Chatto and Windus.

Leavis, F.R. (1971) 'Wordsworth: the Creative Conditions', in R.A. Brewer (ed.), *Twentieth Century Literature in Retrospect*. Cambridge, Massachussetts: Harvard University Press.

Leavis, F.R. (1975) *The Living Principle*. London: Chatto and Windus.

Leavis, F.R. and Thompson, D. (1932) *Culture and Environment*. London: Chatto.

Leavis, Q.D. (contributor) (1968) *A Selection from* Scrutiny. Cambridge: Cambridge University Press.

Lessing, D. (1972) *The Golden Notebook* (new edn). London: Granada Press.

Levi, P. (1984) *The Periodic Table*, translation by R. Rosenthal. London: Abacus.

Lipman, M., Sharp, A.M. and Oscanyon, F.S. (1980) *Philosophy in the Classroom*. Philadelphia: Temple University Press.

Livesay, D. (1972) 'The Children's Letters', from *Collected Poems: The Two Seasons*, in S. Gilbert and S. Guber (eds) (1985).

Mac an Ghaill, M. (1988) *Young, Gifted and Black: Student-Teacher Relations in the Schooling of Black Youth*. Milton Keynes: Open University Press.

Macmurray, J. (1962) *Reason and Emotion* (second edn). London: Faber.

Marbach, A. (1992) 'The Teaching of the Mother Tongue', unpublished Ph.D. thesis. Sheffield: University of Sheffield.

Masterman, L. (1985) *Teaching the Media*. London: Routledge.

Meadows, S. (1993) *The Child as Thinker*. London: Routledge.

Meek, M. (1980) 'Prologomena for a Study of Children's Literature', in M. Benton (ed.), *Approaches to Research in Children's Literature*. Southampton: Department of Education, Southampton University, 27–39.

Meek, M. (1982) *Learning to Read*. London: Bodley Head.

Meek, M. (1985) 'Play and Paradoxes: Some Consideration of Imagination and Language' in G. Wells and J. Nicholls (eds) (1985), 41–57.

Meek, M. (1991) *On Being Literate*. London: Bodley Head.

Mercer, E. (1993) 'Disabled Learners' and Teachers' Attitudes to Learning', unpublished M.Ed. thesis. Sheffield: Division of Education, University of Sheffield.

Merleau-Ponty, M. (1962) *The Phenomenology of Perception*. London: Routledge and Kegan Paul.

Middleton-Murray, J. (1972) 'Metaphor', in W. Shibles (1972).

Mill, J. S. (1873) *Autobiography*. Edition by J. Stillinger (1971). London: Oxford University Press.

Mill, J.S. (1973) 'What is Poetry?', in L. Trilling and H. Bloom (eds), *The Oxford Anthology of English Literature. Victorian Prose and Poetry*. New York: Oxford University Press.

Mill, J.S. (1984) Essays on 'Logic', 'Civilization', 'Genius' and 'Liberty', in *Collected Works of John Stuart Mill*. London: Routledge and Kegan Paul.

Millard, E. (1994) *Developing Readers in the Middle Years*. Milton Keynes: Open University Press.

Miller, A. (1981) *The Drama of the Gifted Child: How Narcissistic Parents Form and Deform the Emotional Lives of their Talented Children*. New York: Basic Books.

Montale, E. (1976) *Poet in our Time*. London: Marion Boyars.

Morris, B. (1991) 'The Nature and Role of Educational Therapy', *The Journal of Educational Therapy*, 3/3, 5–14.

Morrison, T. (1989) *Song of Solomon*. London: Picador.

Morrison, T. (1992) *Jazz*. London: Picador.

Mortimer, J. and Blackstone, T. (1982) *Disadvantage and Education. Studies in Deprivation and Disadvantage*. London: Heinemann.

Murray, D. (1984) *Writing to Learn*. New York: Reinhart and Winston.

NATE (1993) *English 5–16 (1993). A Statement*. Sheffield: NATE.

NCC (1993a) *The National Curriculum and its Assessment. An Interim Report* (first Dearing Report). York: NCC.

NCC (1993b) *National Curriculum Consultation Report: English in the National Curriculum*. York: NCC.

National Oracy Project (1993) *Oracy at Forest Gate School*, Occasional Papers in Oracy no. 7. York: NCC.

Ngugi wa Thiong'o (1977) *Petals of Blood*. London: Cox and Wyman.

Ngugi wa Thiong'o (1986) *Decolonising the Mind: The Politics of Language in African Literature*. London: James Currey.

Nichols, G. (1989) *i is a long memoried woman*. London: Karnak House.

Nichols, G. (1990) 'The Battle with Language', in S.R. Cudjoe (ed.), *Caribbean Women Writers. Essays from the First International Conference*. Wellesley: Calaloux Publications.

Nisbet, J. and Shucksmith, J. (1984) 'The Seventh Sense', SCRE publication no. 86. Edinburgh: SCRE.

Norwottny, N. (1962) *The Language Poets Use*. London: Athlone Press.

Ortony, A. (ed.) (1979) *Metaphor and Thought*. Cambridge: Cambridge University Press.

Ortony, A. (1980) 'Some Psycholinguistic Aspects of Metaphor', in R.R. Hoffman and R.P. Honeck (1980), 186–201.

Owen, P. (1992) 'Defining Reading Standards: Establishing the Operational Validity of Assesments', in M. Hayhoe and S. Parker (1992), 94–107.

Perera, K. (1980) 'The Assessment of Linguistic Difficulty in Reading Material', *Educational Review*, 32/2.

Perls, F. (1971) *Gestalt Therapy Now,* ed. J. Fagan and I.L. Shepherd. New York: Harper Colophon.

Piaget, J. (1973) *The Child and Reality: Problems of Genetic Psychology*. Harmondsworth: Penguin.

Piaget, J. (1978) *Success and Understanding*. Cambridge: Harvard University Press.

Polanyi, M. (1958) *Personal Knowledge*. London: Routledge and Kegan Paul.

Polanyi, M. (1969) *Knowing and Being*, edited by M. Grene. London: Routledge and Kegan Paul.

Polanyi, M. (1975) *The Tacit Dimension*. London: Routledge and Kegan Paul.

Ponsonby, A. (1927) *More English Diaries*. London: Methuen.

Popper, K. (1992) 'The Magic of Myths', *The Times Higher Education Supplement*, 24.7.92, 15–19.

Pound, E. (1968) 'In a Station in the Metro', in *Collected Shorter Poems* (second edn). London: Faber.

Protherough, R. (1983) *Developing Response to Fiction*. Milton Keynes: Open University Press.

Quine, W.V. (1981) 'Postscript on Metaphor', in *Theories and Things*. Cambridge, Massachussetts: Harvard University Press, 187–9.

Ranson, S. (1992) 'Towards the Learning Society', *Educational Management and Administration*, 20/2, 68–79.

Reavis, G.H. (1939) 'The Animal School', quoted in Bassett (eds) (1967) *Teaching in the Primary School*. Sydney: Ian Novak Publishing Co.

Reeve, M. and Peel, R. (1993) 'Notions of Selfhood: an H.E. Expository Course', *English in Education*, 27/2, 33–41.

Richards, E. (1992) *Métaphor and Other Non-literal Language in the Primary School Classroom*. University of Birmingham: unpublished Ph.D. thesis.

Ricoeur, P. (1977) *The Rule of Metaphor: Multi-disciplinary Studies of the Creation of Meaning in Language*, translation by R. Czerny, K. McLaughlin and J. Costello of *La Metaphore Vive*. London: Routledge and Kegan Paul.

Ricoeur, P. (1991) *A Ricoeur Reader: Reflection and Imagination*, ed. M.J.

Valdes. Hemel Hempstead: Harvester Wheatsheaf.

Romaine, S. (1989) *Bilingualism*. Oxford: Blackwell.

Romanyshyn, D. (1982) *Psychological Life. From Science to Metaphor*. Milton Keynes: Open University Press.

Rosen, B. (1991) *Shapers and Polishers. Teachers as Storytellers*. London: Mary Glasgow Press.

Rosenthal, J. (1984) *P'Tang Yang Kipperbang*. London: Longman.

Rowland, S. (1993) *The Enquiring Tutor. Exploring the Process of Professional Learning*. London: Falmer.

Rubin, M.L. (1988) 'Adolescence and Autobiographical Fiction. Teaching "Annie John" by Jamaica Kincaid', *Wasafari*, 8, 11–14.

Rubin, M. 'Make Suns' (unpublished paper).

Rummelhart, D.E. (1979) 'Some Problems with the Notion of Literal Meanings in Metaphor and Thought', in A. Ortony (ed.) (1979).

Ryan, J. (1992) 'Foreword', in J. Hladczuk and W. Eller (1992).

Salter, M. (ed.) (1977) *Play. Anthropological Perspectives*. Proceedings of the Association for the Study of Play. West Point, New York: Leisure Press.

Sanders, W. (1986) 'Who Owns Literature?', *Universities Quarterly*, 40/3, 225–68.

Sapir, E. (1921) *Language*. New York: Harcourt Brace.

Sarland, C. (1991) *Young People Reading: Culture and Response*. Milton Keynes: Open University Press.

Sayer, J. (1993) *The Future Governance of Education*. London: Cassell.

Shibles, W. (ed.) (1972) *Essays on Metaphor*. Wisconsin: Language Press.

Simkins, T., Ellison, L. and Garrett, V. (eds) (1992) *Implementing Educational Reform. The Early Lessons*. Harlow: Longman.

Simon, B. (1960) *The New Nations and the Educational Structure, 1780–1870*. London: Lawrence and Wishart.

Simons, J. (1990) *Diaries and Journals of Literary Women from Fanny Burney to Virginia Woolf*. London: Macmillan.

Simpkins, W. (1992) 'Rationality, Feeling and Advocacy in Educational Research', *Journal of Educational Administration*, 28/3, 48–56.

Smith, F. (1978) *Understanding Reading* (second edn). New York: Holt, Rinehart and Winston.

Smith, F. (1982) *Writing and the Writer*. London: Heinemann.

Smith, F., Goelman, H. and Oberg, A. (eds) (1984) *Awakening to Literacy*. London: Heinemann.

Stafford, W. (1963) 'Vacation', in T. Gunn and T. Hughes (eds) *Five American Poets*. London: Faber.

Steedman, C. (1982) *The Tidy House. Little Girls Writing*. London: Virago.

Sternberg, R.J. (1990) *Metaphors of Mind*. Cambridge: Cambridge University Press.

Stevens, W. (1955) *The Collected Works of Wallace Stevens*. London: Faber.

Stibbs, A. (1993) Review article, *The English and Media Magazine*, Autumn issue. London: The English and Media Centre.

216

Stoppard, T. (1972) *Jumpers*. London: Faber.

Stoppard, T. (1984) *The Real Thing*. London: Faber.

Stoppard, T. (1993) Radio Interview, BBC World Service, 7.9.93.

Stubbs, M. (1976) 'Keeping in Touch', in M. Stubbs and S. Delamont (eds) (1976) *Explorations in Classroom Observations*. London: Waley.

Stubbs, M. (1983) *Language, Schools and Classrooms* (second edn). London: Methuen.

Sturrock, J. (1988) 'How the gramnivorous quadruped jumped over the moon: a romantic approach', in K. Egan and D. Nadaner (1982).

Taverner, D. (1990) *Reading within and beyond the Classroom*. Milton Keynes: Open University Press.

Teasdale, J.D. and Barnard, J. (1993) *Affect, Cognition and Change. Remodelling Depressive Thought*. Hove: Lawrence Erlbaum.

The Independent (1993) 'Literacy of College Students Criticised', in *The Independent*, 20.2.93, 1.

Thompson, E.P. (1963) *The Making of the English Working Class*. Harmondsworth: Penguin.

Thornsby, A. (1994) 'An Investigation into Children using Picture Books.' Unpublished paper. Sheffield: Division of Education, University of Sheffield.

Tolstoy, L. (1862) 'The School at Yasnaya Polanya', in *Tolstoy on Education* (1967) edited and translated by J. Weiner. Chicago: University of Chicago Press.

Townsley, R. (1993) *An Investigation into Young Children's Awareness of their Writing*, unpublished Ph.D. thesis. Sheffield: University of Sheffield.

Trevarthen, C. (1993) 'Playing into Reality: Conversations with the Infant Communicator', in *Winnicott Studies*, 7. London: Squiggle Foundation.

Tuma, J. (1989) 'Mental Health Services for Children: The State of the Art', *American Psychologist*, 44, 188–99.

Verbrugge, R.R. (1980) 'Transformation in Knowing', in R.R. Hoffman and R.P. Honeck (eds) (1980).

Vincent, D. (1979) 'Standards and Assessment', in A. Cashdan (ed.) (1979).

Von Tetzchner, S. Siegel, L.S. and Smith, L. (eds) (1989) *The Social and Cognitive Aspects of Normal and Atypical Language Development*. New York: Springer-Verlag.

Vygotsky, L.S. (1962) *Thought and Language*. Cambridge, Massachussetts: MIT Press.

Wade, B. (1985) *Linklove*. Liskeard: Chambers/Peterloo Poets.

Wade, B. (1992) 'English: Running with a Handicap', in K. Bovair, B. Carpenter and G. Upton (eds), *Special Curriculum Needs*. London: David Fulton, 43–55.

Wade, B. and Moore, M. (1993) 'The Test's the Thing: Viewpoints of Students with Special Educational Needs', *Educational Studies*, 1 9/2, 181–91.

Wade. N. (1990) *Visual Allusions*. Hove: Lawrence Erlbaum.

Walsh, B. (1988) *Shut Up! Communication in the Secondary School*. London: Cassell.

Walsh, B. (1989) *My Language, Our Language. Meeting Special Needs in English*. London: Routledge and Kegan Paul.

Ward, T. (1909) *Peeps into the Past. Passages from the Diary of T.A. Ward*, edited by A.B. Bell. London: Leng and Co.

Washe, R.D. (1990) *Every Child Can Write!* New South Wales: Primary English Teaching Association.

Waugh, P. (1984) *Metafiction. The Theory and Practice of Self-conscious Fiction*. London: Routledge.

Warnock, M. (1976) *Imagination*. Berkeley: University of California Press.

Waterland, L. (1985) *Read With Us. An Apprenticeship Approach to Reading*. Stroud: Thimble Press.

Webb, E. (1992) *Literature and Education. Encounter and Experience*. London: Falmer.

Wells, G. (1987) *The Meaning Makers*. London: Hodder and Stoughton.

Wells, G. and Nicholls, J. (eds) (1985) *Language and Learning. An International Perspective*. London: Falmer.

Wheelwright, W. (1972) 'Semantics and Ontology', in W. Shibles (ed.) (1972).

Whitehead, F.S., Capey, A.C., Maddren, W. and Wellings, A. (1977) *Children and their Books*. Basingstoke: Schools Council/ Macmillan Education.

Whitehead, M.R. (1990) *Language and Literacy in the Early Years. An Approach for Education Students*. London: Paul Chapman.

Wilkinson, A. (1965) *Spoken English*. Occasional Publicaton No. 2, *Educational Review*. Birmingham: School of Education, University of Birmingham.

Wilkinson, A. (1975) *Language and Education*. Oxford: Oxford University Press.

Wilkinson, A. (1982) 'The Implications of Oracy', in B. Wade, *Language Perspectives*. London: Heinemann.

Wilkinson, A., Davies, A. and Berrill, D. (eds) (1990) *Spoken English Illuminated*. Milton Keynes: Open University Press.

Willinsky, J. (1991) *The Triumph of Literature/ The Fate of Literacy. English in the Secondary School Curriculum*. Columbia University, New York: Teachers' College Press.

Willis, P., Jones, S. Canaan, J. and Hurd, G. (1990) *Common Culture*. Milton Keynes: Open University Press.

Wilson, G. (1990) *Our Children. Present Issues and Past Values*. Current papers 1. University of Sheffield: Division of Education.

Wilson, J. (1979) *Preface to the Philosophy of Education*. London: Routledge and Kegan Paul.

Winnicott, D. (1971) *Playing and Reality*. London: Tavistock.

Witkin, R.W. (1974) *The Intelligence of Feeling*. London: Heinemann.

Woods, P. (1993) 'Managing Marginality: teacher development through grounded life history', *British Educational Research Journal*, 19 /5, 447–65.

Woolf, V. (1979) *The Diary of Virginia Woolf*, five volumes, edited by A.O. Bell. Harmondsworth: Penguin.

Wray, D. and Medwell, J. (1991) *Literacy and Language in the Primary Years*. London: Routledge.

Zelan, K. (1991) *The Risks of Knowing. Developmental Impediments to School Learning*. New York: Plenum Press.

Index